PREPARING AHEAD

Successful Management of Family Affairs in Later Life

COLIN ASHLEY

Solicitor

Visit us online at www.authorsonline.co.uk

This book is dedicated to my parents from whose lives and deaths my interest in older people arose and to my partner, Bette Stephenson, without whose constant encouragement the book would never have been completed.

CONTENTS

ACKNOWLEDGEMENTS

Thanks are due a vast number of people, some alive, many now dead, who have contributed to this book. Many of those will never know of that contribution since it has been unintentional and has arisen from the circumstances of and the manner in which they lived their lives and, in many cases, the circumstances of and events following their death. Many have been my clients in life or in whose affairs I have become involved following their death.

A great contribution to this book, much of it indirect but nonetheless valuable, has come from members of the staff of Rochdale Metropolitan Borough Council's Social Services Department, both administrative staff and field social workers, and the Rochdale and Middleton Merit Teams with whom I have come into contact over many years.

Social workers regrettably come in for frequent criticism on the grounds that they are damned if they do and damned if they don't. My own experience has been of a group of dedicated people showing much thought and compassion to the service users with whom they work and from whose example I have learned a great deal as also from the examples of good practice set by the two Lord Chancellor's Visitors with whom I have come into contact.

My thanks are due also to the owners, managers and staff of care homes with whom I have dealt in the Rochdale area.

I am grateful to Martyn Warburton and my Associate Solicitor, Jill Waddington, for reading through the text and in Jill's case for so often sweeping up after me in many of my jobs where I have done the fun bit and she has done the tedious bit. My staff member, Pat Stephenson, deserves much credit for the typing of much of the manuscript having had to endure my appalling handwriting and my frequent and often pernickety amendments.

Colin Ashley
Rochdale

22 January 2005

PREFACE

My mother died suddenly of a heart attack; my father died after a number of years in a nursing home. In the course of thirty years in the legal profession I have seen countless children realise that their parents are suddenly starting to age; they have realised that the roles have been reversed; that the parents who have always advised and cared for the child, even well into adulthood, are now the ones who themselves need advice and who need care.

That realisation can be vivid – not least because it also dawns on the child that he/she is the next generation to be in that position.

It is frequently the case that the child simply does not want to face the reality that their parents are not going to be there forever. As with other things in life, there may well be the view that if we avoid thinking about it, if we avoid acknowledging it, the problem will go away. Certainly the view may well be that there is nothing that they can do about it and a prime reason for that may well be ignorance of the issues that may or will need addressing in the future.

Ignorance on the part of the child is not the only difficulty. Lack of knowledge on the parent's part is as great a problem. The fear of the child of discussing with the parent 'late in life issues' is perhaps the biggest problem of all.

This book is not a legal textbook; it is not even a 'How to' book as such – the issues are often too complex and inter-related to be able to provide easy answers. Every case has to be looked at individually and on its own facts.

It has been written because I want to encourage children to think through the issues that will confront them in terms of their parents in later life. I want to prepare them for decisions that may have to be made and so that they enter into that time of life, not as I did totally unprepared, but at least with some knowledge and perhaps with some idea of a plan.

It is written to alert children to what they don't know.

The book has also been written in such a way that the child can commend the book to a parent to read at his or her leisure and so that issues that the child feels he or she could not possibly raise can be raised with the parent by an independent third party – me. It is my experience that often parents worry about some of these issues but like the child do not want to raise them or do not know that there may be answers.

While I will often refer to 'parents' and 'children', the book is relevant to any older people and those who may have to care for them whatever the relationship and whatever the ages may be. It is often the case that someone in their nineties may be being cared for by someone in their sixties or older. Accordingly, the word 'child' has a very wide scope.

The book is written with the average person and family in mind. It does not address in any detail the issues of great wealth and Inheritance Tax planning. It does not address minority or esoteric issues. For that I make no apology. It looks at the very basic issues that could confront any of us.

It is written with the intention of making those who read it think about their own circumstances. It should prompt them to make their own enquiries on particular issues, the generalities of which may have been touched on in the book. It is not intended to be a replacement for individual professional advice which must always be sought where any legal or financial issues are involved.

If the book helps just a few people to avoid some of the trauma that I experienced through lack of forethought or knowledge, it will have been worthwhile.

Finally, whilst it was originally conceived as a book for families, the way it has developed is that it may well prove a useful resource for other professionals such as social workers, hospital staff, GPs, care home owners and staff etc. They may well find it useful to inform them either of some of the issues involved for the first time, or as a reminder of things they knew in the past but have forgotten.

I hope it will assist them to spot problems in the affairs of their service users/patients/clients which may need to be addressed. If your team seeks specialist training in this area please go to **www.theplatinumtrainingpartnership.com**.

Anyone with constructive comments for improvement or additional issues to be addressed in future editions of this book is welcome to email me at **info@preparingahead.com** or may write to me at the address below.

Please feel free to visit my website at **www.preparingahead.com** where additional information and contact details can be found.

My professional website is at **www.ahsutcliffe.co.uk**

Colin Ashley
22 Drake Street
Rochdale
Lancashire
OL16 1TE
22 January 2005

CONVENTIONS ADOPTED IN THE BOOK AND WARNINGS

1. Words in *italics* are defined in the Explanation of Terms (Glossary) in Appendix 1 at the end of the book.

    I have tried to italicise a word on the occasion it first appears and subsequently where it may be helpful.

2. Words in **bold** in the body of the text are for emphasis

3. I have tried to adopt a non-sexist approach within the book and have interchanged 'he' and 'she' and 'his' and 'her' at will. Sometimes I have used the term 'they' even where the person is singular, if it seems appropriate.

4. Instead of a summary at the end of each chapter I have listed key points at the start of most chapters with a view to the reader having an idea where the chapter is heading from the outset.

5. Whilst a few websites are referred to in the text, a list of useful websites is given in Appendix 2 at the end of the book and which is combined with a list of other useful reference sources and names and addresses.

6. **Warning: Whilst the general parts of this book may well be relevant to all parts of the United Kingdom, other parts, especially those dealing with care and benefits, are only relevant for certain in England. Accordingly, readers whose material concerns are outside England, must not rely on this book for those other areas. Future editions of this book may well be extended to take in other areas of the UK.**

7. **Warning: This book is a general work intended only to make people think and consider their own position.   It must not be relied on as definitive.   Law and practice change on an almost daily basis.**

    Every case must be judged on its own particular facts and everyone should seek their own individual legal and other advice for their own circumstances.

CHAPTER 1

PLANNING ISSUES

KEY POINTS

- Each of our circumstances is different. Each case has to be looked at on its own merits.

- A large number of factors affect how we are able to plan for the future and what those plans are.

- Many of those factors will relate to the personality and attitudes of those with whom we find ourselves involved.

- Despite the problems, planning is important.

- Good legal and other forms of advice must be obtained.

- Good advice is unlikely to be cheap. The cost of bad advice is likely to prove very expensive in the long term.

- Caring is stressful. Carers need to look after themselves. Being a dead hero is unproductive.

CHAPTER 1

PLANNING ISSUES

GENERAL POINTS

- The circumstances in which we each find ourselves are probably as many and various as are our fingerprints. There may be an overall similarity but the detail will be different; there will be nuances. In consequence, each case has to be looked at on its own individual facts and the combination of those facts.
- It is for that reason that specific and individual professional advice should be sought where necessary. A slight difference in circumstances will change entirely the decisions which are reached.
- It has been my experience that a slight delay in acting may well affect decisions reached and action taken whether for good or bad.

I have set out below some of the individual factors that children and parents need to have in mind when planning generally for the future.

SPECIFICS

1. Family size

Family size in general and numbers of siblings in particular can play a vital part in forward planning. Who, one has to ask, will there be to take part in the care of parents and in the decision making process? We are now well into the age of small families. A family with four children is now deemed to be large. Two is perhaps more the norm. There are large numbers of people with few, if indeed any, family to support them in later life. Often it may be left to friends or professional people to provide the support.

2. Family location

It is fine having several children to share the load but where are they? Those close at hand are probably the ones upon whom the major caring role will fall. Those, even in this country, but at a distance may be either unable or unwilling to become involved in the care of parents. With even the best will in the world, a child in Cornwall with a parent in the North of England will have almost as much trouble in providing practical help as would a child on the other side of the Atlantic; that should not, however, prevent their lending moral support to those closer at hand.

3. Family attitude

Perhaps the main problem in the satisfactory provision of help for parents by children will be one of attitude. It is one of the saddest and most frustrating parts of my work to see families where care of parents falls upon one child when there are others who not only simply refuse to shoulder any responsibility for care but who cause grief to those who do. Often that grief may not stem from a child themselves but may arise from interference from a husband, wife or partner. I have indeed seen it arising from the interference of a grandchild and from outsiders.

Parents and children have to have in mind that there are, putting it quite strongly but realistically, some manipulative and mischievous people who we have to count as relatives and it is wise that in forward planning the nature and character of relatives should be taken into account.

Parents in particular need to have regard not only to which child sends them the largest Christmas or birthday card but also which child or children invest their time in them and who are prepared to help, so far as they are able, in a practical way. Frequently, a child living out of the area who sends a posh birthday present once a year will be viewed more favourably than will the child who shoulders the unglamorous day to day care of a parent.

4.   Perverseness

Some older people, as well as some younger ones, can be downright perverse.

This may be as a result of illness but often it is down to straightforward bloody-mindedness, stubbornness and unwillingness to consider others.

Whilst children must consider the wishes of parents so also parents must consider their children and their circumstances. Sometimes they must accept that as they become infirm some changes in their living accommodation may become necessary if they are to remain safe and if they are to help their carers (children) to help them.

It is better that this is done in a structured and organised way than to be forced upon them in an emergency as, for example, following an accident or the death of a spouse or partner.

Similarly, in terms of handing over control of their affairs, parents ought to be prepared to delegate the management of their affairs to others, or at any rate put in place appropriate arrangements at an early stage. My question to parents who may read this is "Could you be perverse?"

5. Family trust

A critical factor in forward planning is the trust which exists within the family; the trust that exists between parents and children generally, between parents and individual children and, perhaps above all, between the children themselves. This will have been affected and influenced in many cases by the values of the parents in the past and the values that they have instilled into their children in the past.

Parents must also remember that they themselves can continue to cause problems amongst children by playing one off against the other. Some older people can be manipulative. They should understand that such manipulation is generally counterproductive.

6. Health

The health of family members may play an important part in the extent of the support provided by children. This does not just mean physical health but also mental health.

7. Finance

The financial resources of the children may well affect the level and type of support that children may be able to give to the parents.

8. Work commitments

Clearly the work commitments of individual family members may seriously impact on the level of care which children can provide for parents. This may not only be in terms of time spent at work but also location of that work.

It may be, however, that a child who is 'time poor' may be 'cash rich' and can offer financial assistance even if not practical help. Whilst not being able to provide ongoing care they might be able to provide respite care.

9. Family commitments

Those with young children, disabled children or a disabled partner may clearly have great difficulty in providing much practical help or support for parents.

10. Family abilities.

Children need to consider where their strengths lie. A child may have no financial acumen but may be a brilliant carer. A child may have great ability in organisation, legal and financial issues, but no practical skills. It is important that children should acknowledge their own and others' strengths and weaknesses and prepare to adjust and co-ordinate their activities accordingly.

11. Family history

One of the factors that families often overlook in planning for the future is that of family history. In most families there are skeletons. Parents in particular need to consider whether there is information that needs to be imparted to children or if children think there may be information that they need:

- information about affairs that may have lead to the birth of illegitimate children;
- information as to whether children are of the *whole blood* or only of the *half blood*;
- information about estranged children who may be unknown to others;
- information about previous marriages;
- information about even such things as basic as whether parents are or were actually married to each other;
- information about genetic disorders;
- issues of incestuous or similar relationships.

Parents have to remember that after their death, matters of inheritance may be affected by some of these issues. Additionally, there may be matters of life and death which may be determined by these issues. Science is developing and has in recent years developed procedures undreamed of only ten years ago for creating children and for determining parentage. This can give rise to interesting legal complications and the dredging up of skeletons long since thought to be well and truly buried.

What skeletons are there in your cupboard?

12. Acknowledgement of problems

Clearly where an older person is suffering from mental health problems it may well be impossible for them to appreciate that there is a problem and that they may need help.

However, there are many older people who, whilst admirably trying to maintain their independence, may well cause great anguish to their families by refusing to acknowledge at all that they may need support now or in the future.

There is no easy solution to this.

13. Openness

Following on from the last point many older people play their cards very close to their chests. They are unwilling to divulge any information about, say, their finances to even close family. Whilst failing to give information may well be wise in some families, older people must appreciate it may well cause those looking after them, or who may have to look after them in the future, great difficulty in supporting them; it may well hinder the carer in obtaining all the help and full benefits to which they may be entitled and in managing their affairs generally.

14. Obtaining reliable general help and information

Access to reliable information is vital in the planning process. Sources and quality of information will vary from place to place but generally there are significant amounts of good quality information and advice about if this is sought. The time in researching the various topics may be considerable and it is important that the enquiries should start early and not just when crisis occurs. Trying to make decisions at the same time as experiencing personal trauma and obtaining information is a sure way to get it wrong.

I have set out in Appendix 2 some sources of information.

15. Legal advice

Anyone who has read this book in its entirety will realise that the issues involved can be complex. More to the point many of them are interrelated. I cannot emphasise too strongly the importance of obtaining legal advice specific to your family circumstances. This book is no substitute for individual legal advice.

Many moons ago, in my early days in the law, I read a legal help book on renting property. Every few pages it said it was essential that the reader should obtain 'good' legal advice. As a newly qualified solicitor I felt offended by this expression. Surely all legal help was 'good'. I now know better. I now know that there are many sources of so-called legal help ranging from the man in the pub through legal programmes on television to senior barristers. Some of it is excellent; some of it is not so good. There is much mythology doing the rounds in this area of the law.

You might expect me, as a solicitor, to say that obtaining help from a solicitor is the preferred course and, indeed, I do say that. It is, however, important to find the right solicitor. Recommendation is probably the best course but recommendation should be from a reputable source. Do bear in mind that solicitors and other lawyers (for example, licensed conveyancers) can now pay referral fees to third parties to introduce clients. Such referrals may well be made irrespective of the quality of the service to be provided and irrespective of the expertise of the solicitor concerned. Referrals via this route are probably best avoided.

Dealing with older people and their affairs needs a solicitor who has knowledge of a wide range of legal topics including wills, probate, court of protection procedures, property law and so on. It also needs a solicitor with an understanding of the way in which social services operate, how care is financed, how care homes are run and the standards which should be expected. The solicitor needs to be prepared to adapt his or her approach to the very specific requirements of the older client and who can communicate with an older person in their own terms and at their own speed.

Above all, it is essential that the solicitor should have the integrity and strength of character always to act in the best interests of the older person irrespective of what pressures may be brought to bear on him or her by third parties.

Choose carefully.

Finally, I have emphasised the need for good legal advice. Legal advice can come cheap. Good legal advice does not. As in most areas of life you get what you pay for.

Dealing with the affairs of older people can be time consuming and stressful even for professionals. The responsibility on a solicitor is frequently considerable. If you want the job to be done correctly and professionally be prepared to pay a proper fee. Failure can, in the long term, be very expensive.

16. Clear cut answers

There may be a tendency to expect that in planning for the care of older people all decisions will be clear cut and easily made. For the reasons set out elsewhere in this chapter that may well not be the case. Additionally, however, it must be appreciated that circumstances change both in the long term and in the short term and what may be a good plan today may, because of say, an intervening medical problem, be a bad plan tomorrow.

A willingness to change direction and an acceptance that it may be a few steps forward and one step back, is an important quality.

It must also be understood (a factor that is not taught to law students!) that there are many grey areas in dealing with the affairs of older people both in terms of law and also because we are dealing with human beings who may well have their own agendas and wishes which may not always be honest, logical or wise. This has to be taken into account.

17. A word of warning: Taking care of the carer

For anyone who becomes responsible for looking after an older person and their affairs the responsibility can be onerous. This will particularly be the case where that older person is someone for whom you care deeply and for whom you are keen to do your best.

Frequently, the task will arise not singly but in pairs, if both parents are involved. It may arise in multiples since it is quite possible that in-laws may also be at that time of life when they too need looking after. Indeed, there may even be extended family of aunts and uncles who may need support.

The people who need support may all need it at the same time or they may follow each other in succession over a number of years.

Whichever it is, the toll on the 'carer' can be great.

My experience is that men, in particular, can appear to suffer more than women: not because they care any more but because women are more used to taking on a caring and nurturing role and also because men are less likely to be prepared to admit that they are finding it stressful and be prepared to talk through the issues.

However, whether the carer be male or female, young or old, it is important that he or she should realise and acknowledge the stresses of caring especially when they are themselves holding down a job and possibly dealing also with the following generation.

They must ensure that:

- they pace themselves and consider whether there are any tasks or roles (for example, in outside organisations) that they can drop or suspend while undertaking the caring role but yet without themselves becoming isolated;
- they look for and accept any practical help that can be provided by appropriate outside agencies;
- they consult their GP if they find themselves suffering from stress or depression and be prepared to accept any chemical help or

counselling that they may be offered. There really is no disgrace in accepting that you are human;
- they find someone in whom they can confide about their feelings;
- they consider whether, if finances permit, they can themselves employ help, such as a cleaner and gardener, to do the chores that they would normally do themselves in their own home even if it is only for a few hours each week; having money in the bank is no use once you are dead;
- they are prepared to reconsider promises that they may have made in the past, in better times and when they were younger. The classic example of this is the promise made to mum or dad many years before that 'I will never "put" you in a home'. Most of us, if we are decent, would prefer to see our older relatives living happily, healthily and independently in the community. The reality is that sometimes this simply cannot happen. Sometimes, residential care is the only option.

The important thing is that, where this becomes inevitable, it should be done in a caring and ordered way. There should be few occasions where someone reaches the point where they have to be 'put' (a word I find wholly unacceptable) in care. Wherever possible, it should be a case of it being agreed with the older person that this is an appropriate course of action and the older person should be as actively involved as possible in the decision making and the choice of placement.

The placement should wherever possible be on a trial basis; the possibility of going back home should be left open in case the older person decides to return home; doors should not appear to be permanently closed until either the older person accepts the position, becomes incapable of themselves making a decision, or until financial pressures are such that it becomes necessary to break up the home and sell it or surrender the tenancy;

- they remember that if he or she, as a carer, becomes ill that it helps no-one and simply adds to the problem

CHAPTER 2

MENTAL CAPACITY

KEY POINTS

- For virtually everything we do, we must have not only physical capacity but also mental capacity.

- Failure to have mental capacity may make the action ineffective legally.

- Physical incapacity is not usually a problem.

- Older people are often the victims of financial and other abuse.

- No one can look after the affairs of someone else in lifetime without having been given power to do so by the person concerned signing a *Power of Attorney* or (in the absence of a Power of Attorney, and in the event of the person being mentally incapable of managing his or her own affairs) by the *Court of Protection*). This can only be validly signed when the person has *mental capacity* to do so.

- If you wish to say where your money and property goes and who looks after your affairs after you have died, then make a *will*.

- Make a will whilst you are mentally capable.

- If you wish to guard against unwanted medical treatment if you cease to be able to communicate your wishes, consider making a *Living Will/Advance Directive.*

- Do not let the fact that someone is physically incapable of signing a document deter them from taking action. Physical difficulties can usually be overcome.

CHAPTER 2

MENTAL CAPACITY

THE ISSUES

An early death is now in one's sixties. Many people live well into their eighties. The Office for National Statistics disclosed that in 1971 the population of the UK aged 75 or over was five million. By 2000 this had risen to seven million. In 2002 life expectancy at birth, for females born in the UK, was 81 years compared with 76 years for males. In 1901 this had been 49 years for females and 45 years for males.

Unfortunately, life expectancy does not mean the same as healthy life expectancy. In 1981 the expected time lived in poor health for males, was 6.5 years and for females 10.1 years. In 2001 this had risen to 8.7 years for men and 11.6 years for women.

Physical frailty may be a problem but the far greater problem from a legal point of view, and even from a practical point of view, is that of mental health.

This is because in simple terms, virtually every action that we perform requires us to have *mental capacity*.

Where these actions have a legal context then this is particularly important and if we do not have that capacity then the action will or may be ineffective legally.

It is frequently a source of confusion to the layman that the fact that a person may have the physical capacity to undertake a task, such as sign a document, is not sufficient. (Indeed, for many things the actual physical ability to undertake the task is unnecessary since others may well be able to carry out the action on our behalf with appropriate safeguards.) A person must have mental capacity. He must know and understand what it is that he is doing. He must understand the consequences.

What sorts of things require such understanding and without which will be ineffective?

The following are included:

- the making of a *will*;
- the handing over to others of management of our affairs during lifetime by, for example, signing an *Enduring Power of Attorney*;
- the purchase of a bus ticket;
- marrying;
- entering into a sexual relationship;
- voting;
- making a decision about medical treatment;
- signing a cheque;
- selling a house;
- giving away a house;
- making a gift of money or property;
- selling shares.

It will be seen that the range of 'actions' for which understanding is required is wide from the very simple (purchasing a bus ticket) to the comparatively complex (making a will).

However, there is no one level of understanding that is applicable to all actions. Different types of action may require different levels of understanding. Therefore, the level of understanding needed lawfully to buy a bus ticket will be much less than that required to make a will. Further, the test of whether a person has sufficient understanding to do various things will differ according to the action proposed. Accordingly, the things that a person would have to be shown to have appreciated lawfully to buy a bus ticket will be wholly different to those which would have to be shown to have been appreciated for the purpose of making a will.

Even actions of a broadly similar type (for example, making a will and making an Enduring Power of Attorney) will have different tests of understanding applied to them.

By way of example, what is the test of understanding to make a will?

The question here is 'does the person making the will have "testamentary capacity"?' Many years ago a judge said that it was essential:

(1)   That a *testator* understood the nature of the act (that is making the will) and its effects.

(2)   That a testator understood the extent of the property of which he is disposing in the will.

(3)   That a testator could understand and appreciate the claims of various people to whom he ought to give something; and

(4)   with a view to (3) above the judge said that 'no disorder of mind must poison the testator's affections, pervert his sense of right or prevent the exercise of his natural faculties and that no insane delusion shall influence his will in disposing of his property and bring about a disposal of it which, if the mind had been sound, would not have been made'.

The first two elements (understanding the nature of the act and its effect and the extent of the property being disposed of) involved the testator's understanding.

Does he have the ability to receive and weigh up information which may possibly be given to him by others?

The third test (being able to understand and appreciate the claims of various people to whom he or she ought to give something) extends beyond understanding and requires the person making the will to be able to distinguish and compare potential *beneficiaries* and arrive at some form of judgment. A person making a will can, if he or she is mentally capable, ignore the claims of relatives and other potential beneficiaries.

Everyone has the right to be foolish, biased or prejudiced. The important thing is, does he have the ability to make a decision. The fact that it may not necessarily be a sensible or wise decision is not particularly relevant.

In the case of making an Enduring Power of Attorney the first, and probably the most important, test is 'does an individual have understanding to hand over control of his affairs to someone else by way of a Power of Attorney?'

If the person concerned makes a Power of Attorney and generally lacks understanding to do so, then the Power of Attorney is null and void unless it can be shown that it was signed during a period when the person had, albeit briefly, got that understanding.

In recent cases a judge said that the test of capacity to create an Enduring Power of Attorney was that the *Donor*, the person making the Power of Attorney, understood the nature and effect of the document.

The judge said that there were four pieces of information that any person creating an Enduring Power of Attorney should understand:

(1)   That the *attorney* will be able to assume complete authority over the donor's affairs (if the Power gave him that authority).

(2)   That the attorney will be able to do anything with the donor's property which the donor could have done (if the Power gave him that authority).

(3)   That the authority will continue if the donor should be, or later become, mentally incapable; and

(4)   that if the donor should be, or become, mentally incapable, the Power of Attorney will not be able to be revoked (cancelled) without confirmation by the *Court of Protection*.

It is not a requirement that the donor should himself have sufficient understanding to do all the things that the attorney will be able to do under the Power. The donor only needs to have the capacity to create an Enduring Power of Attorney.

Therefore, if a businessman has executed an Enduring Power of Attorney and he understands the nature and effect of the document, the fact that he may no longer be able to understand a complex financial restructuring of his company is immaterial. It is enough if he understood that he was handing over control of his affairs to someone else.

Why does someone need to have mental capacity?

What is the consequence, in practical terms, for the ordinary man or woman, of this requirement to have mental capacity?

The consequence is simply this: if there is no understanding to do the particular act (for example make a will, sell shares, draw pensions) then its doing will be ineffective and may be capable of challenge by someone affected by it.

It is true to say that if someone with mental health difficulties gets on a bus, hands over a pound coin and tells the driver he wants to go to the next stop and the driver gives that person the ticket and the correct change and the person gets off at the next stop it is highly unlikely that even if, technically, the person did not have capacity to buy the ticket there will be any repercussions. It is unlikely that their carer will demand back the fare on the grounds that the transaction should not have been entered into.

However, if that same person had signed a will giving his assets away on death to particular individuals, then it is possible that that will be challenged following the death of the *testator* if those gifts were to people who would not have been entitled had there been no will (that is, on an *intestacy*) or if there had been an earlier will leaving the assets in some other way and which was made at a time when the *testator* definitely had sufficient understanding to make a will.

There is, of course, another, very practical consequence. That is that lack of mental capacity opens up an individual to the real possibility of financial or other forms of abuse. (See Chapter 3.) This may be abuse during lifetime or, possibly, following death. It also opens up others to the charge (however unjustified) of abuse

Frequently lifetime abuse is because no one has been put properly in charge of the affairs of an older person. The abuse following death may arise because proper arrangements for a will have not been made during lifetime. I emphasise the words 'properly' and 'proper'.

Often some steps may have been taken but those will be at too late a stage in a person's life to be wholly effective. Alternatively, they may simply have been put in place without the certainty:

- that the older person knew and understood what he or she was doing and
- that the arrangements made were made without any pressure on the older person whether that pressure was from others or from their own confused thoughts.

THE SOLUTIONS

The solution in most cases is relatively easy. It is to act early. The older person should be encouraged to take proper steps to organise her affairs at a time when she is in full possession of her faculties and can be clearly seen to be so. She should make those arrangements at a time when she is still her own person; is not beholden to any particular person; when she can clearly make decisions as to the suitability of those to whom she wishes to entrust her affairs. This should be based on her experience of the person or people concerned over a lengthy period of time and not just at the time when someone sees a vulnerable and often confused older person who is ripe for cultivating as a result of infirmity or loneliness and moves in to ingratiate themselves or worse still, to threaten or intimidate the older person.

It is undoubtedly the case that there are those who make a habit of identifying vulnerable people and abusing them.

There are two key solutions to which the older person should give their attention and a further solution which is important and should be addressed if at all possible.

These solutions are as follows:

- making arrangements for someone to manage the person's affairs during his or her lifetime if he or she becomes incapable (whether physically or mentally – albeit that mentally is the greater danger) of doing so himself or herself. This will be by making an Enduring Power of Attorney;
- making arrangements so that his or her affairs are properly looked after on death and that his or her estate goes where he or she wants. This will be by making a will;
- making arrangements so that his or her views as to future medical treatment are expressed, albeit perhaps in general terms, and that he or she expresses a view as to who should be consulted about medical treatment decisions. This may extend also to expressing some views as to arrangements for residential care should the need arise.

These topics are dealt with in detail in subsequent chapters. However, it is worth at this point, making some general comments about the importance of early action and the risks of inaction.

ENDURING POWER OF ATTORNEY (EPA)

There is a misconception that if you are married or have children then your spouse or children can deal with your affairs automatically if you become unable to do so.

This is simply not the case. You have to give *informed consent* for anyone to be able to sign any legal document on your behalf. Family, however close, are no more entitled to do these things than anyone else.

It may be felt that because your affairs are relatively simple, it will be easy to put things in place to sort out your affairs if you become incapable.

Nothing could be further from the truth.

Anyone with any savings and/or a company/*occupational pension* (as opposed to state pension) and/or property that may need to be dealt with will cause very serious problems for those around them if they have not put in place proper arrangements for managing their affairs before mental incapacity arises. By way of example, if a man has an occupational pension of say £50 per week which is paid into a bank account in his sole name then neither his wife nor anyone else will be able to access those monies without an order of the Court of Protection unless an Enduring Power of Attorney is in place. The cost of obtaining such an order can be great.

An EPA cannot be made if the person does not have mental capacity to understand the nature and effects of the document he or she is signing. If mental incapacity has arisen it will be too late. The fact that he or she can physically sign is irrelevant.

Even if someone is mentally capable there may well be substantial difficulty in establishing that fact if their mental state is impaired or if they cannot, as a result of age or illness, communicate that understanding or communicate their wishes. They will also be susceptible to pressure from unscrupulous relatives, friends or strangers as to who to appoint at a time when they are exceedingly vulnerable and dependent on others.

If they have not made and cannot make an EPA then the Court of Protection will become involved in their affairs and a *receiver* (often someone in the family) will be appointed to see to their affairs on a day-to-day basis. This may well be someone with whom the older person would have no wish to be involved.

Alternatively, it may be found that someone, whether with or without malicious intention, may have managed to take over the person's affairs informally and without any formal control.

The answer is to make an EPA when they still have full mental faculties about them

Have in mind that making an EPA will be infinitely cheaper than going to the Court of Protection for the appointment of a *receiver.*

Enduring Powers of Attorney are dealt with in detail in Chapter 4.

THE WILL

Many of the same considerations apply to will-making as to EPAs.

- Failure to make a *will* will result in the person's affairs being managed following their death potentially by someone they may not even know if there are no close family. Even if there are close family, there may be a wish that close family should not be involved.

- Similarly their estate will be dealt with in accordance with the laws of intestacy which may mean that the estate passes to distant family who they would have no wish to inherit or, indeed, in a small number of cases to the Crown.

- Perhaps more worryingly, there may well be people who they positively want to inherit their estate but who, in the absence of a will, simply cannot do so or, in a few cases, who would only do so after a battle to obtain a share in the estate by showing that some provision should have been made for them but has not been.

- Even if a will is made then it would be open to challenge if it has been made in circumstances where there is an issue as to whether the testator had mental capacity to do so or was under pressure or undue influence to do so or to do so in a particular way.

- Again, the emphasis must be on older people (and indeed younger ones) making a will when they are fit to do so and not at a point when they are clearly incapable of doing so or when it may be alleged they were incapable of doing so. They should make the will when they can understand the extent of their estate and for whom they might be expected to make provision. They should make the will when they have an ability to take a long-term view remembering those who have been good to them over many years and who will continue to support them in their declining years rather than to someone who sees a likely prospect of inheriting if they 'play up' to the older person towards the end of their life.

- Older people should be aware that there are provisions for a will to be made for them after they become mentally incapable of doing so themselves if, either they have made an Enduring Power of Attorney which has been registered with the Court of Protection, or where they become subject to the jurisdiction of the Court of Protection. This is known as a *statutory will*. However, because of the cost and complexity of making a statutory will, in reality few are made even if anyone thinks about doing so. A statutory will, however, is the last thing that a person would wish to have made for them since it can only be a guess by others at what is appropriate and what the older person would want.

- For all these reasons, a will should be made at an early stage in life and kept constantly under review.

The subject of Wills is explored in more detail in Chapters 7 to 10

LIVING WILL OR ADVANCE DIRECTIVE

The way our lives will end must be something that flits through all our minds from an early age but increasingly so as we get older.

We may well form quite strong views as to what level of illness or discomfort or distress we would be prepared to tolerate. As was seen in a case in 2002, as long as we have mental ability to do so, we can decide whether we wish to be kept alive on a machine when the prospect of a happy and fulfilled life is not great and this view must be respected and acted upon by doctors. Whilst we cannot request something illegal be done to us nor can we insist that certain basic care is withdrawn, we do nonetheless have a fair degree of control over what treatment we have.

The big problem arises if we do not have mental capacity to make those medical treatment decisions. Who makes them for us? The answer is usually the doctors sometimes in consultation with next-of-kin.

It is, however, open to us to influence those medical decisions by making a Living Will or Advance Directive setting out our wishes and also giving pointers as to whom should be consulted. However, for our wishes to be effective we must make a Living Will or Advance Directive when we are mentally capable of doing so and must meet certain other criteria (such as ensuring it is kept up to date).

As with all the other things in this chapter the key is to do it when we are mentally capable of doing so and when there can be no suggestion that we were being improperly influenced or pressured by others.

The subject of living wills is explored in more detail in Chapter 14.

SUMMARY

Overall, it will be seen that whilst discussion of mental capacity is not something that enters our day-to-day conversation it is something that is affecting our lives from our earliest years through to our death and even sometimes beyond the grave, largely without our even realising it. However, as we grow older (or earlier if we suffer serious illness or injury) the issue of mental capacity is a very important one and one which can have a serious impact on our lives and those who are around us.

CHAPTER 3

MANAGING AFFAIRS
DURING LIFETIME – INTRODUCTION

KEY POINTS

- On average people now live much longer than in the past.

- Their mental faculties often fail them before their physical abilities.

- Older people are often targets of financial and other forms of abuse.

- *Abuse* can be carried out by anyone – friends and family as well as strangers.

- Older people need to put in place mechanisms to guard against abuse.

- They must put these mechanisms in place whilst they are able to do so.

- Often they do not do so for many reasons but lack of information is a main one.

CHAPTER 3

MANAGING AFFAIRS DURING
LIFETIME – INTRODUCTION

THE ISSUES

- Medical science has advanced dramatically in recent years. Many physical conditions, whether arising through old age, illness or accident, which were fatal even only twenty years ago are now often readily treatable and sometimes just minor irritations. Consequently the life expectancy of people in this country has risen dramatically even in my lifetime. Living into one's eighties is now not in the least bit unusual and 'old' can, perhaps, be regarded as being over ninety.

- What, however, has not seen a corresponding dramatic improvement is the ability of doctors similarly to maintain the mental health of people. Whilst our physical health may be maintained as we grow older our mental faculties may deteriorate – often to the point where (even if we can still physically function satisfactorily) we may no longer have the mental capacity to look after ourselves whether in terms of our general well-being or in terms of looking after our own financial affairs. Consequently, we may well need some help. Not only may we need help, but we may also need protection.

- As we become older we become more vulnerable. We become more vulnerable to:

  - physical (and, sadly, occasionally sexual) *abuse*;
  - mental *abuse* and
  - financial *abuse*.

That abuse may be:
  - actual or
  - threatened.

That abuse may come from:
  - relatives;
  - friends;
  - complete strangers;
  - carers.

That abuse may arise:
- at home;
- in sheltered accommodation;
- in hospital;
- in residential care;
- out in the street or other public places.

That abuse may be:
- by a single incident or by repeated incidents;
- carried out by one person or by a number of people;
- institutionalised.

Depending on the type and circumstances of the abuse will depend what steps can be put in place to deter or prevent it or, if it has already happened, to remedy it and/or prevent it happening again in the future.

With some careful planning, the risk – certainly of financial abuse – can be greatly reduced.

PROBLEMS OF ADDRESSING THE ISSUES

As in other areas addressed by this book, there is a very real danger of the ostrich syndrome applying: if we bury our head in the sand then there is no problem, there can be no problem and even if there is a problem then when we pull our head out of the sand the problem will have gone away.

The truth is, however, that this is simply not the case. These issues may well arise and need to be addressed as early as possible and preferably before the necessity of addressing them arises as an emergency.

It is the case that most of us wish to control our own affairs; we like having control; we wish to maintain control for as long as we can. That is right and proper. However, we often fail to acknowledge that the time may come when we will simply not have control.

Unfortunately, if we maintain total control for too long we may leave it too late and we may reach a point where we are no longer able to *delegate* that control to someone else. This inability to delegate may arise as a result of:

- accident;
- illness;
- old age.

The problem may be:

- physical (for example, being physically unable to sign or communicate wishes); or
- mental (for example, not having the ability to understand what is required and what we are doing); or
- both

The reason for not delegating earlier may be because:

- The older person has no-one obvious to whom to *delegate*.
- The person or persons who are obvious are definitely not trusted.
- There is a perceived lack of trustworthiness.
- There is a distrust between the possible candidates themselves (for example amongst siblings).
- There are too many possible candidates and he/she for various reasons cannot decide to whom to delegate. This may be:
    o for fear of upsetting someone to whom delegation is not made;
    o because he or she does not know who to trust.
- He or she doesn't want to put the burden on anyone else.
- He or she doesn't appreciate that they have affairs that need to be managed or that circumstances may arise that require their affairs to be managed.
- He or she doesn't believe that they will at some point not be able to manage their own affairs.
- He or she thinks they will know when they reach a point when they need to delegate and will have time to do it then.
- He or she has a mistaken belief that someone (often their spouse or children) will be able to take over automatically. Frequently this is accompanied by an arrogance that they know all about these things. This is a problem particularly with men of a certain age and/or certain past occupations.
- He or she is downright difficult and perverse and either always has been or has grown so as time has gone on.
- He or she does not have the information available to them of the need for delegation, the possibilities for delegation (whether in terms of how to do it or to whom to delegate) and the consequences of failing to delegate. This is often accompanied by a fear in the family (if any) of raising the issue because:
    o there is a wish not to distress the older person;
    o the older person is simply not the sort of person with whom one can discuss such matters;
    o it is believed that the older person will think the family are

trying to get their hands on their money.

This is in my experience one of the main reasons why people do not delegate.

Frequently it is a combination of reasons.

THE ANSWER

For some of the reasons there may be no solution or certainly no easy solution.

However, we have to eliminate the easily remedied ones and the main one is that of ignorance: simply lack of information.

If we ensure that the older person has the knowledge of the problems that may arise and the possible solutions available then often they will want to put arrangements in place.

One would hope that the knowledge can be imparted by their taking advice from a solicitor or someone else qualified to give that advice. And, if all else fails, then reading this book may remedy this ignorance.

CHAPTER 4

MANAGING AFFAIRS DURING LIFETIME – ENDURING POWERS OF ATTORNEY

KEY POINTS

- Generally one person cannot deal with the affairs of another during that person's lifetime without the authority of that person given when he or she had mental capacity or by order of the *Court of Protection.*

- Authority by the person concerned (the *donor*) is given by a *Power of Attorney.*

- If it is intended that the Power of Attorney shall continue even if mental incapacity arises subsequently then there must be an *Enduring Power of Attorney (EPA)*

- An EPA does not permit the *attorney* to direct where the donor lives nor can the attorney make medical treatment decisions.

- If the donor becomes or starts to become mentally incapable, the EPA must be registered with the Court of Protection.

- The attorney has only limited powers to make gifts or provide for others.

- Having no relatives to act as attorney is not a reason for doing nothing.

- Professional attorneys can be appointed.

- Whilst the preparation of an EPA does not have to be undertaken by a solicitor it is a prudent step in order to ensure that the appointment is not made by someone under pressure and that he or she has mental capacity to do so.

CHAPTER 4

MANAGING AFFAIRS DURING
LIFETIME – ENDURING POWERS OF ATTORNEY

THE ISSUES

One adult cannot simply deal with the affairs of another, however closely they may be related, without some authority to do so either:

- from the person concerned, or
- from the courts, or
- in the case of state benefits, from the *Department for Work and Pensions*

In the case of a mentally competent adult, they themselves must give that authority.

THE ANSWER

The adult wishing to give authority to the other person can do this most effectively by creating a *Power of Attorney.*

WHAT IS A POWER OF ATTORNEY?

A Power of Attorney is a document by which one person (the *donor*) authorises another person or persons (the *attorney* or *attorneys*) to look after some or all of his or her affairs.

Until 1986 there were just two types of Power of Attorney in everyday use:

- what might loosely be called a 'long' form. They were long deeds because the authority of the donor had to be set out in great detail so as to be sure to cover all the things that the donor wanted the attorney to do (but nothing else), whether that was to sell a house, deal with stocks and shares, operate a bank account, deal with pensions or whatever.

- what was called a 'Section 10' power. It was called this because it was created by Section 10 of the Powers of Attorney Act 1971 and could be created by a deed simply referring to Section 10. In a few lines it authorised the attorney or attorneys to do virtually whatever the donor could do but without spelling it out in detail.

(Both these forms still exist and can still be used. However, because of the problems with them as set out below they are now rarely used in the context of someone of advancing years.)

Both types always had to be made when the donor was mentally capable of doing so. If the donor had ceased to be mentally capable he or she could not make the Power. Additionally, and vitally important, it must be appreciated that if the donor became mentally incapable after the power was made then it ceased to have effect immediately. This was frequently just the point when the power was needed: when the donor needed his or her affairs handling because mentally he or she could not do so.

This caused enormous problems for those needing to manage the affairs of a relative etc.

The problem was in large measure solved (or more accurately it was possible for people to solve the problem if they acted in good time) by the establishment by Parliament of a third type of Power of Attorney called an *Enduring Power of Attorney* by the Enduring Powers of Attorney Act 1985.

ENDURING POWERS OF ATTORNEY

Use

An Enduring Power of Attorney is a deed by which one person (the *donor*) can appoint one or more other people (the *attorney* or the *attorneys*) to manage some or all of his affairs

The Power can be completely open or it can be subject to limitations or restrictions. The donor can be quite specific as to what the attorney/s can do or it can be left in such a way that the attorney/s can do virtually anything that the donor could do with his or her property and affairs. This would include:

- drawing pensions;
- selling or buying property;
- managing investments;
- operating bank accounts;
- managing a business.

The donor could specify in the power things that the attorney could not do, for example, sell his or her house.

There are some things that the attorney/s are restricted/prohibited from doing:

- the granting of an EPA does not give the attorney 'power over the person'. In other words it gives the attorney no power:
  - to direct where the donor should live, even if he or she cannot make that decision themselves;
  - to make medical treatment decisions for the donor;
- the attorney/s are severely restricted as to the extent that they can make gifts from the donor's assets whether to themselves or to others. Despite these restrictions a donor should consider carefully whether greater restriction needs to be placed on the attorney in terms of the power of the attorney to make gifts. This is examined in more detail in the section 'Gifts' below.

Number of Attorneys

As indicated, the donor can appoint more than one attorney. If he does then they can act either:

- jointly which means that they must do everything together (for example, they must all sign withdrawal forms); or
- jointly and severally in which case they can either act together in all things or they can act independently of one another.

There are pros and cons for each.

Advantages of acting jointly

- some measure of protection is afforded to the donor in that to abuse their position, both/all attorneys would have to be parties to the abuse, for example, wrongly withdrawing money from an account.

Disadvantages of acting jointly:

- if any one of the attorneys

  - dies;
  - becomes bankrupt;
  - becomes mentally incapable;

  then the power ceases and none of the attorneys can act;

28

- if one of the attorneys goes to prison, is out of the country or is otherwise unavailable then the operation of the power during such periods could be very difficult in practice;

- even if attorneys are in the country but a distance apart the operation of a joint power can be difficult because of the very great controls imposed and/or adopted by banks etc. in operating bank accounts for fear of breaching *money laundering* regulations.

Advantages of a joint and several appointment:

- flexibility – if any of the situations above occur then the other attorney or attorneys can continue to act;

- there can be advantages where a property has to be sold and where one or more of the attorneys is the other (of two) co-owner of the property or where a property has to be sold and the same two or more attorneys are the attorneys for two co-owners (for example husband and wife) neither of whom can themselves sign the transfer deed.

Disadvantages of a joint and several appointment:

- if one of the attorneys wishes to do something dishonest or irregular then they may be able to do so and there would be no restraint by the other attorney or attorneys if the other attorney or attorneys knew nothing of the dishonesty or irregularity.

Other options

There is nothing to stop:

- one or more attorneys being appointed in one deed with a second deed being created at the same time by which other attorneys could be appointed but who would only act if those in the first deed could not, or would not, act

- different lots of attorneys could be appointed to act at the same time but doing different things. For example, one lot of attorneys could deal with the donor's business affairs and another lot could deal with the donor's personal affairs. The important thing would be to ensure that the dividing line was clear and also that there were no gaps. Everything must be covered but without conflict.

Professional Attorneys

Many people, especially as they grow older, experience difficulty in finding a fit and reliable person (or persons) to act as their attorney.

If that is the case then professional people, such as solicitors, will be prepared to take on the role.

Just occasionally, people will attempt to appoint a casual acquaintance or visiting tradesman to be the attorney. Whilst there is nothing wrong in this, a donor does need to ask what would happen if something went wrong and either through negligence or dishonesty their money was lost. If there was no-one close who can act, then a professional person used to dealing with such matters would be a wiser choice. A professional person will also be insured against negligence and in the case of a solicitor, the Law Society's Compensation Fund could potentially be called upon to make good a loss in the unlikely event of dishonesty.

Charges

An attorney can only charge his or her out of pocket expenses for acting unless a specific provision is included permitting the attorney to charge for his or her services. It is unlikely that a professional attorney would take on the role unless he or she was permitted to charge and therefore a charging clause is essential.

There is, however, a problem with a charging clause. How are the charges to be assessed?

Once the power is registered with the Court of Protection (see below in the section 'Registration with the Court of Protection') then there are provisions to permit directions to be given on the question of costs but this does not apply until the power is registered. Even with solicitors there may be a problem in that, whilst a solicitor's charges must be fair and reasonable, the solicitor could be in a difficult position with a vulnerable client who may well accept any bill presented by the solicitor. Unless the solicitor submits his bill to himself as attorney and is then prepared to require himself to obtain a Remuneration Certificate from the Law Society to verify that the bill is fair and reasonable then there is no other way of controlling the costs other than to require the bill to be approved by some third party. Presumably the solicitor would not wish to challenge his own bill since he must consider it fair and reasonable in the first place. Trust in one's solicitor in such circumstances is therefore very important.

Accounts

A further problem with Powers of Attorney is that there is no routine procedure for checking up on what the attorney is doing with the donor's money. The attorney is not required to produce accounts. There are, however, some points to be made here to qualify that:

- as long as the donor is mentally capable then there is nothing to stop the donor requiring the attorney to produce accounts and evidence in support to the donor to show what has been going on;
- once the power has been registered with the Court of Protection (see above) then the court does have a right to demand accounts from the attorney but this would only happen if a complaint was made to the Court;
- one precaution that could be taken would be to provide in the Power that the attorney does have to produce accounts at intervals to some independent third party. Therefore, where there was a non-professional as the attorney, there could be a requirement to produce accounts to a solicitor or accountant for approval.

Registration with the Court of Protection

There is a safeguard built into the Enduring Powers of Attorney Act that requires the registration of the Power with the Court of Protection in certain circumstances. It must be emphasised that this is an entirely different procedure to making an application to the Court of Protection for the appointment of a Receiver as described in Chapter 5.

Application to register the power must be made if the donor:

- has become mentally incapable of managing his property and affairs; or
- is becoming mentally incapable of managing his property and affairs

The decision as to whether registration is required is that of the attorney. If the attorney has any doubts as to the donor's capacity then he or she would be prudent to consider obtaining a medical report if a doctor is prepared to give such a report without the donor's consent.

Sometimes an EPA is made and is immediately registered. The fact that a person is becoming mentally incapable of managing his affairs does not necessarily prevent him making the EPA as long as at the time he understands its nature and effect.

Failure to Register

If the donor has become, or starts to become, mentally incapable of managing his or her own affairs and the power is not registered then the attorney's powers are severely restricted until registration is effected.

The attorney can only:

- take steps to preserve the donor's estate (for example, to protect the donor's house from deteriorating);
- maintain the donor. It is assumed that this would include drawing money from a bank to pay nursing home fees but it would not be possible to, say, sell a property;
- maintain himself or other persons in so far as the Enduring Powers of Attorney Act 1985 permits him to do so. Curiously the power to maintain himself or other persons appears to be suspended during the registration process itself. It is a valid exercise of powers before registration and after registration but not during registration.

The power for the attorney to maintain himself and others is, in any event, limited.

Procedure for Registration

- In outline, the procedure for registration is that notice has to be given to the following individuals:

  a) the donor of the Power. Notice to the person who granted the Power of Attorney has to be given in *prescribed form* and the notice must be served personally on the donor, that is, it cannot be sent by post. This may sound traumatic. In reality it isn't. As long as no big deal is made of it, most older people readily accept a simple explanation of why they are being given the piece of paper concerned.

  b) the Co-Attorney. If one of a number of attorneys is registering, notice has to be given to the other attorney or attorneys in *prescribed form*.

  c) Relatives. Notice in *prescribed form* has to be given to at least three near relatives (if any). Included in the three to whom notice is given can be the attorney or attorneys if they are one/some of the relatives. To make up the number, if notice is given to one member of a class (for example children) then notice has to be

32

given to all members of that class (that is all the children). Therefore, if the *spouse* of the donor is given notice and to make up the three, notice is given to two children and there are a total of six children then all six children in addition to the spouse must be given notice.

There is an order of priority in respect of which notice must be given starting with the donor's spouse (which would include a separated but not divorced spouse) and finishing up with the children of the donor's uncles and aunts of the *whole blood.*

Relatives in a class who are under eighteen years old, or who are mentally incapable, or whose name and address is unknown and cannot be reasonably ascertained are not entitled to be notified.

Notice has to be given by first class post and is treated as given on the day when it is posted.

There are time limits within which notices have to be given to the various parties.

- Application for registration has to be lodged with the Court of Protection in *prescribed form* not later than ten days after notice has been given to the donor and every relative entitled to receive notice and every co-attorney.

- A fee of £220 must be paid. The Court has some powers to waive the fee.

- If no *valid objection* is received by the Court within five weeks and if no receiver has been appointed for the donor then automatic registration takes place and the Court then sends out the original Enduring Power of Attorney bearing the seal of the Court of Protection showing that it has been registered.

After Registration

After Registration with the Court of Protection the Enduring Power of Attorney must be registered with any financial institutions with which the attorney is going to have to deal on behalf of the donor.

The attorney can then proceed to deal with the affairs of the donor.

The registration of the power still confers no 'power over the person' either on the attorney or on the Court of Protection

When the donor dies, notice of that death must be given to the Court of Protection and the original power of attorney sent in for cancellation.

Gifts

A major issue closely tied in with Enduring Powers of Attorney is that of the ability of attorneys to make gifts of the donor's money or other property either to themselves or to others. It is frequently the case that when I am asked by relatives to advise on the subject of EPAs for their older relatives I am simultaneously asked for advice on the transfer of the donor's house or other money usually in the context of avoiding payment of home fees.

The position is relatively clear: an attorney can use the donor's property to make gifts in the following circumstances only:

- to make gifts of a seasonal nature to someone who is related to or connected with the donor ('seasonal' means seasonal according to the traditions of the community);
- to make gifts at the time of a birth or marriage, or on the anniversary of a birth or marriage, to someone who is related to or connected with the donor;
- to any charity to whom the donor has made or might be expected to make gifts.

These powers are subject to:

- the gift not being unreasonable having regard to all the circumstances and in particular the size of the donor's estate. In other words, a gift of £25 on the occasion of the birthday of a child of the donor where the donor only has £1000 might be unreasonable but the gift of £500 in similar circumstances from the estate of someone with £500,000 may not

- there being no restriction placed on making gifts in the power.

These cannot be extended in the power of attorney and if it were desired to make gifts greater than these or in other circumstances then this would have to be done personally by the donor if he or she is mentally capable of doing so.

After mental incapacity arises and the EPA has been registered, then it is open to the attorney to apply to the Court of Protection for permission to make a gift or gifts outside those narrow circumstances. It is, however, clear that the court will only give that permission if the gift is in the interest of the donor. Frequently such proposed gifts will not be in the interest of the donor but may well be in the interests of the person to whom it is proposed to make the gift.

The Court will consider applications to make gifts where these are being made with a view to Inheritance Tax planning although consent will only be granted if it is satisfied that the donor would wish to do so and can afford to make the gift.

As indicated, whilst the power to make gifts cannot be extended by the Power of Attorney the power to make gifts can be restricted.

In all cases a donor should discuss with his or her solicitor at the time of making the Power of Attorney whether there should be a limit placed on the ability of the attorney to make gifts.

It should be noted that there is a further provision that allows the attorney to benefit himself or others if the donor might be expected to provide for that person's needs and may do whatever the donor might be expected to do to meet those needs. The power can be exercised both before and after mental incapacity arises. The key word here appears to be 'needs' and not just 'wishes' and whether such provision is lawful will depend on all the circumstances. In my view, an attorney who makes such provision would need to consider the situation carefully since someone may well try to challenge the provision.

Donors should certainly consider imposing a restriction on the power to make such provision especially where the attorney is related to the donor or the attorney is related to a relative of the donor.

Making the Power

So having read the above, how does one go about making an Enduring Power of Attorney?

The making of an Enduring Power of Attorney is highly recommended in appropriate circumstances and is a step which can in the long term save the donor a significant amount of money and can save an enormous amount of distress, especially for the donor's family and friends.

However, as I have already made clear, the making of a power of attorney is a step that should not be treated lightly by the donor. It is important therefore that the donor makes that power when he or she is fit to make the power and is able to think clearly and without feeling pressured by circumstances and without feeling or, more importantly, being pressured by anyone else. It is also important that in making the power he or she has all the facts before him or her about the options for the making of the power including the options as to who should be appointed.

It is for this reason that while, as with most legal issues, the donor can make the power without legal assistance, it is highly inadvisable to do so.

It is clearly advisable from the donor's point of view to have the benefit of advice from an independent solicitor acting only on his or her behalf. It is also advisable from the attorney's point of view that such advice should be taken since there may be a serious risk that if an EPA is made without that advice, the attorney's actions could be questioned later, perhaps by an aggrieved or jealous or purely vindictive member of the family (or following the death of the donor, by a beneficiary of his or her estate). This will particularly be the case where the donor is old, ill or otherwise vulnerable at the time the power is made. Not only will the donor have the benefit of the advice of the solicitor, but any competent solicitor will, if need be, consider bringing in medical advice to certify as to the donor's capacity to make the power.

Relatives who consult solicitors about the making of a power of attorney by one of their family must understand that if the solicitor does take on the work then the client of the solicitor will be the donor and not the person making the enquiry and the solicitor will be expected to take proper precautions to ensure that the donor:

- is mentally capable of making the EPA;
- wants to make the EPA;
- is not under any pressure as to whether to make the power;
- is not under any pressure as to who to appoint; and
- generally considers the various options as to the provisions in the power of attorney.

As in all issues relating to older people, it is prudent to ensure that the solicitor who attends to see the older person should have experience in this area of work. The solicitor should not only know about EPAs but should also have an ability to relate to older people so that he or she can speak to them in a way which they can understand without being patronising and can also spot problems. It is often the case that an inexperienced solicitor may not only miss problems but also may see problems that are not there and may deny the older person the opportunity to make the power where he or she may not be totally free from mental health problems but does have sufficient capacity to make the power.

The solicitor must ensure that he or she sees the donor alone on at least one occasion so as to satisfy himself or herself that the donor is acting of his or her own free will. In my case I endeavour to see the donor twice alone: once to take instructions and discuss the options with the donor and on a second occasion to obtain the signature of the donor to the power. Wherever possible, and where time and the condition of the donor permits, I endeavour to send a copy of the proposed power of attorney to the donor along with some explanatory notes written in layman's terms in between the two visits. This allows the donor to consider the instructions given at his or her leisure and without any pressure. I always make it clear that the donor can change his or her mind. This is particularly important where I am being appointed the attorney.

It would be wholly inappropriate for a solicitor to prepare an Enduring Power of Attorney for an older client who the solicitor never sees.

It should be noted that to be valid, a donor has to read or have read to him or her the Notes on the front page of the prescribed form of the Enduring Power of Attorney. These notes are tedious and while they are allegedly in layman's language they are certainly not, especially when they have to be read to a frail older person who simply wants to hand over control of his or her affairs to someone else.

Following signature by the donor, the EPA also has to be signed by the attorney or attorneys.

After the EPA has been made

On the assumption that the Power of Attorney is not registered with the Court of Protection immediately after it has been made, then the power can either :

- be put away and forgotten until either the older person decides it is time to hand over control of his/her affairs or until the older person reaches a point where it has to be activated, or

- be brought into force immediately.

Whenever it is brought into force the EPA will have to be registered with any financial institutions with which the older person has dealings and with whom the Attorney(s) need to deal.

Readers should be aware that a few financial institutions are known to cause problems when it comes to registering Powers of Attorney. One bank is in the habit of insisting that if the Power of Attorney has not been registered with them within six months of being made (and has not been registered with the Court of Protection) then a letter from the donor must be produced confirming that the Power of Attorney is still to be treated as effective.

A building society has recently been known to assert that an Enduring Power of Attorney which has not been registered with the Court of Protection is ineffective for dealing with particular sorts of investments.

Our experience has been that standing one's ground with these institutions and, if need be, threatening to take legal action usually has the desired effect.

Always ask for their 'legal authority' for making such assertions.

Furthermore some financial institutions, despite what often junior staff may say, do not need to see the original EPA. It is sufficient if they see a certified photocopy. A 'certified copy' is one usually provided by a solicitor who certifies that each page is a true copy of the corresponding page of the original, and on the final page, also certifies that the whole document is a true and complete copy of the original document.

It is not possible to submit copies of certified photocopies unless those too are similarly certified.

Certified copies should be returned to the Attorney(s) after registration. Therefore, in most cases, no more than two or three certified copies are likely to be needed.

As long as the donor remains mentally capable of managing his or her own affairs there is nothing to stop the donor continuing to deal with his or her own affairs as well as the attorney. However, in practical terms, this is unwise since confusion may result and, indeed, the attorney may be exposed to allegations of improper conduct.

SUMMARY

- All older people should consider making an Enduring Power of Attorney.
- They should make it early when they clearly have mental capacity.
- They should think carefully about who they want to appoint and if more than one whether they should act jointly or jointly and severally.
- They should think carefully about the extent of the power they wish to give to the Attorney.
- They should consider restricting the Attorney's power to make gifts.
- They should only make an Enduring Power of Attorney after having the benefit of independent legal advice given to them in private.

CHAPTER 5

MANAGING AFFAIRS DURING LIFETIME – COURT OF PROTECTION AND APPOINTEESHIP

KEY POINTS

- A person who is mentally incapable of managing his or her own affairs and who has not made a valid Enduring Power of Attorney will need to have someone appointed to look after his or her financial affairs unless those affairs are minimal.

- If the person has only state benefits to be managed then a relative or friend can be made the *appointee* – but only in respect of state benefits.

- For all other matters a *Receiver* appointed by the Court of Protection will be needed.

- The receiver's and the court's powers only apply during the lifetime of the person concerned and relate only to his or her financial and related affairs.

- Neither the receiver nor the court can direct where the person shall live nor give directions as to medical treatment.

- Receivers must be mentally fit to undertake the task and be of integrity.

- A professional person such as a solicitor can be appointed as receiver.

- Patients are visited on occasions by the *Lord Chancellor's Visitor.*

- Significant changes in Court of Protection issues are on the way.

CHAPTER 5

MANAGING AFFAIRS DURING LIFETIME – COURT OF PROTECTION AND APPOINTEESHIP

THE ISSUE

We have already seen that if someone needs or may need their affairs handling on their behalf then they can, if they wish, sign an Enduring Power of Attorney. However, as we have also seen, to do this he or she must want to do it (and there is no power which can compel someone to do so who does not wish to do so) and they must have the mental capacity to do so.

If they have capacity and refuse to do so then that is the end of the matter. If, however, they have no mental capacity to make an EPA and if they are mentally incapable of managing their affairs then the jurisdiction of the Court of Protection can be invoked. However, Court of Protection involvement will only be needed if there is a property to be dealt with or if there are bank accounts, building society accounts or other forms of investment or other financial matters to be dealt with over and above state benefits.

If the only items to be dealt with are state benefits, then a procedure known as *Appointeeship* is available.

THE SOLUTION

1.   APPOINTEESHIP

If the only financial matters to be dealt with are state benefits such as State Retirement Pension and Attendance Allowance, Pension credit etc. then an appropriate person (a relative, friend etc.) can apply to the Department for Work and Pensions (DWP) for their appointment as '*Appointee*'. When they make that application they will be interviewed by an Officer from the DWP to ensure that they are a proper person to be able to receive state benefits on behalf of an incapacitated person and if approved as the appointee they will become responsible for all issues in connection with the older person's state benefits and will be able to draw the benefits and make application for other benefits on behalf of the older person. They will be responsible for notifying changes in the older person's circumstances to the DWP.

Appointeeship can be a useful means of accessing some monies even whilst an application to the Court of Protection is proceeding.

Once a Court of Protection Order is made then it supersedes the appointeeship and the powers of the appointee come to an end. It may well be the case that the Receiver would be told by the DWP that the appointee has to consent to the change of responsibility.

This is not the case. The DWP's own rules are clear in that Receivership (and indeed a Power of Attorney) supersedes automatically the appointeeship. This can be important if someone has been made the appointee and someone else, perhaps in a move to properly manage the older person's affairs, becomes the Receiver.

2.   THE COURT OF PROTECTION

The Court of Protection is a little known branch of the Supreme Court which deals with the financial affairs of the mentally disordered. It is based in London.

Its administrative arm is the *Public Guardianship Office (PGO)* (formerly the Public Trust Office) and it is this office with which most contact is had when the Court of Protection becomes involved in a person's affairs.

Even as one who has a great deal of contact with the court, I have not been able to clearly identify where the dividing lines between responsibilities fall.

It has to be said that the Court of Protection (and by this term I include the whole of the organisation) has not had a good press over many years. The reasons for this are unclear but the root cause is probably under-funding resulting in under-staffing and inadequately experienced and trained staff.

At the time of writing there have been signs of significant improvement. (Regrettably, the Court may well experience further turmoil now that it is likely to be revamped as a result of the Mental Capacity Bill currently passing through Parliament.) Nonetheless, no one should be under the impression that acting as a receiver is easy. Many clients have told me that they would never again take on receivership.

It is perhaps appropriate at this point to say that before taking on appointment as a receiver you should be entirely sure that:

- you have the time to give to it;
- you are physically and mentally capable of undertaking the role;
- you are emotionally capable of taking on the role;
- you are not responsible for the affairs or well-being of too many other friends/relatives at the time;

- there is nothing in your background which would make you unfit for taking on the role, such as a criminal record.

Above all, you should not take on the role simply because you feel that you 'ought'.

Have in mind that if you take on the role and later find out that you can no longer continue, then a new receiver will have to be appointed at some considerable expense to the person whose affairs you are managing and at some considerable disruption to the management of those affairs.

The Application

The starting point for an application to the court is the obtaining of a medical report. This is obtained on a form prescribed by the court and almost always has to be provided by a Registered Medical Practitioner who can be either the patient's GP or hospital doctor or specialist. By 'patient' is meant the person who is mentally incapable.

Some doctors are superb when asked to provide reports.

Regrettably, there are others who are quite appalling even when their palms are greased with silver. In many instances, I suspect this is due to fear of committing themselves. (The fee recommended by the British Medical Association for providing a medical report in these circumstances is (in April 2003) £100.50 where an examination is required and £50.00 where no examination is necessary).

In the rare case that an attending doctor simply declines to provide a report then it is possible to obtain one from any Registered Medical Practitioner who is prepared to provide one.

Having obtained the report (and on the assumption that the doctor confirms that the '*patient*' is mentally incapable of managing his or her affairs) the next step is the completion of:

1. The *Statement of Client's Assets and Income* which is a lengthy document prescribed by the court requiring the insertion of full details of the client's financial affairs, both income and capital, and debts and information of a more personal nature such as religion, involvement in religious activity, possession of driving licence etc. The completion of this form can be difficult. Frequently, those making applications to the court lack even quite basic information about the patient's financial affairs. This can be the case even where they are quite

closely connected. This can arise:

- because the patient still lives at home and maintains an often obsessive control of their paperwork;
- because the patient has always been 'discreet' about financial matters even with his or her closest family;
- because of the chaotic nature of the patient's affairs either because that is how he or she has always lived his or her life or because as their mental state has deteriorated their affairs have become increasingly disorganised;
- because information and documents have been taken from the patient or the patient's house by others, either with the patient's alleged authority or without it. This may have happened in good faith and in a genuine attempt to help the patient. It may have been done as part of a course of financial abuse. It may simply have been done to prevent others having control of the patient's affairs;
- because virtually every institution has become terrified of giving information for fear of breaching the Data Protection Act. Unfortunately, there is no consistency in approach by institutions. Some are more terrified of the Act than others. I have recently encountered an electricity supplier who would not supply a direct debiting mandate for payment for supply to a mentally incapacitated customer without production of an order of the court, claiming that to do so would be in breach of the Act. Others readily supply such documents. The cynical may say that the latter is concern for profits above respect for the law; I would prefer to call it realistic.

It follows from the above that those who are getting older need to give careful consideration to ensuring that they write down and keep up to date (so far as they are able) information about their assets and life which may well be relevant to those who ultimately have to assume responsibility for their affairs. They do not need to disclose the information prematurely – simply commit it to paper and keep it or deposit it where it can be found. I have included in Appendix 3 a list of information which older people should consider writing down for reference by others

This list is not exhaustive. Each person must think about his or her own circumstances.

The Statement of Client's Assets and Income is completed by the person making the application to the court whether or not he or she is seeking his or her own appointment as receiver.

2. The *Receiver's Declaration*. This is completed by the person who it is proposed should be appointed receiver. It is again in a form prescribed by the court, giving personal information and information as to their suitability for appointment as receiver. This form also requires the proposed receiver to give various undertakings to the court about they way in which he or she will conduct themselves.

As indicated above, appointment as receiver can be a burdensome obligation, particularly for those of advancing years or who suffer from ill-health, and this form tries to ensure that the proposed receiver understands what he or she is taking on and that they do have the ability to undertake the tasks.

3. *Notification letters*. These are 'letters', again in a form prescribed by the court, which have to be sent to all relatives and close associates of the patient informing them of the intention to apply to the court for the appointment of the receiver and giving them the chance to object. The letters also list all those to whom notice is being given.

The Statement of Clients Assets and Income, the Receiver's Declaration and the Medical Certificate are then sent to the court along with a copy of the patient's will and a cheque for the court fee (currently £230) and often an additional fee of (currently) £160 where an order for the sale of property is being requested.

The Public Guardianship Office does have power to waive its fees in certain circumstances.

Following the submission the Public Guardianship Office will send a letter to the applicant addressed to the patient that informs the patient of the intention to appoint a receiver. It gives the patient the opportunity to make representations to the court about the appointment of a receiver and the proposed receiver in particular. It is the job of the applicant to arrange for the letter to be served on the patient. The applicant does not have to do this himself or herself but the letter does have to be handed to the patient in person. It has to be left with him or her. The person serving the letter will then have to sign a *Certificate of Service* giving details of the time and place of service and an indication of whether it appeared that the patient had understood the implications of the letter. This latter point is of fairly recent origin. That certificate has to be sent to the court.

Whilst a date for the hearing of the application is given by the Court it is rare for the applicant or anyone else to have to attend.

During this period the PGO may well ask for additional information about the patient's affairs. How much further information is requested at this stage will depend on how well the original application has been prepared.

Also during this period the court may give 'interim directions' for any urgent steps that may need to be taken in respect of the person's affairs.

The Making of the Order

- On the assumption that there are no objections the court will make an order appointing the receiver. However, before the order is issued the court will usually require the receiver to give security to guarantee performance of his or her obligations. This is effectively an insurance policy to guard against default by the receiver. The receiver can make his or her own arrangements for this or can adopt a simplified procedure arranged by the court with HSBC Insurance Brokers. This involves the receiver signing an application and paying the premium for the 'bond' to the insurers and the insurers notify the court that the bond is in place. Bonds are required in virtually every case.

- The court then issues the order (known as the *First General Order*). Copies of the order are then sent to the receiver and the receiver must then implement the terms of the order. The receiver can only do such things as are permitted by the order. He or she cannot simply go off on a frolic of his or her own.

  A further fee (currently £300) is now payable.

This implementation of the terms of the order will usually involve:

- sending an *office copy* of the order to each financial institution with which the patient has dealings. An office copy can be identified because it bears the impressed seal of the Court in the bottom right hand corner;

- withdrawing monies from those institutions where the court has ordered they be withdrawn and sending them to the Court Funds Office in London for investment by the court;

- withdrawing monies ordered by the court and using them for the patient's benefit;

- arranging for the opening of a *receivership bank account* into which it is advisable that all incoming monies are paid and from which any bills are paid;

- arranging (where permitted by the court and where necessary and appropriate) for the clearance of the patient's house and the disposal of the contents (see below for further comment on this);

- terminating any tenancy under which the patient's house is held where the patient is not going to continue to live there;

- selling the patient's house (see below for further comment on this);

- arranging to receive any benefits to which the patient is entitled – this may include state retirement pension, attendance allowance, disability living allowance, pension credit etc.;

- arranging to receive any occupational pensions to which the patient may be entitled;

- dealing with the patient's tax affairs (an office copy of the *First General Order* will need to be sent to the Inland Revenue);

- thereafter generally managing the patient's financial affairs on a day-to-day basis and where necessary referring issues to the court for decision. Such issues may be the incurring of unusual expenditure such as holidays, private health treatment etc.

The Lord Chancellor's Visitor

Within a month or so of the making of the order it is likely that the patient will receive a visit from the Lord Chancellor's Visitor. This is an official from the Court of Protection who checks on the general well-being of the patient and makes sure that his or her living accommodation is satisfactory and that he or she is receiving the appropriate state benefits and that his or her needs are being provided for. The receiver will be notified of the visit and is welcome to attend but this is not compulsory. Receivers may well find it useful to be present and will find the Visitor supportive. The Visitor may well only visit once or may keep the patient on his or her list and visit again subsequently especially where there are any ongoing issues about the patient or where the patient has no other regular visitors.

Annual Accounts

Every year the receiver will have to complete a detailed Annual Account to show what he or she has done with the patient's money. It is for this reason that paying all monies received into the *receivership bank account* and paying all monies from the account is invaluable.

Ending of the Receivership on death

It is important to note that the powers of the receiver and the court end at the moment the patient dies. The responsibility for the patient's affairs then passes to the patient's *executor* or *administrator*. The receiver will in all probability have to prepare, and have approved by the court, accounts for the final period up to the date of death and the court, on production of a grant of probate or letters of administration, will hand over any monies which may have been paid into court during the receivership. If solicitors have been involved any outstanding costs that are owed to them will need either to be agreed with the executor or administrator or will need to be assessed by the court.

Miscellaneous points

The choice of receiver

Having outlined the steps in the receivership and it having become apparent that receivership is no easy task it is worth again reiterating that receivership should not be undertaken lightly or by anyone who does not have the stamina, especially mental stamina, to complete it. The receiver must be someone of integrity; who can read and write to a reasonable level and who is organised. He or she should be able to resist pressure, possibly from the patient or from the family or others, to do things which may be inappropriate. A person who has been bankrupt or who has a track record of poor financial management would probably not be appointed. If the proposed receiver knows that he or she does not have the appropriate qualities then he or she should not seek appointment. Unnecessary costs will be incurred if he or she has to give up the receivership and another receiver has to be appointed.

The person who makes the application

It should be emphasised that the person who makes the application to the court does not have to be the person appointed. Anyone who is aware that the affairs of someone need managing can make the application but can ask for the appointment of someone else as receiver. If there is no one to be appointed then the court can appoint a *Panel Receiver* who is very often a solicitor who has indicated a willingness to act as a receiver in cases where there is no one else available. Sometimes, however, this will not be necessary since the person making the application, or who has concerns about the affairs of someone else, will consult a local solicitor who will themselves make the application and will seek his or her own appointment as receiver. It should be stressed, however, that by no means all solicitors are prepared to take on Court of Protection matters and it is important that a person looking for a solicitor to deal with a Court of Protection matter should ensure that the solicitor does have some experience of such matters.

The solicitor's charges for dealing with such matters are paid out of the estate of the patient and it must be borne in mind that the solicitor is the patient's solicitor – not the receiver's solicitor. At all times the duty of solicitor lies to the patient and not the receiver

The powers of the receiver and the court

The powers of the receiver and the court relate only to the patient's financial affairs. They do not relate directly to the care of the patient or to the patient's medical treatment or to where the patient should live. However, in reality, the receiver may have some influence on these matters. This is because the receiver is responsible for the proper management of the patient's finances and thus does ultimately have some responsibility for the care of the patient to the extent of ensuring that the patient is properly provided for. The court also can have some indirect influence on the patient's care because the court must ensure that the patient is properly provided for and would need to be consulted on issues of major expenditure such as to the provision of private health care.

As made clear elsewhere in this book, actual decisions as to treatment will be made by doctors taking into account any informed wishes which the patient is able to express or which the patient may have properly recorded prior to him or her becoming ill in the form of an *Advance Directive or Living Will*. If the patient has expressed a wish for a particular person to be consulted then the doctors may well take into account the views of that person. In the event of any controversy as to treatment or if there is any question of the lawfulness of any particular treatment then the matter may well have to be referred to the High Court for a decision when all parties will be entitled to be represented including someone appointed to act on behalf of the patient.

Orders to investigate and report

In cases where there is missing information as to a patient's affairs, as soon as the medical certificate has been filed at Court it is open to the Court to make directions authorising someone to investigate the patient's affairs and to report to the Court as a preliminary to the making of full application for receivership.

In appropriate circumstances and where there is a clear urgency the Court can make an Order appointing a receiver ad interim in order that that person can take steps to secure the estate of the patient again prior to a full application for receivership having been made. This step may be useful where there is a suspicion of fraud or urgent steps need to be taken in other directions to protect the affairs of the patient.

Interim directions

Once an application for receivership has been made, the Court can be asked to make interim directions. This can be useful where access to monies is needed in order to pay home fees whilst a fuller and substantive application for receivership is progressing. Interim directions can also be made authorising the sale of a property or, for example, for the termination of a tenancy and the disposal of assets or authorising the re-direction of post or, in one case in which the writer was involved, the uplifting of a motor vehicle which was parked outside the patient's house and was owned by the patient and which was in danger of being vandalised.

Costs

On the assumption that solicitors have been instructed to make the application to the Court for receivership then their costs will be payable out of the patient's estate.

The solicitors can elect either to take fixed costs or to have their costs assessed by the Court. It is likely that the solicitors will take fixed costs in a simple matter in an amount laid down by the Court. If, however, the solicitors are of the view that they have done more work than would be covered by the fixed amount of costs then they can have their costs assessed by the Court.

The court does have power to waive its own fees in certain limited cases.

Short orders

In some cases, usually where a patient's assets are small, the Court may make a Short Order. This is an order addressed to an individual authorising him or her to take certain limited steps to deal with the patient's affairs. This could, for example, be to access money to pay outstanding debts and thereafter to open a bank account and to use the remaining monies for the patient's benefit.

Unfortunately, for a short order to be made the basic procedure to be followed and the requirement for documents to be submitted is essentially the same as for a full receivership.

Sale of Property

This is often the reason why people consult solicitors about their older relative's affairs: they need to sell the property.

It is prudent to ensure that the Court of Protection application is under way before the property is put on the market since otherwise a buyer may be found and the sale is delayed whilst waiting for the Court of Protection Orders to follow.

It should be noted that estate agents fees for selling property are restricted. These can only be exceeded with permission.

As estate agent should be made aware that it is a Court of Protection matter before engagement.

It should also be noted that before a sale price will be authorised by the Court, a Certificate of Value from a suitably qualified/experienced valuer will be required.
This may cause some difficulties where a private sale is negotiated.

CHAPTER 6

INFORMATION AND SKELETONS

KEY POINTS

- Most families have a skeleton or two in their cupboard.

- Older people need to appreciate that the time may come, whether in lifetime or in death, when his or her affairs need to be dealt with by other people.

- To deal with those affairs efficiently and properly the person who undertakes the task must have full information.

- Older people should ensure that they disclose for the benefit of those managing their affairs all skeletons in their past and all information about their finances that may be relevant or may have an impact on the way in which their affairs are dealt with.

- If need be, such information could be kept in such a way that it would only come to light following the older person's death.

CHAPTER 6

INFORMATION AND SKELETONS

THE ISSUES

An issue that solicitors often see arising is that of what can loosely be described as 'lack of information' and sometimes may be described as 'lack of delicate information'.

Most families have a skeleton in the cupboard: in some cases there can be numerous skeletons. It is often late in life or even still later, at the time of a death, that these skeletons have a habit of emerging.

At a basic level, those who will be responsible for looking after someone's affairs during their lifetime will need all manner of information ranging from the date of birth of the person concerned through to precise details of their finances. Failure to have that information can lead to a great deal of wasted time and money. Financial resources which may be available may go unclaimed.

Following a death, information is needed for various reasons.

The death will have to be registered. Information about the deceased will be needed for that purpose. That information needs to be accurate.

Information will be needed about precisely what financial assets and liabilities the deceased had.

Additionally, if there is no will and consequently an *intestacy*, it will have to be decided who receives the estate. In many instances, where there is a small and compact family, this does not cause a problem. In other cases where it appears there are no relatives, much time and vast expense is often incurred in an attempt to track down any relatives who will be entitled. Frequently these relatives will have been completely unknown to the deceased. Sometimes there can be very close relatives who are 'missing', for example:

- the illegitimate child born to the deceased when she was very young and the child was informally adopted and never mentioned again;
- the child fathered as the result of a 'one night stand';
- the child estranged from the parents in a bitter row years before and never seen or heard from again.

All these (and many others) are the potential source of enormous problems after death.

I would like to say that the making of a will solves or avoids these problems in all cases. I can't and it won't. In many cases the problem will be solved by making a will but only if there is a full and frank disclosure of the facts at the time the will is made even if the information is not made known to the family until after death.

PROBLEMS OF ADDRESSING THE ISSUE

Some of us live our lives completely openly with no secrets.

On the other hand there are those who are 'private'. This may arise for various reasons including:

- When we are young our image is important and we don't want to give anything away about ourselves for fear that it will tarnish our image or make us vulnerable to attack. Hopefully, as we grow older we will lose this and say 'sod it'.
- There are those who have had to adopt a cloak of secrecy and discretion for their own preservation or the protection of their families. This is particularly evident in many older people from Eastern European backgrounds who came to the UK after the war and may have a 'history' which they would rather keep confidential. Frequently, they have wives and families in Eastern Europe who are in the past and who they wish for whatever reason not to mention. This may well be repeated as asylum seekers come to the UK from unstable or violent regimes.
- They have some perceived skeleton in the background such as an illegitimacy, a family feud, a criminal record, a bankruptcy, an early and short marriage (and possibly one which has never been properly brought to an end) a bigamous marriage and so on.
- They come from an era when to be private was the norm and discussion of such issues as illegitimacy was simply unacceptable.
- Many people are very guarded about their finances. They simple do not discuss 'money' or allow anyone, however close, to know anything about their finances.

Depending upon the circumstances, they may simply have never discussed the relevant facts with anyone else or may have sworn to secrecy those who know the facts. They certainly may not want to tell their close family the facts or they may not want to let them be known outside the close family.

It is not for us to question their feelings or their reasons. It is for us to try to make sure that we do have the facts wherever possible and wherever we may possibly need the information for the purpose of properly dealing with their affairs.

THE ANSWER

From the point of the view of the 'child' who reads this book, the simple and, indeed, simplistic answer is to gather together the information that will be necessary for him or her to deal with the parents' (or indeed, of course, any other relevant relatives') affairs:

- as they grow older and become unable to manage their own affairs; and/or
- on their deaths.

That, of course, may be much easier said than done if there is reluctance on the child's part to ask or on the parent's part to tell.

There is also, of course, the problem that the child does not necessarily know that he or she doesn't know what he or she ought and needs to know! In other words the child may not know of the existence of the skeleton.

To get round some of these problems I have set out in the Appendix 3 of this book a list of information that an older person should make known, and which 'a child' ought to have and which he or she should try to obtain as early as possible and before the parent either lapses into mental incapacity or dies. Much of this information is innocent but some is delicate.

But how does the child deal with the problem of the questions that he or she doesn't know to ask and the parent doesn't volunteer? I have no perfect solution to this. Much will depend on what access the child has to the parent's more confidential papers. If there is access to such papers then a careful study of such things as:

- birth, marriage, death and baptismal certificates;
- old wills;
- grants of probate and grants of letters of administration;
- estate and distribution accounts from solicitors or banks following a death;
- family photographs;
- family bibles containing details of family events;
- newspaper cuttings;
- employment or service records;

may well prove fruitful.

A careful examination of such documents tying in dates and names etc. may provide useful clues to 'missing' relatives. One example is the fact that a birth certificate showing a time of birth (in addition to the date of birth) would indicate a multiple birth (for example, twins).

However, it is not only what is there but also what is not there that might be interesting:

- Is there, for instance, a surprising lack of documents? Most people have a box, a briefcase or a drawer where these things are kept.
- Is there, for instance, no marriage certificate? Does this indicate that the parents were not married?
- Is there only a short form birth certificate? Does this indicate a possible illegitimacy because a full one would disclose that the father is not named or is someone other than the man the child believes is the father?
- Are pages missing from documents such as bibles or address books?
- Is there a great deal of information about one child but none or only a little about another?

Conversations now or half remembered conversations in the past with parents or other relatives may give clues to possible secrets. Has there been a reluctance to talk about the past or a particular period in the past or about particular people? Has the conversation been changed when particular topics have been raised? Are there any gaps in the parental history? Without becoming paranoid is there anything which arouses suspicion?

In addition to asking about such issues there may of course be other ways of filling in the gaps:

- a look back at *electoral records* for a particular period might disclose someone additional living at an address (or, indeed, someone not living at an address when they should have been);
- normal family history research using birth, death, baptism and marriage records;
- in serious cases the employment of genealogists to do family research may assist.

You will recall, from the blurb surrounding this book and from the preface that this book is not just intended to be read by children. It is also hoped that parents may read it, perhaps at the request or invitation of children. It may well be that a parent reading this book and these words in particular may realise the importance of coming clean and disclosing information which has been kept hidden. This will:

- make the lives of their children easier when they have to deal with the parental affairs;
- make sure that their estate goes where they want it to go or where it should go rather than leaving it to the vagaries of the law;
- fill in gaps in their children's life histories and about which they may yearn to know but have been afraid to ask;
- fill in information which may (in its absence) have medical consequences for their children such as possible genetic disorders. This could perhaps arise where a 'father' is not in fact the father of the child and the true father has some genetic condition which may cause problems when the child comes to have children of his or her own – this might arise from issues of illegitimacy or *AID* (Artificial Insemination by Donor);
- fill in information which in its absence may lead the child into what would be an unknowing but unlawful relationship such as incest or a marriage within the prohibited degrees; this is an ever-increasing risk not just because of hidden relationships in the past but also because of the recent developments in medical science and fertility treatments; it is interesting to note that there are now two thousand births each year arising from *AID* where the donor is anonymous; a child born prior to 1990 by such methods had no right to any information about the donor and even after that date the information which can be given is only sufficient for the child to ensure that he or she is not marrying within the prohibited degrees; in consequence, a full and frank disclosure by those who know the facts could at least provide the child with the basic information he or she needs about his or her past.

FINALLY

Although I have stressed the need for disclosure of information, it may well be that there is some information which the older person simply cannot bear to disclose to family during lifetime. Whilst it is regrettable in this day and age that this should be the case, nonetheless it may be so. In that event the older person should consider disclosing information in such a way that it does not come to light until after death or until as late in life as possible.

This could be achieved by writing the information down, sealing it in an envelope and keeping it with one's personal papers but in such a way that it can be found and will not be overlooked. As an alternative, the envelope can be placed – possibly along with your other papers, such as your Will and/or your Deeds etc.– with solicitors with a direction that it should be opened only in certain circumstances.

As long as those solicitors are known about and are contacted when the need arises it should solve the problem.

What if an older person is concerned as to whether a piece of information is likely to be relevant? The answer here is to consult solicitors and discuss that with them in confidence. Preferably the solicitor concerned should be someone experienced in dealing with the affairs of older people and who will appreciate the possible significance of what the older person is troubled by and its practical effects on how that person's affairs are ultimately dealt with.

CHAPTER 7

THE WILL – INTRODUCTION

KEY POINTS

- For various (often illogical) reasons people fail or refuse to make a will.

- Wills deals with a range of issues – not just giving away your belongings and money.

- Failure to make a will may well result in your assets going to people you do not want them to go to and not going to the people you do want them to go to.

- Failure to make a will may well mean that someone wholly inappropriate or dishonest looks after your affairs following your death.

- You must be mentally capable of making a will and you must make it of your own free will.

- Home made wills are dangerous. A competent solicitor preparing a will will ensure that you are mentally capable and not making it under any pressure and will ensure it is correctly prepared, signed and witnessed.

- Failure to follow the rules of signing and witnessing a will can invalidate the will.

CHAPTER 7

THE WILL – INTRODUCTION

THE ISSUE

The issue here is straightforward: we all have some property that we will leave behind when we die, however little it may be. For most of us there will be a sum that will improve the lot of whoever we choose to leave it to. If we fail to make a will the law will operate and provide how our estate will pass. This may or may not be what we would want. We may well leave behind great bitterness within our family. We may well do great injustice. We may well deprive those who ought to receive our estate from receiving anything at all. We may well finish up allowing those who should not on any sensible ground receive anything at all to receive everything. But it is not only just about how our estate will pass. The making of wills is about a range of other matters where, if we do not make provision, the law will step in and make provision or we will simply leave behind a problem.

An important point

Husbands and wives tend to assume that everything they have will pass to the other. In the absence of a will, that is not necessarily the case. If a husband dies then (setting aside any assets in the joint names of himself and his wife) his wife will receive

(a)   the *personal chattels*;
(b)   £125,000;
(c)   a life interest in half the remainder (that is, the income for life from half of any other assets);
         the other half of the remainder goes to the children as will the half in which the wife has a life interest when she dies.

Additionally, inheritance tax may well be payable on that part of the estate which goes to the children.

If there are no children then the wife will get

(a)   the personal chattels;
(b)   £200,000;
(c)   half the remainder absolutely.

The parents, if alive, take the other half of the remainder absolutely and in equal shares if both survive.

If there are no children and no parents then the wife will take

(a)   the personal chattels;
(b)   £200,000;
(c)   half the remainder absolutely.

The brothers and sisters (and issue of predeceased brothers and sisters) of the whole blood take the other half of the remainder absolutely.

PROBLEMS OF ADDRESSING THE ISSUE

People fail to make wills for a number of reasons:

- they mistakenly believe they have nothing worthwhile with which to deal;
- they fail to appreciate that wills deal with things other than just money and property;
- they do not understand the laws of *intestacy* (that is, what will happen if there is no will);
- they believe that making a will tempts providence and they will die;
- they think that it is expensive to do;
- they think they are too young;
- they never think about it;
- they are simply perverse.

THE ANSWER

Make a will.

In the following chapters we will look at the essential issues that a will should address but before doing so we will look at what a will is and how it should be made.

WHAT IS A WILL?

A will can be defined as: 'a declaration in [prescribed form] of the intention of the person making it of the [matters] which he wishes to take effect [on or after his death] until which time it is [revocable]'.

Points from the definition

(a)   It has to be in prescribed form. The Law lays down how it should be prepared:

(i)   It must be in writing.

(ii) It must be signed at the foot or end.

(iii) The signature must be witnessed by two adult witnesses who do not benefit under the will and are not close relatives of someone who does benefit.

(iv) The signatures of the person making the will (the testator) and the two witnesses must be made in each other's presence.

Two points emerge out of these requirements:

(i)   If someone is to benefit under the will neither he nor she nor anyone closely related should witness the testator's signature on the will.

(ii) Always ensure that the witnesses and the *testator* are all together when they each sign on the will. In other words the *testator* arranges for two independent witnesses to be present with him or her. The *testator* signs; the first witness signs; the second witness signs. Only then do the parties go their separate ways.

(b) It deals with 'matters'. That is, it is not confined solely to giving away property. It should deal with other things as well. The usual things that it will deal with are as follows:

- making provision for people to be able to use your house or other items for a limited period. This may be to permit your unmarried son or daughter (or, indeed any other person) to live in your house for a time after your death and before the house is sold and the proceeds divided between all your children or other beneficiaries;
- the appointment of executors. Executors are the people who will look after your affairs after you have died;
- the appointment of guardians. Guardians are the people who would assume legal responsibility for any of your children who are under eighteen years old at the time of your death;
- laying down how your money should be invested for anyone not entitled to receive it absolutely immediately following your death (that is, if it is for any reason held in trust for someone whether that be children under eighteen years old or others);
- setting out what should happen to any animals you have at the time of your death;
- giving funeral directions;
- giving other directions to your executors on issues following your death.

(c) It only operates on death. It is important to keep in mind that it cannot affect the lifetime position. It can only operate on the position as found at death. For example, if you made a will in 1995 and made a gift of a stamp collection in that will to cousin Billy and then in 1998 you sold the stamp collection and if you were to die in 2002 Billy will not get the stamp collection or the money representing it. This is commonsense but it is easily forgotten.

(d) It is revocable until death. As long as you have mental capacity to do so then you can revoke the will at any time before you die.

WHO CAN MAKE A WILL?

There are only two requirements as to who can make a will:

(a) The first requirement is that a person must be eighteen years of age or over.
(b) The second requirement is that he or she must have an intention to make a will.

This second point is most critical.

(a) You must be mentally capable of making a will.

In other words the testator must be of 'sound disposing mind'.

Testamentary capacity can be affected obviously by simple mental incapacity or it could be affected by drugs.

In either case you may well not be able to make a will.

This emphasises the need for early action before the *testator* becomes so ill that he is not able to make the will.

It must be appreciated that if a testator makes a will and those who would have benefited under the laws of intestacy had no will been made (or those who benefited under a previous will but who do not benefit under the existing will) may well challenge the will after the death of the *testator* and claim that the *testator* was not up to making the will.

What steps can be taken to avoid this challenge?

It is important that wills should be made by solicitors. A competent solicitor will consider carefully whether the *testator* has clear mental capacity to make the will and if he has any doubts at all will obtain advice from a doctor and, if need be, a psychiatrist. He may well think it prudent to have the *testator's* signature to the will witnessed by one doctor and possibly two.

and

(b) It must be made of your own free will, that is, not under pressure.

This calls for great care.

This is one of the reasons why homemade wills are treated with some suspicion. There may be little evidence of the circumstances in which the will came to be made even if the signing and witnessing has been properly carried out. Who is to know that a person has not been bullied into making the will? It is not only unscrupulous relatives who may press someone into making a will. I have seen instances of clergymen exercising malevolent influence over their flock. *Dr Shipman* of course resorted to outright forgery in his activities.

A solicitor taking instructions for a will will be on the look out for advantage being taken of aged, sick or otherwise vulnerable testators. A competent solicitor will want to see the *testator* at least once entirely on their own without anyone else being present except possibly (all other things being equal) their husband or wife.

A competent solicitor would use the services of an independent and able interpreter if the testator did not have a good command of English or who communicated by sign language.

Virtually any reputable relative would want to ensure that a solicitor had prepared the documentation and was present when it was signed. Most responsible solicitors would be loath to prepare such a document and not see it signed themselves. Relatives and others who try to persuade *testators* to make a will without professional involvement (or who take the older person to someone who is not their regular solicitor where the testator has had a recent or ongoing relationship with that solicitor) must be viewed with suspicion.

HOME MADE WILLS

There is no requirement that solicitors should be instructed by someone who wishes to make a will.

As with most jobs undertaken by professionals or tradesman there will inevitably be those who do not think that it is necessary to employ a professional to carry out the work because they feel that they are capable of undertaking the task themselves or who simply do not want to pay for a professional to do the work.

There are, however, very clear reasons why a solicitor should be employed, some of which we have already touched on:

a)   A competent solicitor will be on the look out for possible lack of *testamentary capacity* on the part of the testator. If the will is called into question the solicitor should be able to give evidence as to why he or she considered the testator had capacity. If the testator has made the will themselves there may be no such evidence available. This may lead to the will being overturned.

b)   A competent solicitor will be on the look out for a testator being under pressure to make the will. Again hopefully, the competent solicitor will have taken reasonable steps to try to satisfy himself or herself that the testator was making the will of his or her own free will and will be able to give evidence as to those circumstances. Again where a testator has made his or her own will there may well be no-one who can give independent evidence as to the circumstances in which the will came to be made and that the will was made free from pressure. This may lead to the will being overturned.

c)   In taking instructions for a will, a solicitor will be listening carefully to what he or she is told and will be asking relevant questions to try to ensure that the will which is being made is the will which is most appropriate taking into account not only the testator's wishes but also the testator's circumstances. The solicitor will, for example, be alive to the possible challenges of the will by a former spouse, or others, who may be entitled to challenge the will under the Inheritance (Provision for Family and Dependants) Act 1975 (as subsequently amended) and be able to advise the testator on what, if any, steps are open to him or her to try to reduce the chances of such a challenge.

d)   The solicitor will take into account the circumstances of property ownership by the testator and whether bricks and mortar are actually owned by the testator in his or her sole name or in joint names and if it is held in joint names precisely how it is held. This too may have an impact on the way in which the will is prepared.

e)   The solicitor will have experience of the use of particular terminology. The solicitor will know that certain terms have precise meanings in law and will either avoid using those terms or alternatively use them quite deliberately to achieve the desired result.

The layman is unlikely to have knowledge of such terms.

f)   Even highly intelligent layman can, when it comes to setting out their thoughts clearly and in a way which are not capable of ambiguous interpretation, have some difficulty.

g)   The opportunity of talking through one's circumstances and requirements with a totally disinterested third party, who has only your interests at heart, can be a very worthwhile experience. It can prompt you to think about things which you would not otherwise have thought of or think about things in a way in which you would not have done.

h)   Solicitors should be able to provide you with a means of storing your will safely once it has been made.

i)   A solicitor will ensure that the will is signed in the correct and effective way.

j)   Solicitors are insured against any acts of negligence that they may commit in making the will.

Overall have in mind that there is a real danger that attempting to make a will yourself may result in the whole of your wishes being thwarted, possibly, by a simple error. Consider carefully, therefore, whether it is prudent to try to make the will yourself. Family should consider whether it is really worth encouraging their older relatives to make a will without the assistance of a solicitor just to save a few pounds.

CHAPTER 8

THE WILL – THE EXECUTORS

KEY POINTS

- Executors are the people who will deal with your affairs on your death.

- The choice of Executors is often as important as to whom you leave your estate.

- Executors should be local, mentally and physically capable (including at the time you die), preferably younger than you (and this is particularly important as you get older) and above all, be honest and have integrity.

- In addition to friends and relatives, banks and professional people such as solicitors can be appointed.

- Beneficiaries under the will can be Executors although sometimes it is not appropriate.

- The number of Executors appointed is a matter of choice. Two is a good number. Substitutes should be provided in case the first die or are unavailable.

- Executors have no power or rights or responsibilities until the testator has died.

CHAPTER 8

THE WILL – THE EXECUTORS

We turn now to one of the other 'issues' which should be considered when thinking about making a will – the choice of *executors*

Executors are the people who are appointed in a will to look after the affairs of the *testator* after he or she has died.

The importance of the appointment of *executors* in the process of will making is frequently underrated. The layman thinking of making a will may spend a great deal of time thinking about how to divide his or her estate amongst beneficiaries. He or she will, however, often give little real thought to the choice of *executors* who may, in appropriate circumstances, have to exercise considerable discretion in the administration of the estate and possibly extending over many years where a trust is created.

SO, WHAT DOES SOMEONE MAKING A WILL HAVE TO CONSIDER ABOUT EXECUTORS?

Much will depend upon what there is in the estate, who is to benefit and when and who there are available to act as executors.

Let's nail two myths.

- There is a common misunderstanding that someone who is a beneficiary under the terms of the will cannot be an executor. That is wrong. It is the witnesses to the *testator's* signature on the will who cannot and must not be beneficiaries or, put more realistically, beneficiaries and those closely related to them must not witness the testator's signature.

In practice, a beneficiary will more often than not be one of the *executors.*

Whether that is always a good idea is a different matter and in some instances it may well be better to have completely independent executors.

We will look at this again later.

- An executor has no power, rights or responsibilities until the testator has died. Some people believe that because they are named as executors in a person's will it gives them rights to direct what should happen to the testator or testator's affairs whilst still alive. This is simply wrong. The will only operates from death; the executor's powers only arise on the death of the testator.

What happens if there are no executors?

The answer is that the law will dictate who looks after the deceased's affairs. In broad terms this would be some or all of those who will be entitled to the estate either under the terms of the will if there is a will but no [surviving] executors or under the laws of intestacy if there is no will.

This may be fine if the person who is eligible for appointment is someone:

- who has the mental ability to handle the affairs of the deceased taking into account the personalities involved and the complexities (if any) of the estate (could the executor be bullied?);
- who has the integrity to handle the affairs of the deceased properly especially where more than he or she is entitled to the estate;
- who has the impartiality to deal with the estate.

What happens if the person concerned does not have these qualities? What if the person is not trustworthy?

- There are likely to be conflicts with beneficiaries.
- The estate may not be distributed in the way the will or (in the case of intestacy) the law directs.

By far the best course is for the testator to choose his or her own *executors.*

What do executors do exactly?

I have said they are the people with legal responsibility for looking after the affairs of the testator after the testator has died. What exactly do I mean by that? Much depends on the size and composition of the estate of the person who has died but in a typical estate it will involve:

- taking responsibility for registering the death;
- making the funeral arrangements;
- finding out, by looking at the deceased's papers and by searching his or her house, what capital assets and savings he or she has left, what sources of income there are and what debts he or she has left;
- probably instructing solicitors to deal with the paperwork and the legal side of administering the estate;
- preparing and signing the papers to lead to the grant of probate

including the papers involved with any Inheritance Tax issues and also paying any Inheritance Tax;

- gathering in the assets by signing withdrawal forms for the savings etc.;
- making decisions about how various assets should be dealt with or disposed of;
- clearing the deceased's house and disposing of all the contents;
- instructing solicitors and then signing the contract and the transfer for the sale of any houses or other properties that the deceased had or, if appropriate, arranging for them to be rented out;
- paying any income tax and capital gains tax following the deceased's death and if need be claiming any refunds;
- stopping any state benefits or other pensions that the deceased received and claiming any arrears or refunding any overpayments;
- if the deceased was in receipt of any means tested benefits, making sure there has been no overpayment based on inaccurate declarations by the deceased or anyone on his or her behalf and dealing with queries from the Department for Work and Pensions;
- dealing with any court proceedings that the deceased was involved in at the date of death;
- paying any debts;
- dealing with any claims against the estate, for example, by disgruntled relatives;
- generally implementing the terms of the deceased's will including:

  o complying with any instructions about the future of any animals owned by the deceased;
  o arranging the distribution of the estate amongst those entitled to it under the terms of the will;
  o investing any money that is to be held in trust for any beneficiaries, if the executors are also trustees (as they usually are); this could be because beneficiaries are under the age at which the testator has said they can have the money and it must be looked after until the beneficiaries reach that age; if the monies are to be held in trust for someone to have only the income for life (and not the capital from which the income comes) then the executors (if they are the trustees) will look after those monies; these duties can go on for many years;
  o if properties are not to be sold but instead let or occupied by someone authorised to do so by the deceased, then keeping an eye on them and making sure they are kept in repair and insured.

It is of course the case that very frequently solicitors will be instructed to do the paperwork and advise on procedure. In the cases involving Inheritance

Tax in practical terms, it can be difficult to raise the money to pay the tax if solicitors are not involved since some, if not all, has to be paid before the *Grant of Probate* is issued. Financial institutions often refuse to release money from the deceased's assets before the Grant of Probate is issued even to pay Inheritance Tax.

Even if solicitors are instructed, it must always be realised that the ultimate responsibility for the estate is that of the executors and that often, if wrong decisions are made, it will be the executors who carry the can.

How many executors?

The number of executors who should be appointed is again dependent upon the circumstances.

Four is the maximum number that can be appointed and act at the same time. Except in the case of husband and wife (where the survivor may be the only one necessary) two is a good number. If there is only one there is a risk that:

- he or she may die;
- one could get up to jiggery-pokery (see below about 'honesty and integrity') with the estate especially if solicitors are not involved.

If there are more than two the administration can become ungainly since all will have to be involved in decision-making and will have to sign all documentation such as withdrawal forms etc.

It is of course always possible to appoint substitutes in case one or more of those first appointed later dies before the testator.

It is also the case that, if two, three or four are appointed in the first place any of them can act and any can choose not to act. It is a matter for their agreement.

Special cases

It is possible (although in normal cases unusual) to appoint different executors to deal with different parts of the estate. This applies often where the testator is a writer and has literary assets to be dealt with in which case special literary executors may be appointed.

Solicitors who are sole practitioners sometimes consider appointing special executors to look after their practice if they die leaving the general executors to manage the 'personal' part of the estate.

Who do you choose?

That is a like asking how long is a piece of string. However, in general terms the choice will be between:

- relatives;
- friends;
- a professional person such as a solicitor;
- a trust corporation – usually a bank;
- or a combination of these options.

Let us look at a few points on some of these options.

Relatives

For many people there will be no debate. They will appoint one or more of their relatives to be their executors.

For some, however, the prospect of letting their relatives loose amongst their personal papers and their money would be an appalling idea.

Some simply have no relatives to appoint.

For some the appointment of one or more relatives to the exclusion of others would cause real problems. The appointment of an outsider would be a safer option.

In some cases a *testator* is quite happy for a relative to share in the estate but he or she would simply not trust that relative to behave honourably towards other beneficiaries or would not have confidence in the ability of that one to take on-board the responsibilities of executorship.

In modern times the geographic spread of families is great. It may simply not be possible for a geographically distant relative to undertake the practical aspects of dealing with the estate especially if this involved an international dimension and possibly with it a complete lack of understanding of the English legal and other procedures involved.

It is worth making the point that it is fine for husband and wife to appoint each other to be their sole executor. However, there is a potential problem with this in that there is always the risk that the *spouse* may be physically, mentally or, simply, emotionally incapable of dealing with the administration especially where their partner has just died, perhaps, after a long marriage

It may well be appropriate to appoint some or all of the children to act along with the surviving spouse (if any). They can then decide between themselves, at the time of the death of the first to die, which of them is to act.

Those who live together without being married (whether heterosexual or homosexual) need to remember that his or her partner will almost certainly not administer the estate unless he or she is a principal beneficiary. A testator who wants his or her partner to be an executor should appoint him or her specifically.

Friends

There is not much to be said about friends.

For many of advancing years the appointment of friends can be difficult because their friends are likely to be of similar vintage and therefore there is a distinct possibility that the friends will die before the testator or simply not be up to dealing with such matters.

If there are family who could have been chosen, the appointment of a friend could cause resentment within the family and the friend could have practical difficulty in administering the estate, for example, because the relatives obstruct them in gaining access to the assets or information about the assets.

Sometimes friends do not have sufficient information about the deceased to be able easily to administer the estate especially if there are decisions to be made which involve a close knowledge of the deceased such as his or her funeral wishes. It is curious that in many instances friends are appointed who really do not consider themselves as friends of the deceased or who have never been asked to be an executor and who simply do not want the job – even if they stand to gain financially from the estate.

Professionals

For many the appointment of a professional person, such as a solicitor, has much to commend it especially if the older person has no family or have family but who they do not want poking about amongst their most intimate papers and possessions. They may well prefer the emotional detachment of a professional especially if it is a professional with whom they have established a close relationship during lifetime and for whom they have a respect.

As with the appointment of friends, the appointment of a professional, especially if the professional is appointed to act alone, can cause some resentment and again the professional can find him or herself having difficulty in gaining access to the assets and to information if close family remain at the deceased's home.

The appointment of a professional with a relative or friend can have some advantages because the professional can act as either a support for, or a restraining influence on, the relative or friend. On the other hand, the professional's ethical and professional constraints can lead to friction with a co-executor who does not have those considerations. I have had to resign from an executorship on one occasion where I came into conflict with my co-executor who was a member of the family. It was a matter of regret that that occurred since I knew that the deceased did not trust her only daughter to manage money bequeathed for the granddaughter.

A true professional executor, such as a solicitor, will be insured against any mistakes that he or she may make in the administration and, in the unlikely event of a professional behaving dishonestly, a professional organisation, such as the Law Society's Compensation Fund, may make good any loss sustained.

A professional executor will charge for his or her services. Solicitors' charges are based on many factors but will always be based primarily on the time that they spend on the matter and are usually supplemented by a percentage of the value of the estate. If the solicitors are going to be undertaking most of the work in the estate on behalf of lay executors then the appointment of solicitors themselves as the executors should not add greatly to the cost except where they are going to have to do a great deal of additional work which lay executors might be expected to do themselves. This might be such things as searching the house, arranging the funeral and the like.

Banks

Ah! Banks. Yes. Appointing a bank has the advantage that it is always there. It never dies. Additionally, it is independent. However, that independence can be a disadvantage in that it is likely to be very bureaucratic and will not have the ability to 'bend' the rules where that is appropriate and proper. Additionally, many people who have experienced a bank administering an estate complain of the inordinate length of time it takes to complete the administration and the very large charges which are levied by the bank.

For anyone minded to appoint a bank it would be prudent to obtain that bank's current charging policy. Apply it to your circumstances and estate taking into account what provisions about the administration that you will put in your will and you will probably decide not to appoint the bank

A look at one major bank's website says simply in relation to their charges,

'These will be based on the degree of responsibility and the amount of work involved'.

It should also be noted that sometimes banks agree to be appointed executors but when the time comes, if they decide there is insufficient to justify them taking on the task, they *renounce* (that is refuse to be executors) resulting in family or beneficiaries still having to undertake the task.

The notion that your friendly local Bank Manager (does he or she still exist?) will administer your estate is also a misguided one. Whilst most banks will use their local branch to obtain basic information, the actual administration itself is more than likely to be dealt with at the bank's Head or Regional Office.

Other considerations

Age

Appointing executors of the same or similar age as you grow older is not a good idea since:

- the executors may die before you;
- the executors may become (physically and/or mentally) unable to deal with your affairs.

Location

Appointing executors at the other end of the country is not a good idea if there are suitable executors nearby. Appointing executors outside the country is definitely not a good idea since not only may they have great practical difficulties in administering the estate but they will also be out of reach of the English courts if anything goes wrong and they have to be brought to heel whether because of negligence or dishonesty.

Honesty and Integrity

This is probably the most important aspect of the appointment of executors. If the executor is the only beneficiary then it does not matter how dishonest he or she is. The only person who can be cheated is him or herself as long as the executor pays all liabilities and pays all the taxes due. However, if there is another beneficiary the risk of dishonesty becomes a possibility.

In my own firm recently we have had two instances where executors have variously simply taken the will and administered the estate themselves or, once we had gathered in the assets the executors simply took the assets to distribute. In both those cases we had serious concerns that there was dishonesty in prospect. This risk of dishonesty is particularly live where there are gifts in the will to people who would not expect provision to be made for them (particularly people outside the family) and would not therefore be suspicious if no gift was received.

In consequence, it is vital that a testator should wholly trust those appointed. If there is any doubt at all (either generally or because the testator knows the executor will be unhappy with the way the estate has been left) then it would be preferable not to appoint the person concerned or at the very least some precautions need to be built in. These could be:

- by appointing one or more other executors and requiring a minimum number to prove the will;
- by depositing the will with solicitors and imposing a requirement that the solicitors on releasing the will, following the death, should write to the beneficiaries informing them of the bequests and making it clear that such work should be paid for by the *executors* out of the estate;
- by imposing a requirement that solicitors must be instructed to act in the administration of the estate and should be responsible for making the actual distribution of the estate.

I have referred not only to honesty but also to integrity. This I see as wider than honesty. It encompasses generally the way in which the executors conduct themselves. It encompasses the way in which they exercise their discretions in the course of the administration.

Sadly, often testators look at their families through rose-tinted spectacles. They sometimes overlook even the most obvious signs of lack of integrity or greed. Before appointing executors testators should think very carefully about those they are thinking of appointing and exclude anyone about whom they have misgivings.

CHAPTER 9

THE WILL – GIFTS

KEY POINTS

- Who you leave your estate to is your decision.

- The will only operates on the position as it is at death.

- Many factors will influence how you decide to distribute your estate.

- Care has to be exercised in making gifts of particular items or classes of items to adequately describe them.

- A gift of Residuary Estate (that is anything left over after all specific bequests etc. have been made) must be made in the will.

- Careful consideration must be given to the destination of assets if the first named beneficiary dies before the testator.

- Care must be taken to insert substitute beneficiaries where necessary especially for the Residuary Estate.

- Special provision in the form of a Discretionary Trust may be necessary for beneficiaries who are physically and/or mentally incapacitated or for aged beneficiaries or for those who may be subject to financial abuse.

- Provision may need to be made for people to occupy a house for a period after the death of the testator even if they are not actually given the house.

CHAPTER 9

THE WILL – GIFTS

This is probably the bit you expected to come first when discussing wills. This section, the giving away part, is what most people see as the reason for a will.

It is not possible in a book of this sort to delve into the subject in great depth and, indeed, I would not wish to do so since the way in which a person disposes of his or her estate is a matter for each individual and will be dependent upon so many factors including:

- the value of the *estate;*
- how it is made up e.g. house, premium bonds, savings etc.;
- whether there may be Inheritance Tax issues;
- the extent of the family who stand to inherit;
- the respective financial assets which individual family members have in their own right;
- the respective needs of individual family members;
- the health of family members;
- issues of disability;
- considerations of the effect that gifts will have on the state benefits being received (or which might in the future be received) by family members;
- the age of family members;
- the life opportunities (such as education) which family members have had;
- the provision that may already have been made for them by the *testator* during lifetime or the provision made for them in lifetime or on death by others;
- the personality of family members;
- the lifestyles of family members and how the testator feels about those lifestyles;
- the care and consideration shown by individuals to the *testator* during the whole of his or her lifetime and not, perhaps, just in later years and not, perhaps, just in earlier years when he or she was vibrant and active and not dependent;
- in the case of those without family or family who they do not wish to benefit, then the extent of their circle of friends; similar factors will come into play here as with family.

I propose to give some pointers as to the general strategy in which the making of gifts under the will may be approached and then move on to look at miscellaneous factors that I have found influence the way in which gifts may be approached.

THE OVERALL STRATEGY

SPECIFIC BEQUESTS

By specific bequests I mean gifts of particular items such as paintings, pieces of china, a stamp collection, a collection of football memorabilia etc. which a testator may wish to give to individuals.

In making such gifts the following points should be borne in mind:

- an adequate description should be given in the will of the item concerned so that there can be no question of its being confused with another similar item; one must keep in mind that because you have always referred to 'granddad's chair' those who are responsible for administering the estate (especially if they are not family members) may not know what you are talking about;
- a common problem area is the gift of jewellery, which really must be properly described in such a way that there cannot only be no risk of confusion between items but also so that an *executor* knows with certainty that the item being handed over really is the one that the *testator* intended. Reference to a professionally prepared valuation could be invaluable for this purpose since a description of an item by a skilled jeweller would be capable of differentiating the item from all others;
- the issue of description can also be a problem if, after making the will, you acquire a further item which could be confused with something mentioned in the will;
- if, after the will is made, you give away or sell the item given in the will then the person to whom it is bequeathed will not receive it nor will they receive its value;
- do make sure that you own the item that you purport to give away; have in mind that if you jointly own an item the chances are that it will pass to the other co-owner in the event of your prior death irrespective of anything in your will.

Frequently *testators* like to allow people to have a choice of items. This can be a problem and needs to be accompanied by clear directions as to:

- the order in which people can chose;
- the range of items they can chose from;
- the time scale in which the choice is to be made;
- the number of items they can each take;
- whether one item can comprise a collection;
- how any disputes are to be resolved; this can often be achieved by giving the executors the power to settle disputes but this can only be done where the executors are not themselves benefiting nor are they closely involved with anyone who is benefiting so that their independence and impartiality could be compromised;
- who is to bear the costs of transporting the gift/s to the beneficiary and of insuring it/them in transit.

BEQUESTS OF ACCOUNTS, SHARES ETC.

A not infrequent suggestion of testators is that they propose to leave a gift of a particular account at a bank or building society to a beneficiary or shares in a particular company or some other very precise gift. There are problems with this.

- What happens if the financial institution changes its name?
- What happens if the bank or other financial institutions changes the account number?
- What happens if you simply move the monies into a higher interest rate account and the number changes?
- If you give a particular number of shares to someone and there is a Rights Issue or a restructuring of the company which leads to a change in the number of shares owned a question will arise about what was intended;
- What happens if you name a building society and it converts to a bank?
- What if a company changes its name?

These and other questions (including the very basic one of what happens if you get rid of the asset entirely) can lead to difficulties. Whilst some of these problems can be overcome by careful drafting of the will, some of them can only be got round if, when a change takes place, the testator alters his or her will to take into account the change which has taken place. The problem here is that the testator may not then be mentally competent to undertake such a change or may simply forget to do so or may have forgotten the terms of the gift in the will.

Overall whilst these gifts can be made, great care is needed and if there is an alternative way of dealing with the matter then it should be adopted.

GIFTS OF CLASSES OF ITEMS

Often testators will want to give one or more people, say, their furniture or their household ornaments or items of some other similar description.

The use of these terms can be problematic. It is vital to ensure that the term includes what the testator wishes to give and excludes what he or she does not want to give.

One common term which lawyers use is *'personal chattels'*. This term is useful because it can be closely defined by reference to Section 55 (1)(x) of the Administration of Estates Act 1925. This is an archaic definition but nonetheless it does its job. The section defines 'personal chattels' as:

> ...carriages, horses, stable furniture and effects (not used for business purposes), motorcars and accessories (not used for business purposes), garden effects, domestic animals, plate, plated articles, linen, china, glass, books, pictures, prints, furniture, jewellery, articles of household or personal use or ornament, musical and scientific instruments and apparatus, wines, liquors and consumable stores, but does not include any chattels used at the death of the intestate for business purposes nor money or securities for money.

However, in using the term one has to make sure it accurately represents the testator's wishes.

It must be ensured that the use of such a term does not conflict with other provisions in the will, so, if for example, there is a gift of a car somewhere else in the will it would need to be ensured that that gift was to take priority over a general gift of personal chattels.

Similarly if there are any items owned by the testator which do not clearly seem to fit within the definition of personal chattels it should be clarified what is or is not to be included.

An example of this would be as to whether an unmounted diamond is to be treated as jewellery and therefore included within the gift of either personal chattels or jewellery. Testators need to think clearly about their possessions and whether they do have any unusual items.

Similarly they need to consider whether there any items of great value which they would not wish to be included in a general gift of say furniture or personal chattels.

It is particularly important to make it clear whether a general term applies to collections of items.

GIFT OF A HOUSE

If a gift of a house is made then it will need to be made clear which house this refers to. Is it just the house that the testator owned at the time the will was made or can it apply to whatever house the testator has at the date of death? What happens if at the date of death the testator has two houses? Which one is meant?

If the property has a mortgage on it then is the gift to be free of mortgage (that is, the mortgage paid off out of other money in the estate) or is the gift taken subject to the mortgage (that is, the beneficiary can have the house but takes over responsibility for the outstanding mortgage)?

Another issue is whether the house is being given as a house or as a home. If it is given as a home is it appropriate to provide for the furniture to go with it? If it is, how are we to define what is to be included?

This could be a particular problem if there is uncertainty as to what furniture the testator actually owns and which might be joint or belong to someone else.

Testators planning to make a gift of a house or an interest in a house need to check carefully that it is theirs to give. This is especially so if the property is or has in the past been jointly owned with someone else.

It is possible for property to be owned by two or more people either as 'joint tenants' or as 'tenants in common'.

In the case of a joint tenancy on the death of the first owner the whole property passes to the other co-owner(s) automatically irrespective of anything in the will of the first to die.

In the case of a tenancy in common each is treated as owning a distinct share in the property which may or may not pass to the other co-owner(s) on the death of the first to die. It will depend on the terms of the will of the first to die or the laws of intestacy. Furthermore, the fact that a property starts out held as joint tenants does not mean it ends up as such and may finish up by 'severance' of the joint tenancy becoming a tenancy in common. The reverse may also be true, but much less frequently.

It is essential that good legal advice is sought to determine the status of such a property before the will is made.

GIFTS OF MONEY OR PECUNIARY LEGACIES

Often testators wish to give sums of money to beneficiaries. There are two associated problems:

- unless the testator is very confident as to his position, the issue will be whether he will have sufficient money to satisfy the legacies at the time of death. This is particularly relevant in days when one has to pay residential care home fees which rapidly deplete savings;
- the second issue is that if a large pecuniary legacy is given there may be sufficient to pay the legacy but what will that leave for the residuary beneficiaries who may in fact be the people the testator wants to receive the bulk of the estate? This again can be the result of a serious reduction in the value of the estate because of payment of home fees.

Accordingly, gifts of specific cash sums should be avoided unless purely nominal. If it were desired to give a sizeable cash gift then this would be better achieved by giving a percentage of the residuary estate. This has the advantage that the gift will decrease proportionately with the decrease in value of the estate as a whole. It also has what may be viewed as a further advantage in that the gift will increase proportionately if the testator's estate increases before death. Some older people play the National Lottery. Many older people own Premium Bonds.

THE RESIDUARY ESTATE

This will be the final gift in the will.

It is of whatever is left over after all the other gifts have been made.

Occasionally a testator will say that he or she does not wish to make a gift of residue because he or she has given away everything that they have in the earlier parts of the will. Sometimes they need considerable persuasion that almost inevitably they will have something left over even if it is only some arrears of pension and some provision must be made for it. Failure to do so will mean that the person dies *partially intestate* with all the problems that may flow from that. Great effort may be needed to locate the people entitled to the residue. This may well undo the advantages of having made the will.

The testator also needs to have in mind that if any earlier gift fails, because, for example, a beneficiary has died before the testator, and there is no provision for what is to happen to the gift then the gift may well fall into residue and will need disposing of.

Residue will either be given to one beneficiary or will be divided between a number of beneficiaries.

This division may either be in equal parts or it may be in unequal parts.

In each case the testator has to ask what will happen if the person or persons to whom a particular share has been given dies before the testator? Alternative gifts need to be made. Similarly, if a gift is made to someone which they only get at a certain age, what happens if they survive the testator but die before reaching the age at which they are entitled to the gift? Again provision needs to be made as to what is to happen to the share.

In drafting a will I try to persuade testators to continue making provisions in the will until they reach a point where a gift of residue is made to someone who will not be in the same house, on the same aircraft, or in the same car as the earlier beneficiaries.

Sometimes this may involve a gift to a charity or outside the family. Sometimes it may simply not be possible for a testator to reach that point and a sensible position has to be adopted. If it is that the only time they would all be together would be for lunch on Christmas Day, then the testator may decide it is an acceptable risk that they could all die if there is a gas explosion or whatever.

MISCELLANEOUS POINTS

I will turn now to look at miscellaneous matters to which thought may need to be given.

Aged beneficiaries

The idea of leaving one's contemporaries a share of one's estate is an appealing idea for most of us but this may not be such a good idea as one gets older.

One has to ask the question as to whether the contemporary will actually derive some benefit from the gift? Will it actually improve their quality of life by, for example, enabling them to afford a holiday or holidays that would otherwise be beyond their means? May it not simply finish up falling into the hands of their relatives or go to pay nursing home fees? If so, is there not a better use to which it could be put?

Disabled beneficiaries

The subject of disabled beneficiaries is one that is complex. The main problem is the issue of the effect that an outright gift will have on any state benefits which the beneficiary may be entitled to receive whether in terms of cash benefits or payment of home fees. *Testators* need to have in mind that the gift may well serve simply to remove the right to benefits until the money has been used up and when that happens the beneficiary will probably go back onto benefit without actually having had the quality of his or her life enhanced by the gift and will certainly not have any lasting benefit from the monies.

A further issue is that often a disabled beneficiary, especially one with learning or mental health difficulties, may well be vulnerable to financial abuse or may have no understanding of how to handle large sums of money.

Accordingly, there may be steps that can be taken to try to ensure that the money is put into a trust in such a way that the trustees can use the money to benefit the beneficiary over many years but without giving the beneficiary any legal right to the money in such a way that it will affect his or her benefits or in such a way that the beneficiary could fritter it away or be abused because of the money. This is called a *discretionary trust*. It is something upon which careful legal advice will be needed not least to discuss the appointment of *trustees*.

Trustees under a discretionary trust really must be independent and not stand to benefit themselves under the trust especially if such a benefit could mean that the trustee fails to exercise his or her discretion in the true interests of the disabled person. This can be a difficult decision since people are often seen as appropriate to be appointed as trustees because they are closely related to the disabled person and therefore can identify his or her needs. Unfortunately, that closeness means that they too are likely to be potential beneficiaries if the trust monies are not exhausted in making payments to or for the disabled person. By way of example, if a widow has three adult children and one of whom suffers from learning difficulties, it may be desired to provide that the share of that child should go into a Discretionary Trust with the other two children as the trustees to decide exactly what if anything is paid over to the child with the difficulty. (Indeed, the other two children may also be potential beneficiaries under the terms of the trust even if the disabled child is intended to be the main object of the trust.) It is likely that the parent will want to provide for the other two children to receive any monies in the Discretionary Trust if the child with difficulty dies. It is also likely that the parent will want the other children to be the trustees. This is not a good idea. There is a risk that the other two children, as the trustees, would not be as generous to the disabled child as they should in the knowledge that the less paid to the child with difficulty will mean more for the two children when the Discretionary Trust comes to an end or as potential beneficiaries during the life of the trust.

The same considerations can apply to children who are wasteful or who may be in a dubious marriage or who have, say, a drug problem.

It is normal, where a Discretionary Trust is created, for the parent making the will to put with the will a letter addressed to the trustees setting out in general terms how they would like the trust to be administered. They will normally set out their wish for it primarily to benefit the disabled child but once that child's needs have been met, then for the trust to benefit others. It will also be likely to set out how the parent envisages the monies actually being used for the child, for example, stressing the importance of using the monies in such a way that it least affects state benefits. It is important that any such letter of wishes is precisely that: a letter of wishes. It must not compel the trustees to do any particular act, since otherwise there is a danger that the trust ceases to be discretionary and whole object of creating the trust may be frustrated.

There can be punitive tax charges relating to discretionary trusts.

Unmarried children

It is well established that children now tend to remain living at home longer than in the past. This does not cause a problem from a will point of view except where there is more than one child and one or more of whom may be living at home at the time of the parent's death but where one or more of whom may have flown the nest.

On the assumption that the parent wants the children to share equally in the estate and on the assumption that the parent's means are not such as to be able to make provision for the children away from home without including the family home, then there may be a problem.

The parent has to decide whether the child (or children) who is living at home at the time the parent dies should be able to continue living in the house after the parent's death. The following issues arise:

- if the parent dies without making any provision then there is every chance that the child(ren) living at home will have to leave the house and it will have to be sold to pay out the non-resident children;
- this may be at a critical time in the child's life, for example, the approach to examinations or at a time of illness.

It is open to the parent to provide that the child or children can continue to live in the house after the parent's death and the following points should be considered:

- the child could be allowed to live in the house until a specific date, if it is known when it would be safe for him or her to be required to move out, for example, at the end of a fixed period of training/education;
- the child could be allowed to live in the house for a particular period of time after the death sufficient to allow him or her to make alternative arrangements; the length of time will probably depend on his or her circumstances;
- the child could be allowed to live in the house until the first of a series of events occurs. Those events might be:

  o the death of the child;
  o the marriage of the child;
  o the child voluntarily vacating the property;
  o the child starting to cohabit. This is tricky to define since who determines what amounts to cohabitation?

The parent will have to decide whether:

- the right applies just to the house the parent lives in at the date the will is made;
- the right applies to whichever house the parent lives in at the date of death;
- the child could, after the parent has died, be allowed to have the house sold and a new (possibly smaller) one bought using the money from the first but to be held upon the same terms of occupation as the first;
- the child should be required to maintain and insure the house and pay all the outgoings. If this is not made a condition then the parent will have to ensure that monies are set aside from the rest of the estate for that purpose. That may be very difficult. It would also be an unusual provision in the average will.

A further supplementary issue will be that of the furniture.

- Should the child be given the right to use the furniture while he lives in the house and afterwards the furniture be divided between the other children?
- If the child has lived at home for many years after starting earning, there could be problems in determining which items of furniture belong to the parent and which belong to the child. There could well be merit in the parent giving the furniture absolutely to the child to avoid any argument.

Others who live in the house

It may be that two sisters live together following the death of their respective partners. The house may belong to one of them. That one may have a child or children to whom she wants her estate to go on death. If she fails to make provision then her sister may well be turfed out of the house by the nephews or nieces on their mother's death. Accordingly, similar considerations will need to be borne in mind as given in the section dealing with 'Unmarried children'.

The same could apply to other relationships, including husbands/wives where the *testator* is in a second marriage (or relationship) and wants the surviving second spouse (or partner) to be able to live in the house but wants the proceeds eventually to go to the children from the first marriage.

Charities

Children or other relatives of *testators* may well not be best pleased by my referring to the possibility of gifts being made by *testators* to charities (and I use this term in the widest possible sense to include gifts to churches, hospitals, hospices and the like) but of course some people do wish to make gifts to charities even where they have close relatives either to the exclusion of those relatives or in addition to gifts to relatives.

I have to declare a personal bias against some charities in that some of them, especially some larger charities with very substantial assets, show extreme greed in their attitude to bequests. (See also Chapter 10 in respect of terms of the will to deal with avaricious charities.) In particular, they have a habit of writing to *executors* very shortly after the death essentially trying to find out what they are going to get and when they are going to get it. *Testators* should carefully investigate the charities who may be the objects of their bounty both in terms of their attitude to bequests and also whether a particular charity actually needs the money. For my own part I find that local charities are often more deserving and needy than national organisations.

Most solicitors will have access to guides to charities but often these tend to concentrate on larger charities.

Testators should consider research on the Charity Commission website to see what local and/or smaller specialist charities are around and which may benefit from a bequest.

Testators may also wish to consider what chance there is of a charity 'folding' and what would happen to any gifts made to it? It may well be prudent for there to be inserted in the will a provision for another charity to get the gift.

It would be useful to allow the executor discretion as to whether a particular charity has ceased to exist – as long as, of course, the executor does not stand to benefit from that decision!

CHAPTER 10

THE WILL – MISCELLANEOUS

KEY POINTS

- Wills deal with more than giving away our possessions.

- In appropriate cases, where the testator has children under eighteen, he or she may wish to appoint guardians for those children if under eighteen at the date of the testator's death.

- A parent may not have a right to appoint a guardian. Appropriate advice should be sought especially where the parents were not married at the date of the child's birth.

- Testators with pets should consider what is to happen to those on death.

- Many people never talk about death and their funeral arrangements. Something should be said in the will about the basic funeral arrangements especially if there is any possibility of argument between those left behind.

- Beneficiaries (including some charities) may show considerable greed following a death. Appropriate restraints should be included in the will.

- Personal papers, photographs, computer data etc. may need to be the subject of specific provisions in the will if they are not to fall into the wrong hands.

CHAPTER 10

THE WILL – MISCELLANEOUS

There will be other miscellaneous provisions in the will. I will touch on those in this chapter.

GUARDIANS

By 'guardian' I mean the person who has legal responsibility for a child.

A guardian has to be someone other than a parent of the child.

Issues of guardianship are unlikely to arise in the circumstances that this book addresses. However, it is not impossible, especially in the case of a man who late in life fathers a child or with men or women who experience early onset dementia and accordingly brief mention is to be made of it for completeness.

Parents may wish to express in their wills who is to act as guardians of their children on their death. However, parents are not necessarily treated equally where the appointment of guardians is concerned.

On the death of either of the parents it has to be determined who has 'parental responsibility' for the child. According to the Children Act 1989 this means who has 'all rights, duties, powers, responsibilities and authority which by law a parent has in relation to the child and his property'. Once a guardian is validly appointed and the appointment takes effect, the guardian has parental responsibility with all that that entails.

Where a child's parents were married to each other at the date of the child's birth (the reference to the date of a child's birth is not straightforward and can include the period between conception and birth and the parents can be treated as married at the time of birth if the child is treated as legitimate or is legitimated or adopted) each has parental responsibility. If they were not married to each other at the time of his birth then the mother has parental responsibility but the father does not unless he has acquired it under the Children Act. This can be acquired either by an order of a court or by agreement between the parents.

In principal only a parent with parental responsibility can appoint a guardian to act in the event of his or her death.

If the parent who survives is the one with parental responsibility then that continues. If, when the appointing parent dies, there is no surviving parent with parental responsibility, the appointment takes effect on the death of the appointing parent. However, if there is a surviving parent with parental responsibility, the appointment will only take effect when there is no surviving parent with parental responsibility.

Where the appointing parent at his death is the only parent with a 'residence order' in his/her favour or where the appointing parent is the only one who has care and control under a court order then, in those exceptional circumstances alone, does an appointment take effect on the death of the appointing parent even if the other surviving parent has parental responsibility. In this case the appointed guardian and the surviving parent will both have parental responsibility.

It will be seen that the position is quite involved and anyone with children (especially where they were not married at the child's birth) should take advice on this issue after a full disclosure of all material facts has been made known to the adviser. Then if there is any risk that an appointment will not be valid and if this is a matter of concern, appropriate steps may be able to be taken to put things on a proper basis, possibly by an application to the court for a parental responsibility order to be made.

PETS

Pets play an important part in the lives of many people.

One of the things to which thought should be given is the future of any animals that you may own at the time of death.

For many the prospect of directing that the animal should be put down would be akin to heresy. However, that is the view of some, especially where the animal is old or crotchety or is a 'one man' animal. If that is the view then it should be expressed clearly in the will.

If on the other hand the testator wants the animal to go to someone in particular then this should be specified since there is a risk that otherwise the animal would pass either as part of *personal chattels* (if that term has been used in the will – see the definition in Chapter 9) or as part of the *residuary estate*.

As an alternative to being specific about the destination of the animal it may be desired simply that the animal be re-homed and in that event that responsibility should perhaps be cast upon the executors to arrange this.

Making provision for the maintenance of an animal after death can be tricky. Bear in mind that there is a risk that someone may only take the animal to get the money that goes with it. If such a provision is to be made it should be a condition that the executor does not disclose to the person taking the animal that a sum of money goes with it until after the person has agreed to take the animal.

Regrettably, some animal charities have been known to give the impression that they are reluctant to take animals unless some cash accompanies them. My experience has been that, if this is the case, a threat to destroy the animal sometimes concentrates their minds wonderfully.

FUNERAL ARRANGEMENTS

This book deals with issues of funeral planning elsewhere in detail. It may be desired to express the essential wishes as to the funeral in the will. I feel that this is useful especially if there is a risk of disagreement between those purportedly close to the deceased. This may be especially useful where there may be a conflict between true relatives, for example children from a first marriage on the one hand and 'partner' on the other. Such disputes can arise through sheer bloody mindedness or genuinely held differing views, for example, over religious issues.

The will could perhaps just deal with:

- burial or cremation;
- the place of cremation or the place of burial (including the plot);
- denomination of the *officiant* (for example, Church of England, Roman Catholic, Muslim, Humanist etc.);
- disposal of ashes;
- flowers.

It needs to be borne in mind that the will may well only be 'read' after the funeral has taken place. It is important therefore that the detailed funeral wishes be made known to those around the testator in such a way as to be certain to come to light promptly when the time arises. I will suggest some housekeeping steps in Chapter 15.

GRASPING RELATIVES AND CHARITIES

In my time in the law one of the saddest things I have seen is the way that beneficiaries under a will or on an intestacy behave. Both individuals and some charities display appalling greed following a death. They are frequently chasing the executors and the solicitors within weeks of the death demanding access to the money. A remarkable number of individuals commit themselves to the purchase of a new car or house or a villa in Spain within days of a death and then press for the release of monies from the estate.

It is my suggestion to testators now that they should make provision in the will that beneficiaries should not be entitled to any information about the progress of the administration for a set period after the death in order to allow the executors and the solicitors to get on with the administration without being hounded by beneficiaries. So far no beneficiary to whom I have suggested such a clause has objected. If it were left to me I would go on to provide that enquiries about progress should debar the beneficiary from receiving any gift at all or should delay their entitlement for a further and lengthy period.

A further innovation that I have recently incorporated into some wills is a request to beneficiaries to behave decently following a death. It is hoped that such a request to beneficiaries might just have some impact on their conscience.

I have suggested in Appendix 4 some clauses that a testator might like to propose to their solicitors for inclusion in the will. Whether my fellow lawyers will go along with these is open to debate.

INVESTMENTS

If monies will or may have to be invested following a death then a decision will need to be made concerning the investment powers of the trustees. This may either be needed because:

- there are children who may benefit under the will but where the monies are to be held on trust until they attain a certain age, for example, eighteen or twenty-one;
- there is a provision that a beneficiary is able to have only the income for life and then the capital passes to someone else;
- there is a *discretionary trust.*

The trustees may:

- be given a very specific direction as to how to invest, for example, in a building society;
- be given a very wide power to invest – in anything the trustees consider appropriate;
- simply be left to rely on the provisions from time to time laid down by statute for trustee investments which at the present time as a result of recent legislation are very wide.

PERSONAL PAPERS

One issue which is rarely mentioned in wills is what is to happen to our photographs, transparencies, home made videos, tape recordings and nowadays, computer data (all of which I shall call 'media').

Setting aside anything that may be of questionable legality, there may well be media which contain intimate images or thoughts which we would simply not want to fall into the hands of others at all or into the hands of particular individuals or the world at large. Accordingly, careful thought needs to be given as to what is to happen to such items and suitable provision made in the will.

It may be that a testator would simply direct the executor to destroy all or any such items. Alternatively, the testator may well wish items to be given to family or friends or, in appropriate circumstances, to a library, museum or sound/video/photographic archive. If there are any items which could be published it may well be appropriate to make this clear and possibly appoint literary executors specifically to deal with such items. Whatever decision the testator reaches it would be wise to commit it to writing preferably in the will and not simply to lump it all in with 'personal chattels' or as part of residue.

OCCUPATIONAL PENSION

The time you make a will is also the time for resolving pension issues. It is important to make enquiries with your employers/former employers/pension providers as to what happens to any pension right you may have on your death. It is more than likely that any lump sums will not form part of your estate and, therefore, will not pass under your will. It may be open to you to nominate the person or persons who are to receive your pension rights on death by signing a nomination form provided by the Trustees of the pension scheme. If you have signed such a nomination it would be preferable not to do anything in the will which would conflict with that.

The important thing is to get authoritative advice from the pension provider as to the position and whether anything needs to be said in your will.

CHAPTER 11

REGULARISING FINANCES

KEY POINTS

- People often enter into deliberate financial arrangements with others which can lead to problems in the long term.

- Often this is done to claim state benefits or to avoid paying care home fees or avoid tax.

- These arrangements may well cause problems for them during lifetime if things go wrong between the parties or if one dies or becomes mentally incapable.

- Finances often become complicated almost by accident by the passage of time or the disintegration of relationships.

- These accidental complexities can cause problems for one or both parties during lifetime especially if one becomes mentally incapable or for those left behind on the death of one or other of them.

- It is important that every one should look at his or her finances and check whether there are any possible complications and if there is any doubt take good legal advice whilst the parties are still mentally capable and alive and capable of taking steps to sort out the complexities.

CHAPTER 11

REGULARISING FINANCES

THE ISSUES

A frequent source of problems as people get older arises from the complexity which can surround their finances. The problems can arise for many reasons but two in particular stand out:

- deliberate financial arrangements that are entered into, by the person concerned, with others;
- when financial issues become complicated simply because of the passage of time and the development or disintegration of relationships.

Dealing firstly with deliberate arrangements.

What do I mean?

A not infrequent source of difficulty can be where the person transfers property or other assets either into the sole name of another person or into the joint names of the *donor* and another.

We see elsewhere in this book the problems which can arise where a person gives away property/other assets to another to avoid care home fees.

Sometimes, however, particularly where money is involved, an older person will transfer money into the name of another person either to avoid the possibility of having to pay home fees in the future or, possibly, to avoid tax or to claim benefits. Sometimes it is done as an informal way of assisting an older person to manage his affairs as age takes its toll.

There are a number of points that the donor (and indeed the donee) needs to have in mind:

- whilst the donor may avoid tax (if that was the motive) the donee will be obliged to pay tax on the income derived from the monies;
- if avoidance of Inheritance Tax is the motive then, of course, unless the donor survives by seven years it is quite possible that the monies which had been given away will still fall to be taxed;
- if the 'gift' is a sham with a view to avoiding tax or avoiding home

fees then, if a dispute arises between donor and donee, a Court may well not look favourably on any attempt by the donor to recover the monies. It may well be a case of 'if you live by the sword, you die by the sword';

- if the donor subsequently becomes mentally incapable who is to know about the monies which have been given away and the circumstances in which they were given?

- if the donor dies then the monies may well be treated as being those of the donee and it may be well nigh impossible for the deceased's executors/administrators to recover those monies so that they form part of the deceased's estate and go in accordance with the terms of his or her will;

- the donor and the donee may be tempted to enter into some form of Trust Deed to show that the donee does not actually own the monies beneficially but is simply holding them on behalf of the donor. Whilst that might ensure that the donor eventually can recover the monies, it would certainly defeat any attempt to avoid home fees or tax;

- if the donee dies before the donor then the monies may well form part of the donee's estate and go in accordance with the donee's will or the laws of intestacy. Once again the donor may well have a very difficult job in trying to show that the monies actually belong to him or her and why they should not simply form part of the deceased's estate and pass to whoever is entitled to his or her estate;

- a similar situation can arise and similar considerations may well be applicable where the donor transfers monies into the joint names of himself and another from his sole name. This may be done with the very best of motives, for example, where perhaps two sisters live together and decide to pool their finances for housekeeping expenses. It may be that one puts in significantly more than the other. If a falling-out occurs how are those monies to be divided? If one of them dies then the principle will be that those monies will pass entirely to the survivor and will not form part of the estate of the one to die unless some very clear evidence can be seen as to how the monies should be divided up, and the intention of the parties was something other than for them to pass to the survivor.

SO WHAT IS THE ANSWER TO ALL THIS?

The answer is not to enter into such relationships in the first instance. If, however, such arrangements have been entered into then steps should be taken whilst the parties are on good terms and are alive and are mentally capable of doing so to regularise the position and for monies to be returned to the true owner. In the case of monies in joint accounts they should be split up properly in accordance with the way in which the parties actually intended them to be split.

If, for the sake of convenience, parties do want to keep a joint account for, say, housekeeping purposes but would want their own estates to take their share of the money if they were to die, then they should ensure that the amount kept in the account is the smallest possible and enter into a formal agreement that in the event of the death of one, the monies are to split equally or in whatever shares is the intention.

The same situation can arise with bricks and mortar although this is less frequent than with savings etc. The circumstances can be many and various. One example would be where the parties for one reason or another chose to buy a property in joint names. They may have contributed to it equally. If the property is bought as *joint tenants* then in the event of one of them dying the property passes to the survivor irrespective of anything in the will of the first to die or if there is no will irrespective of the laws of intestacy. This, depending on the relationship, may be exactly what would be intended. On the other hand the first to die might well have intended that his or her share should pass to his or her family. That is bad enough but what if one of them has put in all or the bulk of the money and that one dies first. His or her family will be pretty disappointed

If for some reason the property has been bought in one name but has been contributed to jointly, then on the death of the one in whose name the property is, the other party may well have serious difficulty in establishing his or her financial interest in the property. The answer to this is to ensure that the property it put into joint names with a declaration of the shares in which they consider that it is owned.

If the property is bought in the joint names of the parties but as *tenants in common* then the parties will each be treated as owning his or her own distinct share in the property. On death it will be split between them in the shares which they declared it was owned at the time of purchase, even if subsequently they contribute to the purchase in some other proportions.

Furthermore the share of each will pass on death to whoever is entitled to that one's estate, either under his or her will or under the laws of intestacy if there is no will. This may or may not be to the other co-owner.

In this case, parties should check to determine the shares in which they own the property and if need be execute a new declaration confirming the shares in which it is owned and they should make wills ensuring that their respective shares go to whoever the individual wants, whether or not that is to the co-owner.

The above are but examples of the situations which can arise and the possible solutions.

Good legal advice should be taken in each case.

Accidental arrangements

The second type of situation are those which arise almost by accident by the passage of time or the disintegration of relationships.

Examples of this would be:

- Husband and wife purchase a house in joint names. The marriage breaks down, they go their separate ways and for one reason or another, possibly through the stubbornness of one or the other, nothing is resolved about the house in which one continues to live. During lifetime there may be issues as to entitlement to the property when one or other goes into care and in assessing their liability to pay fees. On the death of one, issues may well arise with the house in that it might pass automatically to the survivor to the annoyance of the beneficiaries of the one who has died or it may be split between the beneficiaries and the survivor much to the annoyance of the survivor. There may well be problems in determining who is entitled to what share.

- Husband and wife purchase a house but in the name of one only. The marriage breaks down, they go their separate ways and for one reason or another, possibly through the stubbornness of one or the other, nothing is resolved about the house in which one continues to live. The non-occupying spouse registers a *charge* against the property to protect his or her interest. The occupier goes into care and the house has to be sold to pay home fees only for it to be discovered it cannot be sold without the cooperation of the one who had registered the charge. That person is uncooperative or cannot be found.

And so on.

The possibilities are endless. Whilst the examples I give are of husband and wife similar complications can arise in virtually any relationship where there is an asset in which more than one person considers or may consider (or their relatives consider) they have an interest. Whilst a solution may be able to be found it may well cause great anxiety and expense and delay in order to do so and in any event it may not be resolved to everyone's satisfaction.

So what is the answer? The answer is to look at one's finances and relationships and check whether your affairs are in order. This may well involve spending a bit of money in seeking legal advice at an early stage and certainly before mental incapacity or death occurs. It may be that having had that advice you choose to do nothing but at least the issue will have been considered. On the other hand you may well decide to resolve the issues whilst you are still able to do so and while you are still around to explain what has happened and, if need be, to give your side of the story.

Of one thing you can be sure: if you fail to sort things out they will come back to trouble you or, if not you, those you leave behind.

CHAPTER 12

DEATH

KEY POINTS

- Funeral issues should be discussed whilst people are fit and well and their wishes set down.

- Proper enquiries as to what is possible should be made well in advance.

- Squabbles about funeral arrangements are not uncommon.

- Basic wishes should be incorporated in the will. Detailed wishes should be set out elsewhere.

- The wishes should be made known to those who are likely to be involved in the funeral arrangements.

- Executors will be primarily responsible for funeral arrangements.

- Consideration should be given to the cost of the funeral, how it will be paid for and the possibility of pre-payment of the funeral.

- Consider in advance whether, when a loved one dies, you would wish to view the body.

- Express views as to whether you would wish your body to be used for organ donation or medical research. If you think that you may have to make this decision about a relative discuss the matter with them beforehand.

CHAPTER 12

DEATH

THE ISSUES

'It is as natural to die as to be born' wrote Francis Bacon in 1625.

However true this is, most of us steer clear of thinking about the issue of death in any logical way whether in respect of our own death or that of someone close to us and we certainly fail to discuss the issue with those who will be affected.

As a solicitor I almost always try to address the issue of funeral arrangements when I take instructions for a will. It is the opportunity to push people into thinking about the issues and giving directions because:

- it will possibly avoid squabbles when the person dies;

- it will avoid problems if there is a 'mixed' marriage whether that is in terms of religion, culture, race or nationality;

- it will avoid problems if there has been a second marriage and there is a conflict between the surviving spouse and the children from the first marriage;

- it will avoid problems if there is a long term relationship (whether hetero- or homosexual) and there is a possibility of conflict between say children or parents of the deceased on the one hand and the 'partner' on the other;

- it will avoid problems if there is simply conflict in the family;

- it will save the family left behind having to make decisions at a time of great distress and/or exhaustion and possibly after a long period of stress and possibly living to regret decisions made at such times and in such circumstances;

- they may have no-one close with whom to discuss the issue or who will obviously and easily make those decisions;

- it will prompt people to think about the financial aspects of paying for the funeral.

The one time I often do not discuss the issue is when someone is clearly close to death – but even then it depends on the personality with which one is dealing. Oh, how much easier it would be if everyone addressed the issue when hale and hearty.

PROBLEMS OF ADDRESSING THE ISSUE

The problems are these:

- opportunity to discuss it never arises;
- there is fear that it will cause distress to others;
- it is known that it will cause problems when raised;
- there is an illogical belief that discussion will bring it nearer;
- there is an ignorance of the wide range of possible issues to be discussed and the decisions to be made, especially where there have been no near deaths in recent times.

THE ANSWER

The solution is to think through the issues, both practical and emotional, that will arise when your relative dies and try to anticipate them.

In practical terms discuss with your relative(s) their wishes about the funeral arrangements.

Preferably get them to commit them to paper to try to put matters beyond doubt. Try to do this when they are still reasonably well. Try to do it in a light hearted vain. It should, however, be noted that funeral instructions left by the deceased are not actually legally binding but clearly it would be a brave soul who deliberately flouted those instructions without good reason. It should also be noted that in general terms, responsibility for arranging the funeral is that of the executors of the will of the person who has died (if there is a will). If there is no will, then responsibility will be that of the administrators of the estate who will, in general terms, be the next of kin.

There are some curious notions about the term 'next of kin'. I use the term meaning the legal next of kin – not the person who the deceased considers, or refers to, as his next of kin. If a person wishes to appoint someone to be responsible for making funeral arrangements and who is not the legal next of kin then he or she must make a will and appoint an executor or executors. This would be particularly important where there is a 'partner' who the deceased wishes to be responsible for funeral arrangements – otherwise the partner will not be entitled to interfere.

There will be some issues that are entirely decisions which can be made within the family; there will some issues where there will be a legal element to consider.

Especially for anything other than a 'traditional' funeral, the importance of proper enquiries in good time cannot be over emphasised.

A PRELIMINARY POINT

Viewing the body

Death occurs in all manner of circumstances. If death is anticipated you will probably have had chance to contemplate whether you will wish to view the body after death. If, however, death occurs suddenly, for example where your relative suffers a heart attack and you follow the ambulance to hospital only to find that he or she has died, this may well be something you have never contemplated and you may be expected to make a decision very quickly.

It is worth thinking through the scenario in advance. If you make the decision to view the body it will be something you cannot undo. That memory may well be the abiding one you have of your relative and one which you would probably not wish to have. It may well be better to decline to see the body at that time and instead take time to think about how you feel. There is nothing to stop you seeing the body later at the mortuary or later still in the chapel of rest.

One point worthy of mention is the issue of identifying the body.

Sometimes the police or the coroner's officer/coroner's liaison officer may ask you to identify the body to them. This may put you in the position of having to see the body either when you definitely do not wish to do so or when you are uncertain as to whether you wish to do so. It is important to realise that you are under no obligation to do this; no one can force you to do it. There is nothing to stop identification of the body by way of your producing a photograph of the deceased to the police and the police using that to identify the body. Alternatively, someone who knows the deceased but who is more distant can carry out the identification.

THE PRACTICAL ASPECTS

The cost

An important question will always be as to whether there is going to be sufficient money to pay for the funeral.

The cost of funeral arrangements is a first charge on the deceased's estate and may be recovered from it. However, the person ordering the funeral is the contracting party so far as the funeral directors are concerned and that person will be responsible for paying for it even if there is no (or insufficient) money in the estate.

If there is not sufficient then there may be a Social Fund funeral payment available from the Department for Work and Pensions (DWP). The range of people entitled to claim this payment, the financial circumstances of the person, the amount which can be given and what it can cover, is very limited and restricted indeed. If the deceased does not have sufficient assets to pay for the funeral then those responsible should contact the DWP as soon as possible to ascertain if a payment will be available before committing themselves to ordering the funeral unless they are prepared to be responsible for payment themselves. The availability of the benefit depends on the circumstances of the person applying, not those of the person who has died. To all intents and purposes in almost all cases the possibility of a Social Fund funeral payment can be disregarded.

Jobcentre Plus deals with the benefit.

If a person dies in hospital and there is no one available to make funeral arrangements then the hospital must do so or in certain circumstances may pass on responsibility to the local authority. If a death takes place 'in the community' or (in general terms) in a local authority care home and there is no one available to arrange the funeral then the local authority has an obligation to do so. If there is no money available for a full, normal, commercial funeral then the authority will pay for a no-frills public burial. They will be entitled to recover the money paid out from anyone who has an obligation to maintain the deceased under the National Assistance Act 1948 or from any money which the deceased had.

Pre-paid funerals

There is a trend now for people to enter into arrangements whereby they pay for their funeral during their lifetime by way of a pre-paid funeral plan. These can be paid for by a lump sum. Some providers allow for payment by instalments over up to five years.

There are advantages in this, one of which – particularly for those of modest means – is peace of mind that all is settled. A further advantage is that it may well relieve family of decisions in respect of funeral arrangements at a generally distressing time. By the same token there are disadvantages. For example, you may well be tied to a particular funeral director. What happens if you move house? Will another funeral director take the plan?

If it is contemplated entering into such a plan, then it is prudent to enter into such with one of the major providers of funeral plans and care should be taken thoroughly to read and understand the terms of the plan including the small print. It is vital to appreciate that the plan will not cover all the funeral expenses and additional payments may well be needed at the time of death, especially if additional services are required or, for example, the death occurs abroad. There may also be a problem in paying for all the costs of a burial where a new grave is needed.

My own local authority will no longer allow plots to be bought in advance because the local cemetery is running out of space.

Accordingly all that can be done in those circumstances is to pay the basic cost of the funeral in advance but the actual cost of the new grave will have to be paid for at the time it is needed.

Do check carefully as to what is covered.

Maximum care must be exercised when looking at funeral plans offered and administered by individual firms of funeral directors and which are not backed by one of the major providers. Apart from anything else there may well be issues of security of the monies paid. What happens if the funeral director goes out of business? Some information on pre-paid funeral plans can be found in the consumer section of the Office of Fair Trading website

It should be noted that often, if means-tested benefits are claimed during lifetime and because all plan monies may be refundable, the authorities may take the value of the plan into account in assessing means.

Finally if you do take out a plan, do make sure those close to you are aware of the existence of the plan and who it is with.

Burial or cremation?

- The issue of cost may be relevant here. It is likely that if a new grave has to be purchased a burial will be significantly more expensive than cremation.
- If there is an existing grave:
  - will the deceased have a right to be buried in it? Is it known who has ownership of (or more accurately, rights of burial in) the grave? If the deceased does not own the grave then will the person who owns it give permission? How will that be proved? These questions will

need addressing even if there is to be a cremation and only the cremated remains (ashes) are to be interred.

- o Is there sufficient room in the grave?
- o Do you know where the grave is?
- o Do you know where the grave papers are?
- o Is there more than one possible grave? Is there any room for confusion as to which grave is intended?

- In deciding where to bury either a body or ashes, consideration might need to be given to the form of headstone and the inscription on the headstone. Some churches and local authorities have significant restrictions on what can be placed on graves or words/inscriptions that may be used on headstones. It is prudent to enquire of the Vicar or cemetery authority what rules they have.
- Some religious groups, notably, Orthodox Jews and Muslims, forbid cremation.
- For anyone who may wish to put items in the coffin there may well be some restrictions in the case of cremations. Enquiries need to be made. Useful information as to this can be obtained from the Institute of Cemetery and Crematorium Management website. A frequently asked questions section (FAQ) on that website is also valuable.
- Enquiries should, of course, be made of an older person to verify that he or she would not object to cremation. Enquiries should also be made of relatives to make sure that no one else is likely to object to cremation. The person signing the cremation papers will need to certify as to this.
- For those wishing to be buried in a Church of England graveyard then the decision as to whether this will be possible will lie with the incumbent (Vicar). It would be wise to check the position early.

Where is the funeral to take place?

- Did the deceased have any particular wishes as to where the funeral/interment should take place?
- Removal of the body any distance and particularly abroad may well prove costly.
- In the case of removal out of the country there will be a very definite time delay and significant bureaucracy to be gone through.
- Will the location of the interment cause complications for those wishing to visit the grave at a later date? This could be significant even within the UK but it would be particularly relevant if there were to be an international dimension.
- What would the deceased's views be if they he/she were to die abroad? Would they wish to be repatriated? Should there be a cremation abroad and the ashes returned to this country? Anyone who spends periods out of the country and wishes to be repatriated would be well advised to make

enquiries in good time as to procedure and costs involved in case they should die abroad.

The service

- Local facilities will need to be considered here.
- Bear in mind that there will be time limits at Cemetery and Crematorium Chapels. A double 'slot' may have to be booked.
- Are there any absolutes (that is any aspects on which there can be no compromise)?
- Is there to be a religious element?

    o If the answer to this is 'yes' what 'brand' would be involved?
    o Would there be a service in a place of worship as a preliminary and then a short service at the crematorium chapel (if a cremation) or a short service at the graveside if a burial? If so at which place of worship?
    o Would there simply be a service at the crematorium or cemetery chapel?
    o What level of service would be required?
    o Would there be a particular choice of officiant?
    o If there is to be no religious element what will happen?
    o Is there to be a humanist celebration? A humanist celebration is a 'service' without a religious element for those for whom religion is unimportant, or who have made a clear decision to live their lives without it. For them a religious funeral service may seem insincere and bring little comfort. It may not feel the right way to say farewell to someone who did not accept the religious view of life and death. A humanist ceremony is said to have more warmth and meaning for these people.

- Whatever type of service or celebration is to be held, consideration will need to be given to the following:

    o Whether the person conducting the service/celebration is going to have sufficient information to be able to say something meaningful about the person who has died. This will be particularly the case if a professional officiant is to take the service and who has not known the person who has died. It is useful to be able to provide to the person conducting the service some biographical details of the person who has died and in order to ensure that those are accurate, it may be worth while the person themselves preparing their own biographical details. These might include some information about his or her parents, where he or she was born, his or her school days and so on.

Comment might usefully be made on his or her working life, his military service; his interests and hobbies and sports and membership of organisations or churches; any civic appointments he or she has had such as being Magistrate or a Councillor; details of children or other family; details of any awards they may have been given; interests in charities. Even such information as the person's appearance, their height, their weight, hair colour etc. can be invaluable to an officiant along with details as to personality and 'what made him or her tick'.

o   It may also be helpful to have information about any one or anything which should not be mentioned, such as information about any estranged members of the family; information about their later years.

o   A check should be made with the Vicar as to any non-Christian 'service' which may be desired to take place in a Church of England graveyard. Are there any restrictions?

o   Will the family or friends conduct the proceedings? If so, who will do this and what form will it take?

o   It may be that someone in the family, or a friend, may want to give a eulogy. If so, information such as that above will be invaluable. A booklet entitled 'Well chosen words – How to write a eulogy' can be obtained from the Co-operative Funeralcare website.

o   After the service, will it be desired to know who has attended? Will the mourners be invited to complete attendance cards? Who will distribute and collect them?

The music

At most funerals there will be some musical content. The extent will depend upon the place where the funeral is taking place, the practice of the particular religion (if there is to be a religious element) and the facilities available.

Some of the following points may be considered:

- Is there an organ available?
- Can an organist be found? Is some other type of instrument to be played?
- Is there a facility for the playing of cassette tapes or CDs? How many can be played?
- What music is available at the crematorium or chapel?
- If a hymn is to be sung will the congregation be provided with the words?

Will a hymn sheet have to be produced perhaps as part of an order of service? It should be noted that at most cemetery chapels and crematoria a basic service book is provided and does contain the text of the most popular hymns.

- If there is to be a service in a church will there be music whilst the congregation wait?
- What music will be played as the funeral party enters the church or crematorium?
- What music will be played as they leave the church or crematorium?

The body

- How is the body to be dressed – in his/her own clothes or in a dressing gown provided by the funeral directors? There may be restrictions as to the dressing of the body in synthetic clothes especially in the case of a cremation.
- Is jewellery to remain on the body?
- As indicated above, especially in the case of a cremation, there may be restrictions on items to be placed on, or in, the coffin.

Dress

- Will there be any requests for particular dress at the funeral? Some people might choose to ask mourners not to wear black.

Flowers

- Will the issue of flowers be left for each individual to decide or will there be a request for family flowers only with donations to a charity and if so which one?

- Where and by what time will flowers be required?

- What is to happen to flowers after the service? Should they be left behind at the crematorium or should the funeral directors be asked to take them to a church, home or hospital? The decision on this may depend on whether the flowers look as though they have come from a funeral in which case some institutions may prefer not to accept them.

- Consider whether to direct purchase of some flowers at the cost of the estate especially if there may not be many flowers sent by others.

The obituary

- In which newspapers will the obituary be published?
- How many times should it appear? Appearing more than once (even if one of them is after the funeral) can be useful in case someone misses the first notice. It may save an embarrassing incident later.
- What information should be included?
  - Should there be a reference to the deceased's address and if so in how much detail? (Remember, there could be security implications here.)
  - The deceased's age?
  - Which family members or relationships should be mentioned?
  - What terms of endearment should be used (for example beloved, loving, devoted etc.).
  - Which family members should be mentioned?
  - Will family members be mentioned by name or simply by description?
  - Will ex-spouses be mentioned?
  - Will estranged children or other family members be mentioned?
  - Will reference be made to the place of death (for example in hospital)?
  - Will reference be made to the circumstances of death (for example, suddenly, tragically, after a short illness, etc.)?
  - Will reference be made to any particular awards (for example MBE, a doctorate, etc.)?
  - Will reference be made to occupation or past occupation or position in the community (for example former Mayor or Councillor or as local shopkeeper etc.)?

Where should the cortege leave from?

- Will mourners meet at the chapel of rest?
- Will the cortege leave from the deceased's home address? Will the coffin be taken into the home address? (Especially if the cortege is to leave from the home address, consider leaving someone at the property whilst away as a security measure.)
- Will the mourners (or most of them) meet at the church or at the crematorium or cemetery chapel?
- How many cars will be required?
- How will mourners get from the place of worship etc. to the crematorium or cemetery or grave side?

Post funeral refreshments

The issue of post funeral refreshments is one which is very much dependent on all the circumstances.

- Are people coming from far and wide on the day?
- What time of day is the funeral?
- How many people will attend? Is it known, indeed even roughly, how many will attend?
- Will they know each other?
- Are there going to be many acquaintances – perhaps known through some organisation?
- Could there be a family squabble?
- If there is to be a service at a place of worship followed by committal elsewhere will there be refreshments immediately after the service with the family returning to the place of refreshment after a private committal?
- Will the refreshments be provided at the deceased's home or at the home of a family member? If so who will provide them in practical terms?
- If refreshments are to take place at (or indeed if the cortege is to leave from) the deceased's home is there a risk that the 'vultures' may descend and try to remove items?

The acknowledgement

It is of course normal after the funeral to place an acknowledgement in the local newspaper thanking those associated with the deceased in the period leading up to the death and those involved after the death.
In Appendix 5 I have listed some of those who you may wish to mention. The list is not exhaustive.

The ashes

What is to happen to the ashes after the cremation? Much may depend on local facilities. The following points can be made:

- Contrary to popular belief the ashes are those of the individual deceased.
- Cremation takes place as soon as possible after the service and in any event the same day. If there is to be a delay, the person signing the cremation papers will be notified.
- The ashes are normally available for collection within a few days of the funeral. The crematorium normally retains them for a period of time and if no contrary instructions are given they will eventually be buried or scattered at the crematorium.
- Based on my own experience, do not leave it for long after the funeral to deal with the ashes finally since otherwise all the old memories are resurrected when the interment of the ashes comes along.

- Consider whether family are to be present at the interment. Is it desired that a clergyman should be present at that time?
- At some crematoria it is possible to rent a 'niche' in a wall into which an urn containing the ashes may be inserted for a period of years and bearing an appropriate inscription.
- The ashes may well be able to be interred at the crematorium.
- They may be interred in a grave (see above for issues in respect of permission).
- They may be taken away for scattering or burial elsewhere.
- If the ashes are to be buried at sea (as opposed to being scattered on the sea) the consent of a Fisheries Officer of the Department for Environment, Food and Rural Affairs (DEFRA) is required. Embalmed bodies cannot be buried at sea.

Memorials

The type of memorial will depend on local facilities available.

- There may be a Book of Remembrance on display at the crematorium and in which details of the deceased may be entered and which are displayed on the anniversary of the death. At my local authority crematorium the options are for either a two, five or eight line inscription with the first line giving the deceased's name only and thereafter being limited to thirty-five characters per line.
- Some crematoria have the option of purchasing a rose bush or a nameplate in the Garden of Remembrance for a period of time. See earlier for the possibility of a niche being purchased.
- As indicated earlier, thought needs to be given and enquiries made as to whether there are any restrictions as to headstones, inscriptions etc. which can be placed on or near a grave.
- Consideration should be given as to the wording to be placed on the memorial whether that be on a new grave stone or added to an existing grave stone.

Setting it out

As already indicated in Chapter 10, some basic details of the funeral ought to be set out in the will.

The will is frequently the place that those who are charged with making arrangements for a funeral look to see if the testator has any particular wishes.

However, there is a danger that the will may not be seen until after the funeral. Accordingly, it would be wise to write down funeral wishes and place that somewhere safe and where it can be found. It would be wise to give copies to the executors or others who will be responsible for organising the funeral. If the older person is in care it may be wise to put details with their notes at the Home. Care should be taken that conflicting instructions are not given over a period of time to different people. Written instructions should be kept up to date.

Other issues

Body donation

Some people wish their body to be given to medical research.

A number of points need to be considered:

- If this is your wish, do ensure you discuss it with members of your family and your executors.
- There will be no funeral at or around the time of your death. Will this cause problems for the family? Will a memorial service be held instead of a funeral?
- Full arrangements for donations need to be made in good time before death. Forms need to be completed. These can be obtained from a *University Medical School* or from *HM Inspector of Anatomy.*
- There is no guarantee that even if you complete the forms etc. that the University will actually want your body at the time. This may be for a variety of reasons:

  o They are already fully 'stocked'.
  o You die too far away. (This need only be a fairly short distance.)
  o Because you have had an illness or accident etc. which may make your body of no value to them for research purposes.
  o The body has been subject to a post-mortem examination.
  o Organs have been removed for the purpose of organ transplant. The one exception is the removal of corneas.

- The body can be kept only for a limited period at which point the University will arrange and pay for a basic cremation. Anything more will have to be paid for from your estate/by your family. This may have to be provided for in your will and a sum kept back for the purpose.
- Executors and close family and friends who may be responsible for your affairs need to know the position and the procedure to be adopted on your death. Steps will need to be taken to have the body refrigerated until it can be handed over to the Medical School.

- If the donation is refused the responsibility for funeral arrangements reverts to the executors/family and the older person should ensure that they have expressed alternative funeral arrangements in case this happens. They should ensure that adequate money will remain in their estate to pay for the unexpected funeral.

Organ or tissue donation

Many people are now inclined to let parts of their body be used to benefit others following their death.

Organs that can be donated include heart, lungs, kidneys, pancreas, liver and small bowel. Tissue that can be donated includes corneas, skin, bone and heart valves. Unlike organs, tissue can be donated up to twenty-four hours after a person has died and can be stored for longer periods.

The law says that if a person either in writing at any time or orally in the presence of two or more witnesses during his or her last illness, expresses a request that his body or any part be used for therapeutic purposes or for the purposes of medical education or research, the person lawfully in possession of the body may, unless he believes the request was subsequently withdrawn, authorise the removal from the body of any part of it, or, if such is the case, the specified part, for use in accordance with the request.

If this is a person's wish (and irrespective of an oral expression of wish being sufficient) then the person would be well advised to:

- Use a donor card.
- Register their willingness for their body to be used for organ donation with the NHS Organ Donor Register (See under UK Transplant in Appendix 2).
- Make sure that the family and executors are aware and that even if they disagree with the person's wishes, they will respect them.
- Make sure that any home into which the person moves and any hospital or hospice to which they might be admitted is aware of their wishes.

Even if a person has not made such a request then the law allows the person in lawful possession of a body to authorise the removal of any part of the body if, having made reasonable enquiries, he has no reason to believe that the deceased had expressed objection to such removal and had not withdrawn the objection, and has no reason to believe that the surviving spouse or any surviving relative of the deceased objects.

Accordingly, it is essential that if an older person does not wish their body to be used for medical research or for organ donation etc. they should clearly express this wish. This is especially so if they know that their executors or close family members have a strong belief that bodies should be used for such purposes.

Remember:

- Following a death, time for the removal of organs will be of the essence.
- Those who may have to give consent will need to be contacted speedily.
- If someone is in a nursing home etc. then the management of the home, as well as the person's GP should be made aware of the person's wishes and the steps that may need to be taken on their death.

OVERALL

The above items are not intended to be exhaustive. All the circumstances of the individual including their religious beliefs, their culture, their station in life, their financial position and so on and the facilities in the area available at the time of death will need to be considered.

It is important that even if the wishes of the person are discussed and settled that this should not be regarded as a once and for all discussion and decision. People's ideas change as they age and as their circumstances change and plans should be kept up to date.

It is also important to remember that funeral practices change over time. A move to much more informal and personalised funerals has been apparent in recent years. Such funerals may be much more meaningful to those left behind. Those contemplating their own deaths and those who may have to make arrangements should keep their thinking and wishes up-to-date and properly expressed. Useful information and thoughts on modern funerals can be found in 'The Dead Good Funerals Book' published by Welfare State International and from the Natural Death Centre who publish the 'Natural Death Handbook'.

Since to organise a personal funeral might need some time, the need to enquire and plan in advance cannot be over-emphasised.

CHAPTER 13

DISPOSING OF ASSETS

KEY POINTS

- The two main reasons why older people wish to give away their assets is to avoid Inheritance Tax and/or to avoid paying residential care home fees (or in some cases to avoid paying fees for the provision of services at home).

- In the seven years before death the scope for avoiding Inheritance Tax is limited. Specialist Tax advice should be sought.

- For whatever reason assets are given away, you lose control of the asset either totally or partially.

- You cannot give away an asset for one purpose but keep it for another.

- You are not permitted to deliberately deprive yourself of an asset with a significant intention of claiming benefit or reducing accommodation charges.

- In establishing whether there is a deliberate deprivation the authorities take all the circumstances into account especially the time of any transfer.

- If deliberate deprivation is found then the older person will be treated as still owning the asset and may be bankrupted and the asset recovered.

- Those attempting, in their capacity as a donee of an EPA, to give away the assets of someone else, should be warned that they are almost certainly not permitted to do so under the rules governing EPAs unless the Court of Protection can be persuaded to consent to the gift.

- Transfers at an undervalue (that is a transfer to someone of a property or other asset at less than its market value) are treated in the same way as gifts.

CHAPTER 13

DISPOSING OF ASSETS

ISSUES

Frequently people of any age from perhaps fifty-five upwards consult solicitors about transferring assets from their names, whether husband or wife together, or just the survivor of them, into the names of their child or children or sometimes other relatives or friends.

The usual asset that they come to discuss is the house, but often the discussion moves on to other assets such as savings.

Some clients are quite upfront about their motives. Others are quite discreet.

Setting aside those who want to transfer properties to assist in bringing family members into this country from abroad, and those who fear being made bankrupt and wish to divest themselves of assets, the most usual reasons for a transfer of property are:

- avoiding Inheritance Tax on death;
- avoiding having to pay for Residential Care.

INHERITANCE TAX

This book does not purport to deal with issues of Inheritance Tax in any depth. However, the following points can be made:

- Inheritance Tax does not kick-in until the value of the assets on death (and taking into account some gifts made in lifetime) exceed (as at April 2004) £263,000.

  If your estate is below this level Inheritance Tax would not usually be an issue.

- If your estate, (including some gifts made during lifetime) exceeds £263,000 then (unless your estate is going to your husband or wife and you are both domiciled in the UK or to certain charities etc) Inheritance Tax will be payable. ('Husband or wife' does not include unmarried partners.)

- The rate of tax is 40%.

- If you wish to stand any chance of avoiding Inheritance Tax then you will have to dispose of some of your assets more than seven years before death.

- Frequently people try to give their house away to children or others but continue to live in it, rent free, and virtually as before. This will not avoid Inheritance Tax. If there is any element of 'retention of benefit' in any gift, such as continuing to live in the property, then tax will be payable.Only if you pay and continue to pay, for at least seven years from the gift, a full commercial rent and assume the usual responsibilities of a tenant, do you stand any chance of not paying Inheritance Tax in the event of your death within seven years of the gift.

- Additionally, from 6 April 2005 there will be a new tax, the Pre-owned Property Tax, which will levy income tax on the notional rental value of assets (including houses) which are given away but the benefit of which continues to be enjoyed by the person giving the asset away. This will be retrospective and will affect assets given away since 18 March 1986. Whilst there are some limited exemptions from this, anyone with a house in which they continue to live after giving it away, may well find themselves liable to pay annual income tax calculated on the value of the rent which they should pay were they to be a tenant at the property. The same applies to chattels and some other assets which have been given away but from which the donor continues to benefit.

One exemption will be transfers between husband and wife. A further exemption is where the annual value of the benefit retained does not exceed £2500. This is only likely to benefit those who have given away assets of less than approximately £50,000 capital value.

It is important that anyone who has given away assets since 18 March 1986 and from which they continue to benefit, should take legal and/or accountancy advice as soon as possible. They may well be advised to take advantage of an option to bring the asset back into the scope of Inheritance Tax and therefore avoid the new tax. This should be done as soon as possible but in any even the election to bring the asset back must be exercised before January 2007. However, it does still need to be borne in mind that the tax starts to have effect from 6 April 2005.

It is vital that no action should be taken without specific legal and/or accountancy advice.

- There are various tax saving devices that can be adopted. Some of these involve making gifts during lifetime. These include:

  o Wedding gifts of up to £5,000 to each of your children (including step children and adopted children) or the person whom your child is marrying.

  o Wedding gifts up to £2,500 to each grandchild or the person your grandchild is marrying.

  o Wedding gifts of up to £1,000 to anyone else.

  o Payments for the maintenance of your husband or wife, ex-husband or ex-wife, dependant relatives and usually, your children who are under eighteen or in full time education.

  o Other gifts up to a value of £3,000 in any one tax year (the tax year running from 6 April in one year to 5 April in the next year) plus any unused balance of £3,000 from the previous tax year.

  o Outright gifts in any tax year up to a total of £250 each to any number of people but only if the total of all gifts made by you to the recipient in the same tax year does not exceed £250.

The issue here is do you want to give away assets that you may need in the future simply to avoid the tax man on death?

Other strategies involve making a will with provisions for certain gifts the amounts of which will not attract Inheritance Tax. An example of this is:

- A gift to one or more UK registered charities.

The issue here is, again do you want to miss out giving family and friends assets simply to avoid the taxman?

In relation to all Inheritance Tax issues, specialist tax advice is called for either from solicitors with a good knowledge of taxation or an accountant with similar knowledge. Be wary of financial advisors with clever tax saving schemes but who have no idea how to implement them and who may have the commission motive at the back of their minds.

AVOIDING RESIDENTIAL AND OTHER CARE FEES

By far and away the most common motive for the disposal of assets by those in the fifty-five plus age group is the fear of going into residential care and finding that their assets, including their house, have to be used to pay home fees.

The position in respect of home fees and benefits is complex.

In general terms the rule is that in England if you have over £20,000 of capital you will have to pay home fees entirely yourself except for any element of those fees that comprise nursing charges.

If you have between £12,250 and £20,000 then you have to pay a contribution based on five pence per week for each £1 over £12,250 that you have. This is called 'tariff income'. This means that you are not actually treated as having capital but you are treated as having an income from capital.

Only when you drop below £12,250 of capital do fees cease to be payable completely.

Most people, especially those of modest means where perhaps the most significant asset is the house, feel aggrieved that their hard earned assets have to be used to pay home fees when they have contributed to the National Insurance Scheme and have been taxed throughout many years.

It is the wish of most to pass on their assets, and again especially the house, to their children.

In consequence they may well try to pass on their assets (and again this is usually the house) to their child or children, or (occasionally) to others during lifetime so that should they need residential care in the future then they will no longer have assets which can be used to pay the fees.

There are immense problems associated with this and before anyone decides to go along this path they should think very carefully and take good legal advice based on their particular circumstances. However, I will set out some of the main points that must be considered:

- If your intention is to avoid paying home fees you need to have in mind that if the authorities can prove that your disposal of assets has been made with a significant intention of claiming or increasing your claim to benefits then you will continue to be treated as owning those assets for the purpose of determining the level of your contribution to fees. This may well mean that you have no right to help with home fees. The consequences of this may be that, whilst you will not be turfed out of the home, you may be made bankrupt by the local authority who will then 'trace' the assets of which you have disposed even if these have subsequently been disposed of by the person to whom you have given them.

In proving whether you have deliberately disposed of assets for this purpose the authorities look at all the circumstances of the disposal and in particular:

o Your knowledge of the benefits rules. If it can be shown that you knew the financial limits applicable then this may well be fatal.

o How long in advance of going into care did the transfer of the asset take place. If it was only a short time before then there is a real risk that you will be treated as having made the transfer to claim benefits. In consequence it is important that any such transfers should be made well in advance of your going into residential care and indeed before there is a real risk of your going into care. However, you will see from the further points in this section that there are serious risks of effecting the transfer too soon. You have to balance the risk of the authorities getting their hands on your assets against the other risks involved.

• In giving away assets remember that you when you give an asset away you give it away for all purposes; you cannot give it away to defeat the benefits system but not for other reasons. In consequence, you will be unlikely to be able to recover a property from a relative (or other person) to whom you have given it if you change your mind about the wisdom of having given it.

• When you have given away an asset, especially your house, will the person to whom you give it lose interest in you afterwards?

• If you give away your house whilst you are still living in it, the house is no longer yours. Will the new owner (a relative or whoever) decide that they want you out of the house?

• Whilst the new owner may behave properly towards you what will happen if he or she dies before you and the house passes to another more distant family member or indeed out of the family to, say, a charity under the person's will? There must be a real risk that you will be evicted from the property.

- A further risk is as to what will happen if the person to whom you give the property gets into financial difficulty, whether from stupidity or purely bad luck, and his or her creditors look around for assets to seize and discover the property in which you live but which is owned by the debtor. Here again, there must be a real risk of your losing your home

- A property given away to a married child will become a matrimonial asset of that child and will fall to be considered by a court in deciding how to divide the matrimonial assets of the parties should the marriage fall apart. Consider carefully whether you would want your in-law to benefit from your property whilst you were still alive if your child's marriage disintegrated.

- What will happen if, having given away the house, you decide you want to move elsewhere, perhaps to the seaside? The person to whom you have given the house would have to agree to the house being sold and the money being used to buy another house. In other words you have lost your control over the asset. This is a particular risk if you give away the house when you are still comparatively young and active

- I am aware that you will probably think that your family will behave honourably towards you if you give your assets to them. However, it is a sad fact that others have thought this in the past and have been sadly and bitterly disappointed. The family member themselves, may not be the main problem but if they are weak and/or have a strong partner they may be manipulated or pressured into behaving badly.

- I have encountered those in their late fifties who have wanted to give away assets, especially their house, because they fear going into care. Unless the person has a serious health issue it is my view that this is ridiculously early. If people are in good health (and especially where there is a married couple) then real consideration should, in my view, not be given to transferring property until people are in their seventies. Yes, there is a risk; there is always the possibility that the healthiest person in their sixties may have a stroke and be incapacitated and need residential care and the assets of that person may have to be used to pay for care. However, a balance has to be struck between that risk and the risk of giving away to others your house and losing it when you still have need of it.

- It is possible to dispose of the property into an 'interest in possession' Trust whereby the property is transferred to Trustees on trust for named beneficiaries say, your children, but you remain allowed to live in the house for life. It is possible, but inadvisable in case you become mentally incapable, for you to be one of the trustees. This route may well have the advantage of guarding against the excesses of someone to whom the property is given and may also ensure that you are able to live in the house. Nonetheless you still lose control of your asset and it does not get round the risk of the transfer being challenged and possibly set aside on the grounds that it was a deliberate deprivation of capital. It will also not avoid the forthcoming Pre-owned Property Tax.

- Those who are the donees under Enduring Powers of Attorney should not think that they are entitled to transfer to themselves (or others) by way of gift the donor's house. It must be remembered that anything but the most modest of gifts in very restricted circumstances are prohibited unless the power is registered and the Court of Protection approves the gift. Whilst the transfer of a house to a child in order to avoid home fees may well benefit the child, it is hard to see how it can be considered as a benefit to the older person.

- If someone has put in place an EPA which has not been registered with the Court of Protection then the restriction on gifts still applies but it would be open to the donor himself or herself to make the gift as long as he or she has mental capacity to do so. However, the deliberate deprivation provisions may still affect the validity and effect of the gift. For those who may consider transferring their property to a relative etc. but for a figure less than its value, they should be aware that a sale at an undervalue would be treated in much the same way as the gift if the undervalue is discovered.

CONCLUSION

Whilst giving away assets can, in some instances, be distinctly beneficial both in terms of saving Inheritance Tax and avoiding home fees, great care has to be exercised and all the circumstances of the case examined. Older people contemplating such gifts do need to consider carefully all the facts and particularly the personalities of those to whom they contemplate giving the asset. The benefit of good and independent legal advice cannot be underestimated.

If in doubt, keep the asset and pay the tax or the home fees.

CHAPTER 14

ADVANCE DIRECTIVES (LIVING WILLS)

KEY POINTS

- The manner of a person's dying might be more frightening to them than death itself especially if they are or may be unable to communicate their wishes.

- Requests for unlawful treatment or action cannot validly be made.

- English law now accepts that, subject to certain conditions, and with a few exceptions, a person can express in advance what medical treatment he or she would not want at a later date if he or she could not express their view at that time. This is done in an Advance Directive or Living Will.

- Expression of wishes will assist doctors in deciding the course of treatment to be followed.

- Doctors should be consulted before an Advance Directive is made.

- Good legal advice would also be prudent.

- As a supplement to the Advance Directive an extended values history would also be helpful.

- Steps must be taken to ensure that the documents are available at the appropriate time.

- Expressions of wishes as to who should or should not be consulted about medical treatment decisions, whilst not being effective in the same way as an Advance Directive refusing treatment, may well serve a very valuable purpose.

- The law in this area is changing.

CHAPTER 14

ADVANCE DIRECTIVES (LIVING WILLS)

ISSUES

For a few people the idea of death is not a problem – but for a great many more the manner of their dying (and their care generally in later years) causes them concern. This concern is magnified by worry about being unable to control it or express their views if they cease to be mentally capable of doing so.

For some, therefore, the concept of being able to express their view on the subject in some way before they become too ill has a certain appeal and to some extent this can be achieved by the making of an *Advance Directive* (sometimes, and more popularly, called a *Living Will*).

This is an ever-developing area of the law that is being developed largely by case law and not, until recently, by Acts of Parliament. (As a result of the Mental Capacity Bill 2004 significant changes will take place in the not too distant future.) Accordingly no absolute guarantee can be given as to the legal effect of the Living Will or an Advance Directive but as things stand at present as long as the Advance Directive meets some basic criteria it is likely to prove a very useful step in the planning for later life and in the following sections I look at some of the main aspects of Advance Directives.

Before doing that, however, there is one important point which needs to be made: Advance Directives/Living Wills have nothing whatsoever to do with the highly emotive subject of euthanasia often referred to in the tabloid press as 'mercy-killing'. Making an Advance Directive is only about expressing views as to what treatment a person would not wish to undergo or which lawful treatment they would be willing to undergo if they were unable to communicate that view at the time problems arose. Indeed, it must be stressed that any attempt to include a provision for any illegal steps to be taken deliberately to end a life would be wholly ineffective.

This area is a complex one and no one should be under the impression that making an Advance Directive is straightforward notwithstanding that it is possible to buy forms for the purpose.

1.   WHAT IS AN ADVANCE DIRECTIVE?

It is a statement, usually in writing, in which a mentally competent person expresses his or her preferences about medical treatment in the event of he or she becoming incapable of making and communicating a decision about treatment.

Technically, an Advance Directive may be:

(a)   An 'instruction directive' in which the maker gives instructions about the kind of treatment he or she wants (a 'request directive') or does not want (a 'refusal directive').

(b)   A 'proxy directive' in which the maker appoints someone else to make and communicate treatment decisions on his or her behalf.

(c)   A combined instruction and proxy directive.

Advance Directives (and particularly refusal directives) are commonly called 'Living Wills'.

2.   WHAT IS THE LEGAL STATUS OF AN ADVANCE DIRECTIVE?

As a result of recent court decisions it would appear that a refusal directive (as distinct from a request directive or a proxy directive) would be valid and enforceable subject to certain conditions.

These conditions are that:

(a)   It is clearly established.

(b)   It is applicable in the circumstances.

(c)   That the maker was mentally competent when he or she made it.

(d)   The maker was not unduly influenced by someone else.

(e)   The maker contemplated the situation that eventually arose.

(f)   The maker was aware of the consequences of refusing treatment.

(g)   It does not request any unlawful action or omission.

(h)   It does not request treatment that the medical team considers to be clinically inappropriate.

At the moment in English law a proxy directive, in which the maker appoints someone else to make treatment decisions, is not valid or enforceable. Indeed, it should be noted that whilst doctors may choose to discuss treatment decisions with members of the patient's family where the patient cannot express his or her own view, there is no legal requirement to do so and the doctors must act in what they consider to be the best interests of the patient and if they are in doubt it is open to them to go to the court for a decision. However, it is unlikely that a request for a particular individual to be consulted before a treatment decision was made would be ignored by the doctors – but at the end of the day the decision is theirs.

(Note: Where a patient is detained under the Mental Health Act 1983 the contents of any Advance Directive may well be overridden.)

3.   RE-DRAFTING

As long ago as November 1992 the British Medical Association issued a statement on the subject of Advance Directives and made the point that Advance Directives should be redrafted at least every five years but it is now considered that a living will should be redrafted or, at any rate affirmed, every three years. This is clearly very important since it allows regard to be had to the changes in medical science that may have taken place in the intervening period.

If a particular condition is being anticipated and where there are continuing improvements in the treatment available then, in those cases especially, it may be appropriate to redraft much more frequently. It is important that the drafting of the Advance Directive should not be seen as a once and for all act but should be part of a continuing relationship between the doctor and patient. It also follows from this that in the drafting of an Advance Directive the maker of the Advance Directive should consult with their doctor.

4.   LEGAL ADVICE

It is the case that legal advice is not a necessity for an Advance Directive. However, it would be a very prudent step for a number of reasons:

- As with an ordinary will it is vital that the person signing an Advance Directive does so of their own free will and not because of any pressure from family and friends especially where those family or friends stand to gain from the client's estate in the event of his or her death.

- The whole idea of an Advance Directive is so that if the client cannot speak for him or herself at the appropriate time the doctors can refer to the document which the client made when he or she was physically and mentally able to express a view. Accordingly, when the client makes the Advance Directive he or she must be mentally competent to do so. A solicitor would endeavour to ensure that, as with an ordinary will, the client was mentally capable of executing the document. If the client does not have someone reliable and independent to confirm that the wishes were expressed when the client was mentally competent then the validity of the document may be called into question at the time when it is needed. This would particularly be the case if members of the family tried to intervene and interfere with the expressed wishes whether that was due to a genuine disagreement with the client's views (whether for moral or religious reasons or because of selfish motives of wishing the patient to live albeit with a poor quality of life) or because of malicious motives.

- The making of an Advance Directive is by no means a straightforward task and often clients who embark on the task do not appreciate the 'brain power' which they will have to put in to making an Advance Directive and making decisions as to what he or she does or does not want. There is a danger that the Advance Directive on the one hand may be too simple and generalised as to be meaningless or on the other hand that it may be so complex and specific as not to be appropriate or relevant at the time when it is needed. A balance has to be struck. It is the case that Advance Directive forms can be purchased but many of these are highly complex and it may well be better for a 'custom' designed Directive to be prepared but only after some discussion. Discussing the matter with a solicitor may well assist in clarifying the client's thoughts and enable him or her to strike a balance between the two extremes. Whilst a solicitor would almost certainly advise the client to consult his or her own doctor before signing an Advance Directive the reality is that many doctors have little understanding of Advance Directives and in any event would probably have insufficient time to discuss the matter at any length. Accordingly, the solicitor may well be the only detached and professional person with whom the client can discuss the matter

5. OTHER COUNTRIES

Different countries have different laws about Advance Directives.

Those who make an Advance Directive and who travel out of the country especially for prolonged periods should consider whether they should make enquiries of the country to which they travel whether that country (or, indeed, in different states in the USA and possibly other places) will recognise the Advance Directive. It may well be prudent to enter into a new Advance

Directive for the period that the person is abroad and which meets the requirement of the area to which he or she is travelling. Investigation on reliable sites on the internet may prove helpful as would enquiry of the appropriate Embassy etc.

6. CONSULTATION

I have touched on the possibility of a client naming the person who he or she would like to be consulted about treatment decisions. Perhaps as important could be the naming of those who the client would not wish to be consulted. It may well be that the client knows full well that a particular member of the family would not have their best interests at heart in making treatment decisions or that the person concerned would allow irrational or emotional thinking to cloud their decision making. Guidance set out when the patient was able to understand and communicate his or her wishes may well be very helpful to medical staff when deciding whom to consult. As with all things in connection with Advance Directives the importance of keeping this part of the Directive up-to-date cannot be over emphasised. It would be unfortunate if a person, going through a rough patch in a relationship, excluded the other party from decision making and failed to remove that exclusion if the relationship returned to a state of happiness.

7. WAIVING CONFIDENTIALITY

As a result of experiences with a local hospital it has become apparent that another very good reason for making an Advance Directive is to allow a patient to waive his or her rights of confidentiality. Doctors, in common with other professionals, are under a duty to maintain confidentiality about a patient's affairs. This has been strengthened by the Data Protection Legislation.

However, I am of the view that this issue of confidentiality can be carried to extremes and can be used by medical professionals to avoid discussing a patient's condition and treatment with those who have a legitimate reason for knowing. This can cause unnecessary anguish.

Accordingly, one way round this is for the patient to consider including in their Advance Directive a provision waiving their right of confidentiality and expressly permitting the medical team to give full information about the patient's treatment to a named individual or named individuals or to a group of people. This may well also be combined with a direction not to disclose information to others.

I am confident that such a written provision would prevent medical professionals hiding behind the cloak of confidentiality.

8.   INFORMATION TO BE INCLUDED

In drafting an Advance Directive the following information should be included:

- the maker's full name and address;
- date of birth;
- the name address and telephone number of the General Practitioner;
- whether the matter had been discussed with a doctor or doctors and if so who;
- in the event of a wish being expressed as to who should be consulted before any treatment decision is made then the name and address of that person, their relationship to the maker of the Advance Directive and also their home and work and mobile telephone numbers;
- in the event of a wish to direct who should not be consulted then the name and relationship of that person or those persons;
- a waiver of the patient's right of confidentiality;
- a clear statement of the person's wishes; these could be in general terms or specific terms;
- a statement as to the circumstances in which the Advance Directive should be brought into effect; for example, a description of any terminal illness or other conditions which will trigger a particular course of action or inaction;
- a statement of what would be unacceptable treatment e.g. the treatment might be limited to keeping the maker comfortable and free from pain but all other treatment would be refused; it may be for instance that major surgery, kidney dialysis, chemotherapy etc. may be considered unacceptable; it should be noted that 'basic care' (care to maintain bodily cleanliness and to alleviate severe pain) cannot be excluded nor can the provision of direct oral nutrition and hydration; however, there may well be other types of treatment that the maker would wish to express as being acceptable; it must, however, be emphasised that any attempt to request something that would be unlawful would be ineffective;
- it should be dated;
- it should be signed; there might be advantages in having the signature witnessed and as with an ordinary will it would be better if that witness was an independent party;
- it would be useful for provision to be made for the person to re-sign it and re-date it as and when they review it and wish it to continue as drafted.

Additionally, it might be useful for a person to include in the Advance Directive something about their wishes generally and what are described as 'life values'. This might include a statement as to the sort of residential care establishment that they would wish to move to if the need arose including naming any particular care homes or stating if they would wish to be near particular family members or stay in their own particular neighbourhood. Whilst this information could be included in an Advance Directive it may well be better to create a separate document going by various names but often called an 'Extended Values History'.

Finally, it is probably inappropriate for wishes about organ donation to be included in either document but if they are to be included these should be more appropriately included in the Values History than in the Advance Directive. Potential organ donors should carry donor cards or register with the National Organ Donor register (see UK Transplant in Appendix 2).

9. COMMUNICATING THE WISHES

It is important that when the Advance Directive has been made the original should be kept somewhere safe, quite possibly with solicitors, and that a copy should be sent to the patient's doctor and anyone else who may have responsibility for the patient's medical treatment. In the case of a patient who is in residential care, a copy should be made available to the home concerned in order that they can ensure that any doctor, whether General Practitioner or at a hospital, may be made aware of its contents. Patients who are 'in the community' may well consider that it is appropriate to keep a copy on their 'person' in case they should be involved in a medical emergency whilst out and about and when there is no one to alert the doctors to the existence of the Advance Directive. Laminating the Advance Directive may be a useful measure.

10. OTHER BENEFITS

In this chapter I have dwelt on the direct importance to the client themselves of making an Advance Directive. There are two further reasons why making an Advance Directive can be useful. The first of these is that any doctor treating a person who is unable to understand or communicate a decision on treatment will almost certainly find a well-constructed, appropriate and up-to-date expression of views if not invaluable then certainly reassuring that he or she is acting in a way the patient would have wished if it is that the doctor's views and the patient's expressions of wishes coincide. The second reason is that its existence may well eliminate the risk of an unseemly squabble between relatives or friends of the patient. It is not impossible to envisage a situation where a second spouse or a cohabitee are in vicious disagreement with, say, the children from an earlier marriage as to what should or should not happen to their loved one. Such disagreements could happen even between individual children and could happen in any form of relationship. If the client has already expressed clear and appropriate views then it would be a very brave person who went against those views without very good reasons for doing so.

11. THE FUTURE

At the time of writing this section, the Mental Capacity Bill is passing through Parliament. It is not clear when the Bill will become law. A summary of the main changes which it is anticipated will be brought about by the Bill is to be found in Appendix 7.

CHAPTER 15

HOUSEKEEPING

KEY POINTS

- It is important that our affairs should be left in such a way that someone can take them over either during lifetime or on death.

- Your will should be kept up to date. It should be reviewed at frequent intervals.

- Have in mind a will is revoked by marriage.

- Your will, deeds and other papers should be kept safe and where they can be found.

- Never attempt to alter a will after it has been signed and witnessed. It may well be invalidated.

- Make a new will or for minor alterations have a codicil properly prepared.

- Keep an up to date record of your assets and keep it in such a place that it can be found.

- Do not split Title Deeds.

- Keep all documents in respect of your property together. This would include permissions, consents, guarantees, reports etc.

- If you have any particularly valuable assets keep a note of them with your papers.

- Ensure that access can be had to computer data.

- Make it clear what is to happen to personal papers and computer data on your death.

- Keep accessible records of gifts etc. made during your lifetime.

- If there are family secrets consider recording them on paper and leaving them with your will and/or with your solicitor.

CHAPTER 15

HOUSEKEEPING

ISSUES

As a 'hands on' solicitor I have considerable experience not only in administering estates on behalf of executors but also as acting as an executor and having to undertake the very practical steps which have to be taken following a death and the difficulties which can arise if the deceased has not taken proper steps to put his or her affairs in order. This is not only in terms of making and keeping up-to-date a will but also in terms of sorting out their paperwork and belongings, and keeping them sorted out in such a way that grieving relatives (if they are undertaking the task) or a solicitor or other executor (if there are no family or close friends involved) will be able to administer the estate calmly, efficiently, economically, safely and completely.

Clearly the steps that need to be taken in this direction will depend very much on individual circumstances but I have set out below pointers which may be helpful.

1. THE UPDATING OF THE WILL.

If the advice elsewhere in this book has been followed then not only will a will have been made but it will, at the time of death, be an up-to-date document.

Some people will make one will and that will be totally effective and appropriate at their death even if it is many years later.

A classic case will be a will leaving all to husband/wife and in the event of the husband/wife having predeceased then everything to go between the children.

However, for many – especially as a result of the high incidence of marital breakdown and remarriage, the incidence of small families where there are few or no obvious beneficiaries, the incidence of crime and drug addiction affecting family relationships and unreasonable and uncaring behaviour – a will is something which only has a short shelf life and may have to be changed frequently to take account of changing circumstances.

I have set out below some of the circumstances when a new will would be needed:

- On marriage – except in those rare circumstances where a will has been expressly made 'in contemplation of marriage' marriage will revoke a will.

  That revocation does not revive an earlier will. If the person concerned then died then he or she will die intestate and the laws of intestacy will operate. This may, (depending on the value of the Estate and the near relatives) be perfectly satisfactory in the event of a first marriage, but may be totally unsatisfactory following a second marriage. It is, therefore, vital that consideration, at the very least, be given to the making of a new will even if in the same terms as the earlier and revoked will.

- Where the executors (or indeed guardians) of your choice have died or become incapable because of age, illness or infirmity of fulfilling their role, or because the executors have moved out of the area or abroad. Remember, that you may have appointed two or more executors because of their collective ability or responsibility. The loss of one or more may upset the plan.

- Where beneficiaries have died and the gift(s) which they would have received are just going to fall into residue and go where you would not want them to go.

- Where one or more residuary beneficiaries have died and there are no acceptable substitutes in the will.

- Where you no longer have items which you bequeathed in the will and you need to make some alternative provision for the beneficiary who will be disappointed.

- Where you have had a falling out with, or estrangement from, a beneficiary, executor or guardian.

- Where a beneficiary would no longer be able to benefit from a gift for example, a gift to someone who has gone (or may well go) into residential care and if it would serve only to swell his or her estate and go to pay fees.

- Where a gift has been made because a particular beneficiary had particular needs and those needs now no longer exist or have changed.

- A grandchild (or another grandchild) has been born and the existing gifts are to named grandchildren as opposed to grandchildren in particular.

- Where a beneficiary's marriage(s) has fallen apart or is likely to fall apart you may wish to skip a generation.

- Where you have come into significant wealth such that the previous will would no longer be appropriate.

- Where your assets have decreased in value possibly resulting in being unable to meet particular legacies and leave sufficient residue to adequately benefit a possibly main beneficiary.

2. SAFEGUARDING THE WILL

So the will has been made but will it be found on death? Whilst there is a procedure for depositing a will with the Probate Registry before death, the actual take up rate for this facility is very small.

There are also some unofficial schemes for the depositing of wills.

However, by far the majority of wills made in this country are either:

- left with the Solicitors who prepared them;
- kept at home by the testator;
- given to someone else to look after.

From my own point of view, keeping a will at a bank may, apart from problems set out below, result in difficulties of securing its release on death.

Wherever it is decided that the will should be kept it must be ensured:

- that no one who would have benefited under an earlier will, but who does not benefit under the present will or who would benefit on an intestacy but does not benefit under the will, has the opportunity to destroy it, thus thwarting the testator's wishes;

- that the will does, in fact, come to light because the risk is that no one knows where it has been deposited (especially with a bank or solicitor or with someone else). This is especially the case if the testator has moved to a new area and/or changed banks/solicitors;

- that the will does come to light if kept at home. The will itself may well still be in the deceased's possession at death but is simply not found because it has been put 'somewhere safe' or overlooked or is thrown out with volumes of other paper or other rubbish;

- that an old will does not come to light resulting in no one looking for a more recent one.

It is amazing how frequently, especially where there are no really close family, suggestions are made following a death that a deceased has made a further and later will. This can result in many hours and pounds being expended in the hunt for a will which may never have existed.

What is the answer?

There is no right answer in every case. However the following are some useful steps that testators might consider:

- deposit the original of the will with solicitors (or if you feel you must, with a bank);

- have photocopies of the will taken and keep one with your personal papers at home, preferably in a sealed envelope to avoid the attention of prying eyes;

- keep your personal papers altogether in a place where they will be found on death. This would preferably be in a safe but if not, then in something that is fireproof or failing that in a readily identifiable box or briefcase. If a safe is used, the deceased must ensure that the keys (or combination) can be found;

- leave a photocopy with the executor or executors in a sealed envelope which should be endorsed with a note of where the original will can be found or alternatively leave a note with your executors that a will has been made, its date, where it is located and that they are the executors;

- ensure that someone who is going to know of your death (such as a neighbour) also knows that you have made a will and where it is located. Perhaps ask that person to ensure that your solicitors are contacted on your death to notify them of it. Ensure that such a person tells the Police, if they are involved, of the fact that you have made a will and where it will be found;

- in case you give up your home before death, and go into residential care, ensure that those close to you, for example a neighbour, tells the home and any social workers who may be involved that you have made a will and that not only does it go on the records of the home and/or social worker but that any copy of the will in your home

139

follows you to the home and is put in your file, or that you keep it amongst your personal papers in the home;

- ensure that, if you make a new will, all copies of the old will are destroyed and the arrangements for the new one come to light.

Whilst these steps may appear to be somewhat contrived, it is my view that enough care cannot be taken.

If a *Codicil* is made to a will, ensure that copies of that are placed with copies of the original will.

If by chance you simply revoke a will by destroying it (see below) and if you do not (unwisely) make a new one, ensure that the original is destroyed and that all copies are destroyed. Remember that simple physical destruction of a will may not, of itself, revoke it. It must be destroyed with the intention of revoking the will.

Keeping a signed and dated note with your papers recording your having deliberately destroyed and revoked the will, will be a useful precautionary step as would notifying the solicitors who have been involved in its preparation, even if they do not hold the original.

If you do revoke the will with a new one, but instruct new solicitors, do ensure that you obtain from the previous solicitors your original will and arrange for its destruction.

These may be counsels of perfection.

However, even taking these steps does not guarantee that the will, or the correct will, will come to light especially if there are malicious people involved who may stand to benefit from the will not coming to light.

Altering the will

You can only physically alter a will validly by doing so **before** it is signed and witnessed and the testator and witnesses initialling the alterations.

Any attempt to alter a will after it has been signed and witnessed will make it in whole or part invalid. Do not do it. If you want to alter the will make a new one from scratch (or have a proper codicil prepared).

Other safeguards

Never staple, stick or even paper clip anything to the original will. It will leave marks and queries may arise on your death.

If you are unwise enough to make a home-made will, do not be tempted to write out a copy of the will and have that signed and witnessed. If you want a copy then pay for a photocopy to be made. More than once wills have been copied – but not accurately – and problems have arisen after the death as to which was in fact the last will.

3.   SAFEGUARDING YOUR OTHER PAPERS

A constant fear amongst many solicitors who are executors of a will is that they may miss finding assets of the deceased or even if they know that an asset exists being unable to find the documents of title.

This fear can arise because of simply not knowing of the existence of the asset or assets or it can arise from the fact that assets may have been concealed by family/friends/neighbours etc. who get to them before the solicitor.

It is therefore important that you take steps to ensure:

- that your securities are kept safe, but in doing so you must ensure that your assets can be found;

- your assets can be found and are known by those who need to find and know about them.

How to do this depends on your circumstances but the following steps may be prudent:

- keep your papers in a safe or failing that a fire proof box or failing that in one place in a box, brief case, or cabinet;

- keep a separate note of your assets giving details of :

  o institutions (for example, bank, building society etc);
  o account numbers;
  o holders numbers;
  o rough value;
  o the date that the note is made;

- ensure that this note is updated at frequent intervals and earlier ones are destroyed;

- consider keeping the note of assets on computer so that you can keep it up to date easily but do ensure that you print it off regularly so that those who are charged with handling your affairs do not need to worry whether information is buried on the computer;

- ensure that you keep a copy of the note somewhere where it will easily be found but away from your actual securities in case they are stolen;

- consider telling your executors where the list is kept but keep it in a sealed envelope to avoid prying eyes;

- consider having a copy placed with your will.

4.   YOUR DEEDS AND OTHER PROPERTY DOCUMENTS

Generally

- Much the same can be said about your deeds as about other documents.

- Replacing lost title deeds can be expensive and time consuming especially following the death of the owner of a property. This assumes that anyone else knows you [still] own the property especially where you do not live in it.

  Certainly ensure that details of any property you own appear on your list of assets.

- Keep your deeds safe. Again if they are to be kept at home, preferably keep them in a safe but failing that a fireproof box. Try to avoid hiding the deeds in 'a safe place' which may be so safe that you forget where they are and which no one else can find.

- If you deposit them with solicitors or the bank keep a prominent note of that fact with your other personal papers. This is especially important if you move areas and leave your deeds in the area you moved from. Keep carefully any receipts given to you for their deposit.

- If a property is in mortgage, and the deeds are therefore with the lender, keep a careful note of that fact. (This will be especially important if your mortgage has been paid off and a nominal amount is left outstanding to enable you to leave your deeds deposited with the lender.)

- If, because your lender did not require all the deeds to be deposited with them when the mortgage was created, and you have the remainder of the deeds ensure that a note is kept with the remainder that the property is in mortgage. If your solicitors keep the remainder note that fact with your personal papers.

Splitting deeds

Other than in those cases where the property is in mortgage, do keep your deeds together. For some reason some members of the public decide to split up sets of title deeds and take out some of the deeds and keep them apart from the rest without there being any sound legal reason for this. This causes chaos when the property comes to be sold. There is also the risk that an odd deed on its own may be lost or destroyed.

Ground rent

If you pay *ground rent/rentcharge/chief rent* on a property do always ensure you obtain a receipt for the ground rent. This means a receipt and not a demand on which you note that you have paid it. This will become very important when the property comes to be sold. Keep the receipt for just the last payment due. Throw out any receipts for earlier periods.

For those in flats also keep minutes of recent management company meetings and copies of the last few years' service charge accounts and receipts for service charge paid.

Ground landlord's consents

If you ever ask the ground landlord for consent to the carrying out of any work at the property (and remember very often leases require you to obtain such consent) keep such consents carefully and preferably with the deeds. The same can apply to freehold properties sometimes where the consent of a previous owner is necessary.

Planning, Building Regulations and other permissions (including glass replacement approvals).

If you need to carry out any work for which building regulations consent/planning permission/ listed building consent/ conservation area consent/ approval under a tree preservation order/ any other special consent is necessary keep the consents with your title deeds or failing that with your personal papers in such a way that they will be found.

With effect from April 2002, if you replace glass you must have the work carried out by a FENSA (Fenestration Self-Assessment Scheme) approved installer or have the work approved by the local authority. Ensure you keep any certificate issued by the installer or local authority.

From 1 January 2005 much electrical work has to be carried out by a properly qualified person or with the knowledge and approval of the Building Control Department of the Local Authority. Any documents should be carefully preserved. They will be needed when the house is sold.

For any work which you carry out and where you check with the local authority whether building regulations consent/planning permission/glass approval/listed building consent/conservation area consent/approval under a tree preservation order/ any other special consent is required and you are told it is not, then ensure that you obtain that confirmation in writing and keep it with the deeds or your personal papers.

Repairs

Companies carrying out the installation of such things as damp-proof courses, cavity wall-ties, timber treatments etc. frequently give long-term guarantees. Ensure these are kept with your deeds or personal papers. However, frequently these guarantees are only enforceable if you can produce the original guarantee and not just a copy and if you can produce the report and plans (from the contractor who carried out the work) upon the basis of which the work was carried out. The moral is, therefore, to keep the documents with your deeds or your personal papers.

The same general principal also applies to such things as the installation of double-glazing etc.

5   VALUABLE ASSETS

The average home contains many ordinary, and not particularly valuable, items but will have a few items which may have particular worth. Those few items can easily be overlooked amongst the remainder by those who have to deal with your affairs. It is important, therefore, that you keep a note with your papers of any such items explaining why the item is of particular value. You may also like to give an indication of any particular methods of disposing of the item such as through a particular dealer or auctioneer who will have specialist knowledge.

Obviously, there is a risk that identifying such an item may also identify it and its worth to a burglar. In consequence, whilst making a note of its worth, do be discreet about how visible the note is. Perhaps again keep it in a sealed envelope with your will.

6.   COMPUTERS

Information technology is now impinging on the lives of older people in their own homes. Many older people are now getting to grips with computers and using them for maintaining their correspondence and so on.

For those who are maintaining data on computer (and especially where that is crucial data) they need to consider what impact that will have following their deaths or if they become mentally incapable of managing their own affairs and someone has to take over their affairs.

There are at least two aspects to this:

- Will the data be accessible by others should the need arise?
- What is to happen to data on the computer?

Access to the data

Those maintaining their important data on computer do need to think about three things in terms of access to that data by other people:

- Will others know that data is kept on computer?
- Will others be able to find out where on the computer it is kept or, if kept on removable storage media, such as floppy disks, CD-ROMs etc., where they are kept?
- Will others be able to access the data in terms of getting past passwords used to access the computer and/or to protect individual documents

There are no easy answers to this.

If someone thinks that their data is sufficiently sensitive to warrant password protection then presumably they will not be keen for the password to be left around for prying eyes to see. Accordingly, my suggestion would be that for any information that others may need to access in the future the computer owner may well choose one common password for document protection and place that in a sealed envelope with their personal papers remembering to change the detail in the envelope if the password changes. Any system password can also be placed in the envelope.

It is important to remember the need for accuracy and legibility in writing down passwords. Do ensure that:

- spaces are correctly and clearly shown; and
- case (upper or lower) is correctly used as well, of course, as the actual letters/digits.

Placing a copy of such information with your will (again in a sealed envelope) may also be a useful step.

In terms of knowing what data is actually stored on the computer then the only answers to this are to ensure that those close to you know that you do store data on the computer and give them an idea of the nature of that data. Placing a note of what data is stored on your computer with your personal papers would be a good idea.

In terms of others actually being able to locate data on the computer the problem is that it is possible to create 'hidden' files or files that are so well buried in the file structure that without knowing that they are there it would be well-nigh impossible to find them. This problem would be further aggravated by the use of file or folder names that do not accurately represent their contents. Accordingly, it would be wise to keep files that contain important data clearly and obviously named and in clearly marked folders at the top of the structure. Placing in the envelope with the passwords etc. a note of where the files can be found would be wise.

A note should also be kept of any backup arrangements you have made for the protection of data.

Future of the data

The use of computers means that we are able to store vast amounts of data very easily.

That data may be information about our financial affairs. It may be intensely personal and confidential data about others or ourselves. It may be perfectly innocuous but nonetheless personal data such as family photographs. Some of that information, especially such things as digital photographs, might be quite irreplaceable.

What is to happen to that data if we become mentally incapable or following our death? Remember that, during our lifetime, the data remains our personal property and it is not open to anyone else to give that data away or deal with it without an order of the court.
In terms of our lifetime we will have to rely on those who are looking after our affairs to do the right thing. They may, however, be helped in that by our having left some written instructions as to what is to happen to the data should

we become incapable of making our own decisions. It may for instance be a good idea to direct that certain files should be wiped out or that copies of data should be made on removable storage media (floppy disks, CDs etc) and placed in safe custody with someone until a certain point, for example our death, is reached. The will then takes over and the data will become the responsibility of our executors and will have to be dealt with in accordance with the terms of our will (see Chapter 10).

7. RECORD KEEPING

When you die, part of your legacy may well be that you leave a headache to those left behind. This headache can be caused in many ways but ensuring that you keep adequate and up-to-date records can reduce the severity of the headache.

Keeping your paperwork in proper order as outlined above is an important part of this but there may well be much information that will not be current but which must be preserved.

Gifts

One important example of this is information about gifts that you may have made. On death, if you have made any sizeable gifts during lifetime and which are outside the usual exemptions, your personal representatives may well have to inform the Inland Revenue Capital Taxes Office about them even if the estate is not taxable. Accordingly, it is important that you should leave with your papers details of any gifts that you have made especially in the last seven years. You should ensure that the information left behind includes what type of asset was given away (for example, cash, land or buildings, shares, a car etc.), its value, the date of the gift, the person to whom given, where the property/money comprising the gift came from and whether a formal valuation was carried out.

8. FAMILY SECRETS

In Chapter 6, entitled 'Information and Skeletons' I have emphasised the need to make known to family and others any secrets that you may have from the past. If it is that you have not been able to do that during lifetime, do consider writing the information down and leaving it in such a way that it can be found on death. There is no reason why that should not be put in a sealed envelope and given to your solicitors to place with your will. Your solicitors could be instructed only to reveal it in certain circumstances or at a certain time.

9. BANK ACCOUNTS

It may seem odd that I should suggest that an older person should ensure that they have a bank account open. However, that is what I do suggest.

With the advent of tighter money laundering regulations, the banks and building societies have become fanatical and utterly unrealistic and unreasonable when it comes to the precautions to be taken when new accounts are required and this is particularly evident when older people are concerned.

The banks' position is that they expect older people to be able to jump through exactly the same hoops as a younger person by producing the same level of identification evidence and by attending at the bank. They seem to take no account of the fact that an older person may long since have ceased to have a passport and driving licence or similar document and if 'in care' will not have utility bills and credit card statements. Neither do they take into account the fact that they may at least have difficulty attending at the bank and at worst be totally unable to do so. Even an older person with an account already at the bank is likely still to be required to produce themselves and their identification at the bank. When it is suggested that the bank may wish to send out a representative to visit the customer/potential customer they recoil in horror. Any bank which let it be known that it was particularly interested in older people's accounts and would take steps to go the further mile for those customers would see significant numbers of new accounts being opened.

It is perhaps also appropriate to say that care homes are also now experiencing problems in this regard where they have residents whose personal allowances are accruing but the home has problems in keeping these monies for them because of restrictions imposed by the Commission for Social Care Inspection (CSCI).

Accordingly, older people should be encouraged to open, at the very least, a current (cheque) account at a bank which can offer a full range of banking services (including standing order and direct debit facilities) and which can accept direct payments into the account. They may also find it helpful also to open a deposit/savings account paying a higher rate of interest so that 'spare' monies can be put in there.

The accounts should be opened at a time when the older person has the physical capacity to attend at the bank (as well, of course, the mental capacity) to open the account and when they are likely still to be able to furnish adequate identification evidence.

The advantage of opening accounts (even if they keep in the accounts only sufficient to keep them open) is that, if and when they are unable to deal with their affairs (and as long as they signed an Enduring Power of Attorney), someone else will be able to operate the account in the older person's name and without having to open accounts in the attorney's name or risk mixing the attorney's money with that of the older person in order to deal with their affairs.

A secondary but related advantage is that, if the older person goes into care, there will be an account into which the home can pay any spare money for the older person even if (because the older person has not made an Enduring Power of Attorney) no one can get monies out. Further, it will permit an attorney to have the older person's benefits and pensions paid in and contributions to home fees paid out.

If no such accounts are opened then even if an attorney has been appointed they may have great difficulty in making satisfactory banking arrangements.

CHAPTER 16

ACCOMMODATION

KEY POINTS

- A wide range and combination of factors will affect where an older person lives at a particular time.

- Older people should be encouraged to check out the options along with their family at an early stage.

- Older people should try to acknowledge that their needs will change and that it may not be possible to maintain the status quo.

- A wide range of options is available.

- Moving to live with relatives or friends can be a risky business.

- No change in lifestyle or accommodation should be made, wherever possible, within twelve months of bereavement.

- Good legal advice should be sought before becoming financially involved in the purchase of a property with someone else however close.

- Care needs to be exercised before engaging in Right-to-Buy purchase of rented accommodation along with others.

- Care needs to be exercised before engaging in income or capital generation schemes involving an older person's property.

CHAPTER 16

ACCOMMODATION

INTRODUCTION

The subject of accommodation for older people is massively complex.

If we could see into the future it would not be as much so. But we can't.

What accommodation an older person occupies or will occupy will depend upon:

- a large number of individual factors;
- in what combination any number of those factors fit together.

Some of the factors are as follows:

- Is the person alone or one of a couple?
- Do they have anyone living with them?
- Do they live with anyone?
- Do they have children? (In referring to children this could include other younger and/or fitter friends or relatives.)
- Where are those children located?
- What support, practical and/or financial, can the children offer?
- What sort and size of accommodation do the children have?
- What sort of accommodation does the older person occupy?
- Do they own it or rent it?
- Is there a mortgage on the property? If so, how much is outstanding?
- How much does the accommodation cost to run?
- What state of repair is it in?
- Is it too big for the older person?
- Will it be suitable if the older person is or becomes:
  - o physically incapable;
  - o mentally incapable;
  or both?
- Can it be made suitable (at a cost that can be met by the older person with or without any grants or other financial assistance that may be available)?
- What equipment is there available for facilitating someone with a disability remaining at home?

- What is the social support network (friends, relatives, neighbours, social organisations, churches etc.) of the older person in the area?
- What would be the social support network of the older person in another area?
- What provision is there in the area for support in the home from social services or voluntary bodies?
- What other, more suitable, accommodation is there available in the area?
- What other, more suitable, accommodation is there available in another area?
- Is there any specialised accommodation available?
- Are there waiting lists for suitable accommodation? Might there be a waiting list in the future?
- What are the future needs of the older person likely to be? For example, whilst they might only need residential care at the moment, might they need nursing care in the future? Might a second move be necessary?
- What financial resources does the older person have? Does he or she want to take steps to preserve their assets to pass on to others?

The answers to these and other questions will determine what steps an older person needs to take to arrange their accommodation.

UNREALISTIC EXPECTATIONS

Sometimes older people refuse to acknowledge that their needs will change as they get older and frailer and they postpone any thought about the accommodation they will need as they get older. They perhaps make unrealistic demands of their family and friends simply because of stubbornness, fear or lack of information. Things are left until there is a crisis, such as an accident or illness, and decisions then have to be made rapidly and often unsatisfactorily whereas, had some thought been applied to the possibilities earlier, matters may well have been managed much more satisfactorily. It is undoubtedly true that where a move is planned carefully the long-term outcome is much more likely to be positive.

It is possible that the crisis which propels a person into new accommodation may not be a crisis with them. It may be a crisis with a carer – perhaps who is worn out by caring. As I know from my own experience, and the experiences of so many of my clients, the duties of caring for an older person, however close you are to them, can be enormously wearing and debilitating. The guilt associated with the older person moving from his or her own home into a care home or, even sheltered accommodation, can be enormous.

152

FEARS

Many older people who are now in their seventies or older remember or have heard stories of the days of 'the workhouse'. I suspect that many still view 'homes' and, indeed, sheltered accommodation, in the same light as they would have viewed the workhouse. They resist all attempts to persuade them that modern care homes, whilst sometimes leaving things to be desired, and sheltered housing complexes, can provide a better quality of life for them than could be achieved by living alone, often in unsatisfactory accommodation, with the ever present fear of accident, sudden illness, crime and with the daily trauma of having to take care of basic needs such as dressing, cleaning, cooking and shopping and often in acute loneliness.

ANSWERS

There is no easy solution to this but perhaps the best that can be achieved is for those close to the older person to try to discuss with them at an early stage the options for the future and to try to give the person an insight into the possibilities. This is best achieved well in advance of the time when it may be forced on them. Taking the opportunity to visit sheltered accommodation or one of the good care homes, perhaps to visit someone already resident there, would be a good idea. It may plant the seed of an idea especially when the older person sees the advantages that could come from moving to other accommodation. As in other things in this area, ignorance of the possibilities can sometimes be a major factor in a person deciding that they want the status quo to be maintained even when it puts themselves at risk or places an intolerable burden on carers. It has been my experience that if someone moves into a care home, or even into sheltered accommodation, it means that they and family and friends can spend 'quality' time together rather than having to deal with the mundane issues of cleaning, washing and ironing as well as the worry etc. of what is happening to the older person when the cover is not there.

THE OPTIONS

There is now a wide range of options available for accommodation. Availability may well depend on the area and what financial resources the older person has. I will look at some of those options but there can be no substitute for enquiry in the local area.

Staying put

For most older people staying put in their own accommodation, which they may have occupied for many years, is the option of choice. However, to do this might involve spending some money on adaptations and equipment. Much will depend upon the nature of the older person's problems and disabilities. The following are some of the many possibilities:

- installation of additional security features such as a burglar alarm system with panic buttons and CCTV or better perimeter security such as new locks and fencing;
- installation of systems to send an alert if the older person has not taken some positive action within a certain time scale or period;
- door entry phones and locks with video;
- a pendant telephone alarm system so that the older person can summon help via the telephone at the touch of a button;
- the purchase of a microwave oven;
- the lowering of working surfaces;
- adaptation of taps;
- installation of a bath lift;
- installation of a stair lift;
- purchase of new and more suitable chairs;
- installation of a downstairs toilet and shower;
- conversion of a downstairs room to a bedroom;
- installation of ramps and grab rails and handles inside and outside the house;
- removal of steps;
- purchase of aids for specific problems such as liquid level indicators for those with visual impairment;

The range of aids which can be obtained is probably only limited by the imagination of the person thinking about the matter and, to some extent, by the limit of financial resources available. An Occupational Therapist will doubtless be able to advise on such matters and a trawl of the Internet may well discover more specialised equipment even if this can only be purchased abroad.

Move to a different house

Frequently as people get older they realise that remaining in the house in which they have lived for many years is no longer a wise option. This will often be for one or more of different reasons:

- it is simply too big for them; or
- its location is no longer appropriate. This may be because the older person has ceased to drive or because one of a couple has died and the survivor cannot drive and thus access to shops, medical and other

facilities has become (or, if they have foresight to realise it, might become) a problem. This would be the case particularly if the older person lived in a rural area or in a house away from readily available public transport. A move to a smaller house or to a house (whether owned or rented) nearer to facilities may be a good move; or

- the facilities are in the wrong place and cannot be moved or adapted or cannot be moved or adapted at a reasonable price; or
- they may wish to be nearer family whilst still maintaining total independence; or
- the house is in an area which has gone (either actually or from the perspective of the older person) downhill either because of problems with crime, because of an influx of families with young children or because of nearby development etc.

One factor which an older person may wish to have in mind is whether the move to a smaller house may lead to a loss in benefits (whether pension credit or housing benefit [whether council tax or rent rebate]) because they have acquired liquid capital from the sale of the larger property. If they chose to give that capital away to children etc. this would not necessarily prevent the loss of benefits because it may well be treated as a deliberate deprivation of capital (see the section on Charges for residential accommodation in Chapter 18). If at the time, the older person does want to give away some capital and they have not previously claimed benefit then a way round the problem may be for them to give away other capital that they have making sure that the account from which that capital comes is then closed before the claim is made. The profit made from the sale of the house should be put into another account/investment. The reasoning for this is that the authorities do not ask whether you have ever given away capital, they only ask whether you have ever owned a house and if so what has happened to the proceeds of sale. If on the other hand money is withdrawn from an account which remains open then enquiries may be made as to what has happened to capital which can plainly be seen to have been withdrawn. There is, however, still a risk that such disposal may come to light following your death when the Inheritance Tax position comes to be examined.

Move to a bungalow or flat

If living in a house (whether owned or rented) ceases to be an option either because of problems with stairs, because of problems in maintaining the house and/or garden or both (or indeed for the other reasons mentioned in the previous section) then a move to a bungalow or flat (whether owned or rented) may be an attractive option. Some developments, whilst providing totally independent living, may well have restrictions requiring one or more of the occupants to be above a certain age, for example, fifty-five which means that the likelihood of children or noisy young people being on the development is at the least reduced and at best eliminated. Such accommodation may either be a little cheaper if there is little demand for it in the area or may be more expensive if there is a shortage of such accommodation in the area.

Move to some form of supported or assisted living accommodation

There is perhaps immediately a tendency to think that moving from total independence to some form of supported accommodation has to be directly into a care home. This, of course, is no longer the case and has not been so for many years. There are schemes that fall between the two ends of the spectrum.

These types of scheme fall probably into two basic types namely rented sheltered accommodation and purchased assisted living accommodation:

- **Rented sheltered accommodation**

Most people will be familiar with this type of accommodation. It is provided either by:

- local authorities; or
- by some organisations such as Anchor Housing; or
- by voluntary/charitable organisations such as English Churches Housing, St Vincent's or the Abbeyfield Society.

Usually the key element in such accommodation is that each occupier has his or her own front door either straight out into the street/courtyard etc. or into a block of flats thus maintaining his or her independence but with the support of an on-site warden who manages the day-to-day running of the scheme and may coordinate group activities which residents are free to participate in if they so wish. Perhaps the most important role of such a warden is in keeping an eye on the day-to-day welfare of the residents and summoning specialist support where necessary. It is however critical that older people should understand that this is not an alternative to residential care. Wardens usually do not provide any element of personal care and certainly do not perform any nursing functions. Residents must be capable of looking after themselves in large measure whether with or without input from outside caring agencies such as the Home Care service of the local authority or from the GP and district nurse etc.

It is true to say that many wardens do exceed their brief (especially where someone has been resident in the accommodation for many years and may need some additional short-term support) but this is entirely their choice and older people and, even more so, their relatives must understand this. It must also be understood that no one who needs, or is very likely to need in the foreseeable future, residential care should move into sheltered accommodation since a second move may well be required very shortly.

- **Purchased assisted living accommodation**

Some builders, having realised the need for specialised accommodation for older people, have in the last twenty-five years taken advantage of that need and have built developments specially for older people and which can be purchased (often on long leases of say 125 years) as opposed to being rented. In some cases it is possible to part own and part rent.

These schemes vary one to another and it is important that before purchasing such a property careful thought is given as to whether, in principal, it will be right for the person concerned and also to consider the terms of the particular scheme.

The main points of these schemes are as follows:

- A capital sum will be paid for the property just as with any house being purchased.
- Usually the property will be purchased by way of a long lease under the terms of which a ground rent will be paid. Some ground rents nowadays are more than nominal.
- The scheme will provide a range of services that have to be paid for by way of an annual service charge which is divided amongst the owners of the individual units. These services may include:

  o the services of a warden or manager;
  o a care service for when the manager is off duty;
  o security systems such as CCTV, entry phones, fire alarms etc.;
  o the cleaning and lighting and general maintenance of the *common parts* and the grounds as well, of course, of the flats themselves (albeit that usually internal decorations etc. will be the responsibility of individual residents);
  o the provision of a 'sinking fund' or a reserve from which to meet the cost of major repair or replacement costs of, say, lifts;
  o the cost of employment of a management company to manage the flats and to assess and collect the service charge and to employ staff;
  o the provision of a communal lounge and in some cases even a restaurant;

- the provision of a guest suite for the use of visitors;
- insurance of the block;
- sometimes water rates for the block or at least the common facilities;
- possibly other utility services.

It will be appreciated that these costs can be significant and this will be reflected in the service charges. It will, therefore, be essential to know that you will be able to afford the charges on an ongoing basis. It is possible that financial assistance with service charges may be available by way of Housing Benefit and enquiries should be made with the local authority about availability.

- There will almost certainly be restrictions on the age of those who can live in the flat. Usually they will have to be over fifty-five or sixty although it may be possible for someone younger to buy the flat to be occupied by someone older.
- There may well be a fee to be paid to the Management Company when the property changes hands and sometimes the Management Company actually arranges the sale. The property may have to be sold to someone on its waiting list. The fee can run into several thousand pounds and may be a percentage of the sale price. In one instance that I have seen recently there was provision that if the outgoing occupier did not pay the fee within seven days the incoming occupier had to pay it. A competent conveyancing solicitor is essential in these transactions.

Whether a person is to buy a brand new property or take an assignment of an existing property it is important that they study all the documents in respect of the property and make full enquiries about the terms on which the property is held. Appointment of solicitors who you choose is very important. Do not be pointed in the direction of solicitors recommended by the seller or the Management Company. You need to know that the solicitors will be acting totally in your best interests and will make the fullest possible enquiries and will not be influenced by wishing 'to keep in' with builders or sales staff or management companies who want a quick transaction with few questions asked. Don't pressure your solicitors to do the job fast; do pressure them to do it right and follow their advice.

If buying a brand new apartment do be careful about paying a deposit. You must find out and have confirmed in writing whether it is refundable if you cannot proceed. This may, for example, be if you cannot sell your own house. Be aware also that you may well be set a deadline for an exchange of contracts and/or completion of your purchase. Be prepared to come under pressure from the builder to exchange contracts and complete. Have in mind that these builders are in the business of making money and whilst appearing 'fluffy' on the outside may well be hard-nosed businessmen.

Moving to live with relatives or friends

Moving to live with relatives or others as one gets older can have a certain appeal. However, this, like any move needs careful thought.

The following points need to be borne in mind:

- How well do you know the people with whom you plan to live?
- You may get on with your child but what about the in-law?
- While you may get on with the grandchildren in short bursts what about on a long-term basis? More particularly how will they feel about having an older person around the house?
- What happens if the family has to move house or out of the area? Will you be able to go too? How will you feel about leaving behind other friends and family? What about if the family have to move abroad – especially if it is a move forced by work commitments?
- What will happen if your child's marriage breaks down – possibly contributed to by your living there? What if your child wants to remarry?
- What happens if your child dies? Will your in law/ the grandchildren still feel as kindly disposed to you? What if your in-law wishes to remarry? Will the new spouse still want ex parent-in-law in the house?
- Perhaps most importantly great care needs to be taken if you are planning to invest some money in the property in which you are going to live. This may be by contributing to the purchase of a bigger house or contributing to the cost of an extension as a granny flat. It is essential that you receive and act upon independent legal advice to ensure that your monies are protected in case any of the above issues should arise and it proves necessary for you to move out and purchase new accommodation for yourself. It is also important if you wish someone other than or in addition to the child with whom you live to benefit from your estate when you die. Also have in mind what will happen if you subsequently have to go into a care home. Issues could well arise as to what part of the property you live in belongs to you for the purpose of assessing your contribution to care fees. This may not only have an effect on you but also on your family. Good legal advice is essential before entering into such an arrangement and, at the risk of being repetitious, it is essential to emphasise that the older person should have completely independent legal advice from that being given to the family.

Moving to a Care Home

A move to a Care Home is usually the least favourite option for most people. The emphasis must be on the word 'most'. I have had clients who have thought very carefully about going into care and have made plans well in advance – in one notable case putting her name down for a particular care home many years prior to needing such care and in another case simply turning up on the doorstep of a home and demanding to be admitted.

I have devoted a separate chapter (Chapter 17) to choosing a care home and part of a further chapter (Chapter 18) to issues of funding such a placement.

Suffice it to say at this point that the amount and quality of provision of care varies from area to area as does the cost. As stressed elsewhere in this book, advance planning is, if at all possible, highly desirable. Find out about the options in your own area and in the area where relatives live. Find out about the standards that can be found in those areas and the cost of accommodation. Discuss it with the family or those who may have to make decisions for you and let them know your thoughts. Perhaps set down in a document, something akin to a living will, your thoughts on the matter.

MISCELLANEOUS

Right to buy

One point which is worth making, albeit as a side issue, is that frequently older people who are in suitable rented accommodation decide to exercise their right to buy the property at a discount. This may be of their own volition or, frequently, it is at the suggestion of their family who see that within a few years a sizeable profit can be made from the sale of the property when the discount no longer has to be repaid. Often the family will fund the purchase but the property will have to be put in the name of the older person.

It is once again important that the older person and the family should each obtain good and independent legal advice before entering into such a transaction for the following reasons:

- if a family member is to fund the purchase some steps need to be taken to ensure that their money is secured in case:

  o the relationship between the older person and the family member breaks down and there is a dispute as to who is entitled to the house or the proceeds of sale;
  o the older person dies and their estate goes to someone other than the

family member who has provided the funding;

o the older person gets into financial difficulty and the house is seized by his or her creditors;

o the older person goes into care and the local authority considers the house belongs to the older person and is therefore an asset to meet home fees;

- if a family member contributes part of the purchase money with the older person contributing the rest then steps need to be taken to establish which part belongs to whom for the same reasons as outlined above but also to ensure that if the younger person gets into financial difficulties the contribution of the older person to the purchase is clear and cannot be touched;

- the discount which is allowed can be sizeable and is a valuable asset. It needs to be clearly established who is going to be entitled to the share of the proceeds of sale represented by the discount. This may well be of importance not just between the parties themselves but may also be impacted upon by the charging regulations for accommodation in a care home should the older person subsequently find themselves in care.

In all the above cases, what takes place at the time of purchase and how it is documented can have an impact on who ultimately gets what, whether that be if trouble breaks out during lifetime, or if a person has to go into care or on the death of either the older person or the younger person. The parties to such a transaction should ensure that the solicitors involved in the transaction are fully aware of the background to the transaction. If they are not aware of the arrangements then they cannot give proper and full advice on the matter.

Income and Capital Generation Schemes (Equity Release Schemes)

A further issue on which it is appropriate to touch is the issue of the various schemes for income or capital generation from the equity in the home of an older person.

There are large numbers of these schemes around which allow older people to enter into arrangements with financial institutions which allow them either to get a lump sum to spend how they wish whilst they are alive or which can be used to provide an income once it is invested and without ceasing to live in their house. They can be a mixture of both.

David McGrath and Cecil Hinton have written an excellent book on this topic, published by Age Concern and entitled 'Using Your Home as Capital 2002-3' and anyone thinking of entering into one of these schemes would be well advised to read that work. I will confine myself to a few points:

- There are many variations on these schemes and it is essential that an older person takes his or her time to ensure that he or she fully understands the exact implications of these schemes. He or she should take good legal advice from a solicitor who has had chance to see the full details of the scheme and follow the solicitor's advice. Care needs to be taken that the solicitor is completely independent of the financial institution concerned as well as of any Independent Financial Adviser (IFA) who may have arranged the scheme. It needs to be remembered that an IFA may well be deriving commission from the transaction and may well want a solicitor to be involved who does not ask too many questions whether about the deal arranged nor about the title of the property which is involved and which may lead to the older person not proceeding or not being allowed to proceed because of a problem with the title to the property. Remember, some solicitors and other lawyers pay referral fees to get work from IFAs and the like.
- Some schemes have involved transfer of ownership of the property to the lender and with a lease back by the lender to the older person. This can be very frightening for someone older. These are often called Home Reversion plans.
- Another variation is based on the notion that the lender advances money to the older person and then takes a mortgage on the property which will have detailed provisions as to when the capital and accrued interest are repayable which may, for instance, be when the older person dies or moves into permanent care or when he or she vacates for more than a certain period. These schemes are usually known as Lifetime Mortgages.

Whilst these schemes often give the older person the reassurance of a fixed rate of interest, the fact that interest is compounded (that is interest is paid on accrued interest) and nothing is being repaid, means that the amount outstanding can rapidly exceed the value of the property (especially in times of the falling or static house prices) leaving little, if anything, behind for beneficiaries. Theoretically, it could reach a point where, because the amount outstanding exceeds the value of the property, the rest of the older person's estate may have to meet the shortfall. In reality, in most cases there is a no-negative equity guarantee, meaning that as long as the older person has fulfilled their obligations under the terms of the mortgage (for example by ensuring that they keep the property in repair), then the lender agrees not to seek to recover more than the value of the property. Sometimes, on appropriate terms, the lender will agree not to take back more than a specified percentage of the ultimate sale price.

- Some schemes allow the lender to take the whole of the older person's interest in the property when it comes to be sold; some simply take back what is owed; some take back what is owed with an additional percentage of the spare money.
- Most of the schemes will have an impact on what the beneficiaries of the older person will receive from their estate on death and it is very wise for the older person to discuss their proposed plans with their family or other possible beneficiaries so that the beneficiaries do not get any nasty surprises on the death of the older person. This could particularly be the case if the beneficiary had invested some money in the property assuming that they would get it back on the death of the older person or if the beneficiary has done their own financial planning and was relying on monies which he or she would eventually receive on the older person's death by way of inheritance.
- Some of these schemes may well affect housing and other benefits to which the older person may be entitled and it is essential that before entering into such a transaction the older person takes good advice on benefit issues from Citizens Advice Bureau, Solicitors, Housing Benefits Office or a welfare benefits adviser in the local authority.
- Because of some very bad publicity that some of these schemes received in the past they largely disappeared from the scene. In recent times, and after the industry cleaned up its act, they have become more popular and for some people they may be an acceptable means of releasing money from their property during lifetime for whatever purpose the older person requires it.

However, because of the risk involved and the quite complex nature of schemes, reputable lenders now go to great lengths to ensure that potential borrowers do fully understand what they are letting themselves in for and insist that borrowers are represented by independent solicitors. The solicitors are required to certify that they have taken all necessary steps to ensure that the older person understands the risks involved.

Borrowers should not, therefore, be surprised if their solicitor appears to be going to great lengths to ensure that the borrower fully understands what is involved.

- For the reasons set out above, these schemes are certainly not appropriate for someone whose mental faculties are failing and who may have difficulty in grasping and remembering what is involved.
- Finally where someone is thinking of entering into such a scheme then they should consider whether there is some other option open to them by which they can gain access to monies. A few examples of these are as follows:

- Your independent financial advisor should have carried out a general financial health check to ensure that you are getting the largest possible return on your capital, savings and investments, and also should ensure that all means-tested and non-means-tested state benefits are being claimed.

- If you need money to repair or adapt your house, then there may be alternative sources of finance available through your local authority, home improvement agencies, home improvement trusts, the Department for Work and Pensions, charities and possibly, your family.

- Consideration should be given to the possibility of an ordinary loan or mortgage as an alternative to an equity release scheme. High Street lenders will consider giving a normal repayment loan where you repay back the loan and interest, or a loan where interest only is paid. An independent financial advisor should be able to offer advice in respect of this.

- Your immediate family may be able to offer some financial assistance, for example, by way of a gift or loan from their own financial resources, through a loan on their property, or as acting as guarantor on your loan or mortgage. However, before any such arrangements are entered into, it is essential that you and your family each receive independent legal advice for the reasons set out elsewhere in this book arising out of complicated financial arrangements.

- Is there a possibility of your selling part of your home, for example, the garden as a means of raising capital?

- An obvious solution to raising an additional lump sum would be for you to move from your home to alternative accommodation releasing capital in the process. For example, moving to less expensive accommodation, purchasing a property with relatives, moving in with relatives, moving to sheltered or retirement housing or renting. However, do have in mind that once you become entitled to a capital sum, this may remove your entitlement to means tested state benefits. Do also have in mind the warnings given elsewhere in this book about the risks of sharing properties and entering into arrangements with other people as to the purchase of properties. Independent legal advice should always be sought.

- If you have a large house, it may be possible for you to rent out some of the rooms to lodgers, to provide additional income. This arrangement may also have benefits for you in the form of providing company for you, assistance with domestic tasks, the security of the property and looking after the property when you are away. There may also be tax relief available to you on the income you receive. Making arrangements through a reputable organisation would be wise. It may be that some employers may be on the look out for accommodation for their staff. Such organisations may well prove useful in disciplining their staff if they misbehave as lodgers or fail to meet their obligations.

CHAPTER 17

CHOICE OF CARE HOME

KEY POINTS

- Recommendation can play an important part in choosing the home.

- Remember we all have different values. What is important to one, will not be to another.

- Be circumspect about recommendations from those who have or may have a financial incentive to recommend.

- Visit the home more than once and at different times.

- View a number of homes to compare and contrast.

- The older person should, wherever possible, visit the home and be involved in the selection process.

- The selection process should not be rushed.

- Ask questions. Go prepared with questions to ask.

- The culture of a home may be more important than its physical properties.

- Read the last couple of inspection reports.

- Become familiar with the relevant National Care Standards.

- Be involved. Show an interest in what is going on.

- Don't allow standards to slide.

- Establish a good relationship with the home so that you can express your concerns openly whilst being reasonable and supportive.

CHAPTER 17

CHOICE OF CARE HOME

ISSUES

One of the most onerous tasks that a caring child can have to undertake is to have to make arrangements for a parent to go into care.

I have looked elsewhere at how this can come about.

As will become apparent there can be circumstances (where an older person has significant financial resources and will be self-funding) in which a child can find himself or herself effectively having to make the choice of care home entirely themselves with little or no support from social workers. Additionally, there is reluctance on the part of those who know to give frank assessments of the quality of care homes, particularly where a home is poor. Many people 'in the know' are frightened of being too honest. That was the case also when I had to make such a choice. However, two things have changed in the twelve years since I was in that position.

Firstly, there is more guidance available on the issues which those choosing a care home for a relative should be addressing and looking for.

Secondly, the Care Standards Act 2000 has been brought into force. Whilst for many years a system of registration and inspection of care homes has been in existence, the 2000 Act, and the regulations which have been made under it, have strengthened the system of inspection but perhaps more importantly have laid down clear standards which must be adhered to by care homes. These standards are wide ranging and govern the physical standards which a home must comply with, the training which staff must undertake, staffing levels, issues of privacy and dignity, social contact, meals and mealtimes, complaints etc.

Whilst only months after introducing the National Minimum Standards for Care Homes for Older People (NMS), the Department of Health had to introduce amended (and slightly less rigorous) Standards because of the enormous financial burden which homes faced to comply with them, nonetheless the public can now look to the Standards and see what is expected of homes to whom they entrust the care of their older, and very vulnerable, relatives. The Standards can be found, using the Internet, at **www.csci.org.uk**

So how do you go about choosing a care home?

ANSWERS

- The first question will be what sort of home does the older person need? If an assessment has been carried out by social services or by the multi-disciplinary team on hospital discharge then it should be clear if a residential home is required or if nursing care is required or if some specialised unit is required. In every case it would be prudent to arrange for an assessment to be carried out by social services even if the older person is to be self-funding. This will ensure that the level of care provided to the older person is appropriate and not in excess of his or her needs in case in the future the money runs out and the older person has to be moved because the local authority will not pay for care above the level actually required. If money is no object then the home which provides the best level of care in its widest sense will be the main criteria. The older person will also need to decide whether he or she wants a domestic 'family' style home or wants what the NMS describe as a 'hotel' style environment. This may well depend on what he or she has been used to in the past.
- The second issue will be the area in which the home is located. Is the older person to be moved out of his or her own area to be near relatives? Does this mean uprooting the person from their family and friends and their social support network simply to be near one other individual or group of people, however close the blood tie may be? Is this a good idea?
- Having decided those basic issues attention will need to turn to precisely which home is to be chosen.
- Recommendation must play a part in home selection. Enquiring with a wide range of people is essential.

Talking to others who have had relatives in homes is useful but should never be to any great extent the determining factor. Each of us has different values and what one person may see as quite intolerable another may find perfectly acceptable. Thus, for some people the apparent plushness of the accommodation and impeccable decorations may be the most important feature whereas for others (and in my view rightly so) the standard of care and the culture of the home and a caring attitude of staff is much more important.

Try to obtain the view of 'professionals' with whom you come into contact. Social workers and doctors may have a useful insight, as may those who have worked in homes (especially if it is one in which the individual has actually worked). However, be careful again not to rely wholly on the opinion of one professional. Has that individual received any financial inducement to recommend a particular home? Indeed, does that individual actually own the home involved or have some financial interest in it? Some doctors actually own homes! Additionally and crucially, the experience of a particular home must be up-to-date. Standards in a home can change very quickly especially where there has been a change in management or ownership.

Does your solicitor, if specialising in such matters, have any insight?

- Going to visit the home must be a vital part in the selection process. Wherever possible the older person should also go to look at the home and be involved in the decision making process. Indeed, Standard 5.1 of the NMS says that prospective service users should be 'invited to visit the home and to move in on a trial basis, before they and/or their representatives make a decision to stay; unplanned admissions are avoided where possible'. Standard 5.2 says 'prospective service users [should be] given the opportunity for staff to meet them in their own homes or current situation if different'. Presumably this is so staff can see how the prospective resident currently lives and their abilities and capabilities.

It should also be noted that the NMS provides (Standard 3.1) that new service users are to be admitted only on the basis of 'a full assessment undertaken by people trained to do so, and to which the prospective service user, his/her representatives (if any) and relevant professionals have been involved.'

- Where the individual is referred through 'Care management' arrangements (that is where the service user is funded by the local authority or presumably where the person is discharged from hospital or in other circumstances where a Care Management Assessment/Care Plan has been carried out) then the home must obtain 'a summary of the Care Management (Health and Social Services) Assessment and a copy of the Care Plan produced for care management purposes.' (Standard 3.2). For those who are self-funding and without a Care Management Assessment/Care Plan, the home must carry out an assessment covering (Standard 3.3):

  o personal care and physical well-being;
  o diet and weight, including dietary preferences;
  o sight, hearing and communication;
  o oral health;
  o foot care;
  o mobility and dexterity;
  o history of falls;
  o continence;

- o medication usage;
- o mental state and cognition;
- o social interests, hobbies, religious and cultural needs;
- o personal safety and risk;
- o carer and family involvement and other social contacts/relationships.

It is strongly recommended that those close to the service user should always check the Care Management Assessment/Care Plan etc. to ensure that it accurately reflects the facts concerning the patient's needs, likes and dislikes and, more importantly, such critical issues as any known allergies, food intolerance or even such essential information as to whether the service user is allowed anything by mouth. A recent case has come to light where a new resident, having been discharged from hospital, was about to be given a drink of tea by nursing home staff when she was on a regime of nil-by-mouth and would surely have choked. It was discovered, by the timely intervention of a visiting relative, that the care plan sent by the hospital actually said 'X should be offered a drink of tea every hour'.

What to look for.

For those with time to do so, a study of the NMS would be useful to show what is expected of a home following on from the Care Standards Act.

It will be seen that that the range of things to be checked is very wide and there is set out in Appendix 6 to this book a useful check list of things that a prospective service user should be looking for and questions to be asked.

In general terms it would be useful to go to the home on more than one occasion and preferably at different times of the day. Perhaps take the opportunity to try to go at a mealtime to see what the food looks like and what assistance is being given to residents. Ask to see a menu for the week. Consider going when there are likely to be people visiting residents (Sunday afternoon is a good time) and try to engage visitors in conversation to see if you can get a feel for how they view the home.

Use all your senses to make an assessment from the moment you approach the front door. If the door is locked how long does it take for it to be answered? What is the security like? How are you greeted? Is the person who answers the door presentable and professional looking? Is there any unpleasant odour as you enter or in any part of the home? Do the staff appear to be engaging with the residents even as they simply walk through the room? How are other staff dressed? Are they in uniform? Do they look professional and presentable? Are there plenty of staff around? If a resident is being moved in a wheelchair are footrests in place and in use? Does the home exude a relaxed atmosphere? Is there an air of activity around the place?

What information are you given by the home to assist in making your decision?

The first of the NMS says 'prospective users [should] have the information they need to make an informed choice about where to live'. In addition to the other enquiries referred to above, the Standards provide (Standard 1) that certain information must be given to service users. The home must produce and make available to service users:

- an up-to-date statement of purpose setting out the aims, objectives, philosophy of care, services and facilities, and terms and conditions of the home and
- a service users' guide to the home for current and prospective residents.

The service users' guide must be written in plain English and be made available in a language and/or format suitable for intended residents and must include:

- a brief description of the services provided;
- a description of the individual accommodation and communal space provided;
- relevant qualifications and experience of the registered provider (that is, the owner), manager and staff;
- the number of places provided and any special needs or interests catered for;
- a copy of the most recent inspection report;
- a copy of the complaints procedure;
- service users' views of the home;

and

- information for service users and their representatives in writing in a relevant language and format about how to contact the local office of the Commission for Social Care Inspection (previously known as the National Care Standards Commission) and local social services and health care authorities.

Additionally, each service user must be provided (Standard 2) with a statement of terms and conditions at the point of moving into the home. If they are purchasing the care privately they must be provided with a contract.

The statement of terms and conditions must include at least the following:

- rooms to be occupied;
- overall care and services (including food) covered by the fee;
- fees payable and by whom (service user, local or health authority, relative or another);
- additional services (including food and equipment) to be paid for over and above those included in the fees;
- rights and obligations of the service user and registered provider and who is liable if there is a breach of contract;
- terms and conditions of occupancy, including period of notice (for example short/long term, intermediate care/respite).

WARNING: Representatives of service users who are asked to sign Terms and Conditions should be very careful. I have recently seen Terms and Conditions from a National Care Home organisation which attempt to put **personal** responsibility for fees and top-ups on the representative. This is unacceptable.

The representative is precisely that, and should not accept personal responsibility for the observance of the Terms and Conditions except where he or she is paying a top-up for the resident. The personal responsibility should be limited to the top-up.

Relatives, friends and representatives of service users are to be given written information about the home's policy on maintaining relatives' and friends' involvement with service users, at the time of moving into the home.

It is provided in the Standards that residents must be permitted to take personal possessions with them and the extent of this must be agreed prior to admission. Those responsible for arranging admission will doubtless also wish to consider this issue and in particular whether a particular item is suitable and in an appropriate condition to be taken especially if a service user has allowed his or her domestic cleanliness to deteriorate.

For those going into Intermediate Care

The NMS say that service users who are assessed and referred solely to a home for *intermediate care* (rehabilitation) are expected to be helped to maximise their independence and return home and Standard 6 provides that dedicated accommodation must be provided, together with specialised facilities, equipment and staff, to deliver short term intensive rehabilitation and enable service users to return home.

Rehabilitation facilities must be sited in dedicated space and include equipment for therapies and treatment, as well as equipment to promote activities of daily living and mobility.

Staff must be qualified and/or are trained and appropriately supervised to use techniques for rehabilitation including treatment and recovery programmes, promotion of mobility, continence and self-care, and outreach programmes to re-establish community living.

Staff must be deployed, and specialist services from relevant professions, including occupational and physiotherapists are to be provided in sufficient numbers and with sufficient competence and skills, to meet the assessed needs of service users admitted for rehabilitation.

The Standard goes on to provide that the service user placed for intermediate care must not be admitted for long term care unless and until the requirements regarding information, assessment and care planning (Standards 1, 3 and 7) are met.

The Longer Term

In the longer term what is to be expected of a care home?

The NMS sets out the expectations.

Service user care plan

- Standard 7 requires that a service user plan of care must be created. This will be based on the comprehensive assessment required by Standard 3 and is drawn up with each service user. It provides the basis for the care to be delivered. It must be stressed that:

  o it must involve the service user;

  o be recorded in a style accessible to the service user (which presumably means not just on a computer!) and

  o it must be agreed and signed by the service user whenever the service user is capable and/or by the service user's representative (if any);

- it must set out in detail the action which needs to be taken by care staff to ensure that all aspects of the health, personal and social care needs of the service user (see Standard 3) are met;

- it must meet relevant clinical guidelines produced by the relevant professional bodies concerned with the care of older people, and include a risk assessment, with particular attention to prevention of falls;

- the plan must be reviewed by care staff in the home at least once a month, updated to reflect changing needs and current objectives for health and personal care, and actioned.

Where the service user is on the Care Programme Approach (this is the formal process (integrated with Care Management) of assessing needs for services for people with mental health problems prior to and after discharge from hospital) or subject to requirements under the Mental Health Act 1983 the service user's plan must take this fully into account.

Health care issues

- Standard 8 makes it clear that it is the home's responsibility to promote and maintain the resident's health and to ensure access to health care services. Whilst encouraging the resident to care for him or herself, it is the responsibility of the care staff to maintain the personal and oral hygiene of the resident. One specific point of care is the assessment of the risk of *pressure sores* and the taking of steps to prevent them and deal with them should they arise. The incidence of pressure sores and the steps taken to deal with them must be recorded. Appropriate equipment must be provided as must be aids and equipment for the promotion of continence. The psychological mental health of the resident must be monitored on a regular basis and appropriate remedial action taken and care provided.
- Opportunities for appropriate exercise and physical activity must be provided having in mind the risks of falling.
- Nutritional screening must be carried out on admission and periodically afterwards and a record maintained of nutrition, weight gain and loss.
- The resident must be permitted to register with a GP of his or her own choice and access must also be provided to other specialist services, and to appropriate information about health service entitlements and advice. (It should be noted that in reality the choice of GP is severely limited because of the refusal of most GPs to travel any distance. Very often those going into care are forced to change GP.)
- Service users should be encouraged to take responsibility for their own medication where appropriate and in those cases must be provided with a lockable space in which to store medication. Appropriate records must be kept. It should be noted that following a death, medicine must be retained for a period of seven days.

Issues of privacy and dignity

Standard 10 provides that arrangements for health and personal care must ensure that service user's privacy and dignity are maintained at all times especially with regard to:

- personal care-giving, including nursing, bathing, washing, using the toilet or commode;
- consultation with, and examination by, health and social care professionals;
- consultation with legal and financial advisors;
- maintaining social contacts with relatives and friends;
- staff entering bedrooms, toilets and bathrooms;
- following death.

The Standard goes on to provide that:

- medical treatment etc. must be provided in the resident's own room;
- residents must have easy access to a telephone for use in private and receive their mail unopened (regrettably the Standard says nothing about mail being handed over promptly!);
- residents must wear their own clothes at all times. The standard provides no exceptions or excuses for this and neither should those responsible for residents. I have listed in the Information Section at the back of this book some places where labels for clothes can be purchased. If these are purchased and attached to all clothes there should be no excuse for clothes not being returned to their owners;
- where a resident has chosen to share a room with someone else, appropriate screens must be provided for when personal care is being given and at other times.

Issues of death and dying.

Standard 11 provides that:

- The spiritual needs, rites and functions must be observed and the resident's wishes concerning terminal care and after death are discussed and carried out. If the resident wishes, their family and friends should be involved in such planning.
- In keeping with the principal of maintaining privacy and dignity, residents should be able to spend their 'final days' in their own rooms, surrounded by their personal belongings, unless there are strong medical reasons for doing otherwise and relatives and friends should be able to stay with him or her for as long as they wish unless

the resident makes it clear that they do not want them.

- Following death, time must be allowed for family and friends to pay their respects.

Issues of daily life

Standard 12 requires that:

- the daily routines are as flexible as possible to suit the service user's expectations, preferences and capacities and that they can exercise their own choice in such matters as:

  o leisure and social activities and cultural interests;
  o food, meals and mealtimes;
  o routines of daily living;
  o personal and social relationships;
  o religious observance;

- the interests of the residents must be recorded and they must be given opportunities for stimulation through leisure and recreation including provision for those with dementia etc. and those with visual and/or hearing impairment or physical or learning disabilities.

Issues of food

A key element in all our lives is food and Standard 15 emphasises that:

- residents must receive a 'wholesome, appealing and balanced diet';
- in pleasing surroundings at times convenient to them;
- the resident is offered three full meals each day of which at least one must be cooked and at intervals of not more than five hours;
- hot and cold drinks and snacks must be available at all times and offered regularly (presumably it is not up to the resident to ask);
- a snack meal must be offered in the evening and the interval between this and breakfast next day must not exceed twelve hours;
- food, including liquefied meals, must be presented in a manner which is attractive and appealing;
- special diets must be provided when advised including adequate provision of calcium and vitamin D;
- religious or cultural diets should be agreed on admission and must be recorded in the care plan. Food for special occasions should be available;
- menus are to be changed regularly and made available in an appropriate format. They must be read by or read to residents and explained;

- mealtimes must be unhurried and residents given sufficient time to eat;
- assistance in eating must be given where necessary 'discreetly, sensitively and individually' although independent eating should be encouraged.

Issues of visitors

Standard 13 provides that:

- residents must be able to have visitors at any reasonable time and
- to see them in private;
- residents must be able to decide who they do and do not want to see;
- no restrictions must be placed on visits except when requested to do so by the resident and when those wishes are recorded;
- links with the outside world should be maintained to suit the resident.

The Standard does not make clear how homes are expected to deal with those visitors who cause distress to a resident or try to cause mischief but where the resident expresses no wish for the visitor to be prohibited.

Issues of finance etc

- Residents should be allowed to handle their own financial affairs for as long as they wish and are able to do so;
- Residents and their relatives and friends should be told how to contact external agents such as advocates and presumably solicitors and accountants who can act in their interests;
- Access to personal records must be facilitated to residents.

It should however be borne in mind that the interests of residents and relatives etc. may not coincide and it is important that the resident understands (as must also the relatives and friends) that, for instance, solicitors instructed are there to represent the resident and not their family and friends.

Issues of complaints

Complaints about homes is a difficult area.

Relatives etc., who perhaps see things going wrong, may well be reluctant to complain for fear that the resident will be victimised, either generally or by a particular member of staff, if a complaint is made. This is going to be particularly so if the older person is naturally timid or if he or she is suffering from dementia and there may be doubts as to whether their evidence will be believed or if they simply cannot communicate. However, the new regulations lay down extensive rules about complaints and the setting up of complaint procedures.

Homes:

- have to have 'simple, clear and accessible' complaints procedures (Standard 16);
- which include 'the stages and time scales for the process', and that;
- ensure complaints are dealt with promptly and effectively and in any event responded to within 28 days;
- must maintain records of complaints;
- must also provide written information to all residents as to how a complaint can be referred at any stage to the *CSCI*.

Residents could, of course, always make representations to their Care Manager or direct to the CSCI if the complaint is sufficiently serious and they wish to be as discreet as possible. It may well be that in this way the complaint may be able to be addressed anonymously without the home ever knowing the source of the complaint.

Residents Rights

The home is required in general terms to ensure that a resident's legal rights are protected and can be exercised and that they can take part in the civic process, by for example, voting in elections. Presumably all residents should be entered on the electoral roll (Voters List) and that they are encouraged, where appropriate, to register for a postal vote. The fact that a resident may be to some extent mentally incapable does not of itself take away a person's right to vote. It is up to election officials to satisfy themselves whether or not a person has mental capacity to vote.

Protection of residents

Standard 18 requires the home to ensure that residents are protected from 'physical, financial or material, psychological or sexual abuse, neglect, discriminatory abuse or self-harm, inhuman or degrading treatment, through deliberate intent, negligence or ignorance, in accordance with written policies.'

A culture, encouraged by government now exists, for any suspicion of abuse to be dealt with firmly and 'whistleblowers' are now protected by law from the consequences of reporting to authorities improper behaviour.

The Standards are somewhat vague when it comes to the home's policies and practices regarding service users' money and financial affairs and simply require the home to ensure:

- service user's access to their personal financial records;
- safe storage of money and valuables;
- consultation on finances in private;
- advice on personal insurance.

The Standards do, however, require the home's policies to prohibit staff involvement in assisting in the making of, or benefiting from, service users' wills.

Environment

Section 5 of the Standards deals with the physical environment of the home. Owners are required to make clear to their prospective residents precisely what type of residents they aim to cater for and to make sure that the physical environment matches their claims.

The standards do set out in great detail the requirements and I propose to summarise only a few of the specific requirements that may be of interest to prospective residents:

- The use of CCTV cameras is restricted to entrance areas for security purposes only.
- Communal space is available which includes:
  o rooms in which a variety of social, cultural and religious activities can take place;
  o rooms where service users can meet visitors in private;
  o dining room(s) to cater for all service users
  o a smoke-free sitting room;
  o outdoor space for service users, accessible to those in wheelchairs or with other mobility problems, with seating and designed to meet the needs of all service users including those with physical, sensory and cognitive impairments.
- There are accessible toilets for service users, clearly marked, close to lounge and dining areas.
- Each service user has a toilet within close proximity of his/her private accommodation.
- En-suite facilities (at minimum a toilet and hand-basin) are provided to all service users in all newly built homes, extensions and all first time registrations from 1 April 2002.
- Service users must have access to all parts of service users'

communal and private space, through the provision of ramps and passenger lifts, where required to achieve this, or stair/chair lifts where they meet the assessed needs of service users and the appropriate requirements of the Environmental Health departments and the Health and Safety Executive.

- The home must provide grab rails and other aids in corridors, bathrooms, toilets, communal rooms and where necessary in service users' own accommodation.
- Aids, hoists and assisted toilets and baths are installed which are capable of meeting the assessed needs of service users.
- Doorways into communal areas, service users' rooms, bathing and toilet facilities and other spaces to which wheelchair users have access, should be of a width sufficient to allow wheelchair users adequate access. In all newly built homes, new extensions to homes and first time registrations doorways into areas to which wheelchair users have access should have a clear opening of 800 mm.
- Facilities, including communication aids (for example a loop system) and signs must be provided to assist the needs of all service users, taking account of, for example, the needs of those with hearing impairment, visual impairment, dual sensory impairments, learning disabilities or dementia or other cognitive impairment.
- Call systems with an accessible alarm facility are provided in every room.
- Where rooms are shared, they are occupied by no more than two service users who have made a positive choice to share with each other. When a shared place becomes vacant, the remaining service user must have the opportunity to choose not to share, by moving into a different room if necessary.
- The premises must be kept clean, hygienic and free from offensive odours throughout.

Individual accommodation

The home must provide private accommodation for each service user which is furnished and equipped to assure comfort and privacy, and meets the assessed needs of the service user. In the absence of service users' own provision, furnishings for individual rooms must be provided to the minimum as follows:

- the room must be carpeted or equivalent; it must be fitted with locks suited to service users' capabilities and accessible to staff in emergencies. The resident must be provided with keys unless their risk assessment suggests otherwise;
- the room must be centrally heated and heating must be capable of control in the resident's own room;

- a clean comfortable bed, minimum 900 mm wide, at a suitable, safe height for the service user, and bed linen. If the resident is receiving nursing care the bed must be adjustable;
- curtains or blinds;
- mirror;
- overhead and bedside lighting;
- comfortable seating for two people (experience teaches that this is frequently ignored. I often find that I have to sit on a commode when visiting older clients);
- drawers and enclosed space for hanging clothes;
- at least 2 accessible double electric sockets;
- a table to sit at and a bed-side table;
- washbasin (unless an en-suite WC and washbasin are provided).
- each resident must have lockable storage space for medication, money and valuables and is provided with the key that he or she can retain (unless the reason for not doing so is explained in the care plan);
- screening is provided in double rooms to ensure privacy for personal care.

Service Users' Money

There is an overall obligation cast upon homes to ensure that residents' financial interests are safeguarded. Standard 35 lays down some specific requirements:

- Homes must ensures that service users control their own money except where they state that they do not wish to or they lack capacity and that safeguards are in place to protect the interests of the service user.
- Written records of all transactions are maintained.
- Where the money of individual service users is handled, the manager must ensure the personal allowances of these service users are not pooled and appropriate records and receipts are kept.
- The home manager may be appointed as agent for a service user only where no other individual is available. In this case, the manager must ensure that:

  o the registration authority is notified on inspection;
  o records are kept of all incoming and outgoing payments.
  o if the manager is to be an appointee for social security purposes, the DWP is given appropriate notice. (I am not sure how this can be avoided since the DWP make the appointment.)
  o Secure facilities are provided for the safe-keeping of money and

valuables on behalf of the service user.

o Records and receipts are kept of possessions handed over for safe-keeping.

Records

Standard 37 says that service users must have access to their records and information about them held by the home, as well as opportunities to help maintain their personal records.

Generally

I have looked above at what the NMS provide and have given some pointers in this chapter and elsewhere as to the issues to be looked at in choosing a home. It is not an easy process. It is one to be undertaken carefully and above all, and wherever possible, in an ordered sort of way. Sadly, many admissions to care take place at a time of crisis, often following a medical emergency or following a period in hospital and when there will be pressure from the hospital to free up a bed. Often it will not be possible to tell if and when such a situation will arise. However, as with many of the things dealt with in this book, if as a relative gets older and their condition starts to deteriorate, children start to acknowledge the realities and commence looking at possible options and finding out how the system works, they will be in a much better position to organise the care of their relative in the preferred ordered way. This will be likely to have a more satisfactory outcome for them and for their relative.

Longer term relationships with the home

Although perhaps strictly outside the confines of this book, I think that it is worth saying a little about the relationship between the resident/the relatives and the home.

It is my view that both sides should fulfil their obligations to the other. No home is perfect. Issues will arise. If the consumer wishes to be in a position to make demands on the home they must put themselves above reproach. This applies particularly to the relatives. The expectations of the home on the relatives will not be great and should be relatively easy to meet and can be summarised as follows:

• Homes have staff wages to pay and other expenses to meet. Accordingly, they need fees to be paid. In the early stages after an admission there may be problems in doing this especially where someone is paying their own fees in whole or significant part. There may well be problems in accessing money to pay fees especially where the Court of Protection is involved. In my view it is important that before admission the position is made clear to the home especially where there may be any significant delay in paying fees. It is then up to the relatives to make sure that everything which can be done to get fees paid promptly is done and once things are put on a proper basis, fees should be kept up to date.

- Treat staff with courtesy and consideration. Care assistants are often not generously paid, and even if they were, should still be treated in a friendly and proper manner. Things should be asked of them and not demanded.

- Homes are expected to have very flexible visiting times. However, this should not be abused and consideration should be given to the running of the home and the general well being of all residents.

- Close contact should be maintained with the home. Homes do not respect relatives who simply 'dump' an older person on them and show little interest afterwards. The home will generally be glad to have a sensible input from relatives in issues of care. The home will also need to know that should a resident need anything over and above that contracted to be provided by the home there is someone who can be contacted and who will respond to their request for money or items etc. promptly. Regrettably, there are some relatives who simply fail to do this.

These are relatively straightforward issues. In return what should the consumer expect?

- That the resident is cared for properly in every sense of the word and at least in accordance with the NMS. Perfection cannot however be expected and must not be demanded.

- Whilst relatives should expect their loved one to be clean and tidy they must not expect every spill to be cleared immediately.

- One particular expectation and which in the past has frequently been a problem is ensuring that residents are dressed in their own clothes. The NMS make clear that this must happen and it should be non-negotiable. The odd occasion there may be a slip up but this should never be accepted on a regular basis and should be brought to the attention of the home promptly. Relatives can play their part by ensuring that all clothes are properly and permanently marked/labelled.

CHAPTER 18

COMMUNITY CARE SERVICES

KEY POINTS

- Community Care Services fall into two types – non-residential care services provided to a service user in his or her own home and residential care services where someone moves into a *care home.*

- The law in this area, especially in respect of funding services, is complex.

- Unless a service user wishes to arrange and pay for their help entirely themselves, the starting point for obtaining help is an *assessment* by the local authority if the service user is at home or by the multi disciplinary team where a service user is about to be discharged from hospital. A '*Care Plan*' is devised.

- A local authority is obliged to provide an assessment free of charge as soon as they become aware of someone in their area who may be in need of help.

- Assessment opens the door to most other services.

- The local authority does not have to provide services themselves nor in many instances does it have to pay for them. Each authority has its own policies.

- If someone needs help and the local authority arranges the care and the service user has the resources to pay but refuses, then the authority may arrange and pay for the services but sue the service user for the cost.

- Residential care is broadly of two types, namely nursing and personal (for example, help with getting dressed).

- Consequently there are broadly two types of care home, namely nursing and residential.

- If a service user is *'self funding'* they should make their own arrangements for care unless they are unable to do so and have no one to make the arrangements in which case the local authority will do so but the service user will still have to pay for the care provided.

- If a service user is not self funding then the local authority will make the arrangements for care and enter into the contract with the home. The service user may well have a contribution to pay towards the cost.

- Unless a service user is certain that he or she will be self funding for life, it is essential that he or she should have an assessment carried out before going in care to ensure that the level of care is not excessive.

- If a service user is discharged from hospital under Section 117 Mental Health Act 1983 after care will be provided free by the NHS.

- If a person needs continuing nursing care (effectively total nursing care) then home fees will be paid for in full by the NHS. Each *Primary Care Trust* has its own criteria.

- If a person needs care in a Care Home but only requires an element of nursing care then part of the fees will be provided by the NHS (the *Registered Nursing Care Contribution)*

- In all other cases fees are charged to the service user if his or her income/capital is above certain levels.

- Most sources of income and capital (including the service user's house) are taken into account. The house is exempt from inclusion in certain circumstances. The rules are complex.

- All local authorities are obliged to provide welfare benefits advice. Such advice should always be taken.

CHAPTER 18

COMMUNITY CARE SERVICES

OVERVIEW

When the time comes for an older person to need some help in managing their daily life and they approach the local authority for support, they will be seeking 'Community Care Services'.

Community Care Services fall into two basic types:

- non-residential care services which are those provided to a service user in his or her own home (such as home care, respite care, night sitting service, meals on wheels, day care or the provision of practical aids to assist with the tasks of daily life) and
- residential care services where someone moves from his or her own home into a care home.

The law governing the provision of Community Care Services is highly complex.

- It is found in no less than 16 Acts of Parliament and numerous *Statutory Instruments* going back to the National Assistance Act 1948.
- On top of this there are countless pieces of advice, policy guidance, practice guidance and directions from central government as to how legislation should be applied and in recent years there have been numerous cases before the courts which have looked at how the law should be interpreted and applied.

It is further complicated by the fact that a large element of discretion is allowed to local authorities and health care trusts as to:

- the way in which they provide care;
- what care is provided and
- how that care is charged for, if at all.

The fact that some services are funded and/or provided by the local authority and some by the National Health Service and some by contribution from the Department for Work and Pensions does not make things any easier to understand. It is also complicated by reason of the fact that although a particular piece of legislation may have been enacted it may not have been brought into force even many years after the event. All of it is also subject to what funds a particular authority has available and how it chooses to allocate that money between the competing types of *service user*.

Accordingly, it would be well nigh impossible to give a detailed statement in a book of this nature as to the legal position. What I will try to do in this chapter is to highlight some basic principles and, in keeping with the overall notion behind this book, prompt readers to think about their position early and seek specific advice at an early stage.

Service users should be aware that each Social Services Department is obliged, along with the local health authorities and trusts and housing departments to produce a local 'Better Care Higher Standards Charter'. These charters are for anyone over eighteen in England who has difficulties associated with old age, long term illness or disability and for carers who support people in these circumstances. They are expected to tell anyone needing care or support over the longer term in what areas they can expect health, housing and social services to set standards for the services they provide and what to do if the expectations are not met.

Service users and their carers should, at an early stage, obtain a copy from their local authority. Often these are published on the local authority website.

WHERE DO YOU START?

ASSESSMENTS

- The law places on local authorities a duty to conduct an *assessment* (a Community Care Assessment) of the needs of any person [for whom they may have to provide, or arrange to provide, community care services] for community care services and then having carried out that assessment they must decide whether the person's needs call for the provision by the authority of such services and if so what. The carrying out of an assessment is not dependent upon whether or not an individual can pay for care services.
- By community care services is meant either residential care or non-residential care services.
- The local authority's obligation to conduct such an assessment arises as soon as they become aware of someone in their area who may be in need of their help. This may happen in many ways. For example, a referral by a GP or a hospital; a referral by a concerned friend or relative; a referral by the police; a referral by the person themselves.
- **The assessment process is the key which opens the door to help and assistance.**

- The manner of assessment is not currently laid down in detail. It is intended that by April 2005 there should be in place a 'single assessment process' (SAP for Older People). The object is to ensure that an assessment is carried out to assess an older person's health and social care needs and so that the individual needs to provide information only once rather than as is the past having to give the same information to different people. The SAP may be broken down into parts.
- The actual level (the extent or intensity) of the assessment is not laid down but it is provided that the assessment arrangement should normally include an initial screening process to determine the appropriate form of assessment. It may be found that some people need only advice whereas with others the initial screening may uncover the possible need for wide ranging services in which case an in-depth assessment will be called for. The Department of Health suggests that there should be four types of assessment:
    o Contact assessment – obtaining basic personal information and dealing with simple requirements;
    o Overview assessment – where various aspects of care may need to be explored;
    o Specialist assessment – where specific problems are explored;
    o Comprehensive assessment – where there are multiple needs and several agencies may need to be involved.

- Neither is there laid down any time scale in which an assessment should be carried out. It must, however, be 'timely'.
- Local Authorities, however, are generally expected to start an assessment within forty-eight hours of referral with services being in place within twenty-eight days. In the case of those being discharged from hospital, much speedier requirements are imposed. The service user should be told how long they will have to wait for assessment and how long the assessment process will take.
- However, even if an assessment has not been carried out, the authority still has **emergency powers** under which it can provide services until a full assessment has been carried out.
- The assessment does not have to be in writing but usually will be so especially where anything but the most basic and simple needs are identified. The results of the assessment will be made known, so far as possible, to the service user and anyone acting on behalf of the service user as well as anyone who is going to provide care.

There are provisions via the Local Authority's Complaints Procedure for assessments to be challenged if necessary. Furthermore the assessment is not a once and for all process. Reviews for older people should be held after three months and then at least annually.

After the assessment

- Having carried out the assessment, the authority must then decide whether the user's needs require provision to be made by the local Social Services Department having in mind any service which may be available from the National Health Service and the Local Housing Authority always having in mind that the 'lead' authority is the local Social Services Department.
- Have in mind that because a need is identified the Local Authority may not necessarily provide help itself, nor, indeed, will the Authority necessarily pay for the help. The service user himself may have to pay some or all of the cost. A third party, for example, a privately operated Home Care Agency, may provide the service.

Additionally, before any changes in services are made for existing service users, a re-assessment should take place.

- Reviews of service users' needs and circumstances must be carried out routinely and regularly and this may involve a reassessment of an individual's needs. The first review should be three months after help is first provided and then annually or more often if individuals circumstances appear to warrant it. Reviews can be considered at the request of service users, providers of services and other appropriate individuals or agencies.
- The authority makes its decision as to whether it will provide or arrange services for you by comparing your assessed care needs with the eligibility criteria which each individual authority has set for the Community Care Services. It is important to appreciate that this is decided by each local authority. There are no national criteria.
- It should be noted that unlike the case of residential care where a service user needs services in their own home it is the local authority who should arrange the services irrespective of the financial resources or the mental capacity of the service user if that is what the service user wants the council to do.
- It is now established that to a lesser or greater extent, local authorities, in deciding what provision to make for a particular individual, inevitably have to have regard to the financial resources which are available to the authority. The key issue is that they must be seen to abide by proper processes in reaching decisions and must not be seen to act arbitrarily or inconsistently. Once a local authority has established that you fall within its eligibility criteria then it cannot use lack of resources to justify not meeting your needs. Policy and Practice Guidance has been issued in May 2002 by the Department of Health under the title 'Fair Access to Care Services'. From April 2003 authorities must have reviewed, revised and implemented revised eligibility criteria for care services and by April

2004 all the then existing care plans had to have been reviewed. This guidance may be accessed via the Internet at **www.dh.gov.uk**

- Outside the scope of Fair Access Guidance are the provision of services such as travel concessions and disabled parking badges which are covered under Regulations and Guidance under the Road Traffic Act 2000 which sets out who is entitled to such services.

- Once a decision has been taken as to the services to be provided then a **written** '*care plan*' is established and in any but very simple cases a '*care manager*' (usually from social services) will be appointed. The care manager will be responsible for organising the provision of services both from inside and outside the authority and the care manager will be responsible for the implementation of the plan and co-ordinating the various bodies.

- Government guidance says that local authorities should provide services promptly when they have agreed to do so.

- When a council has agreed to supply disability equipment, items costing less than £1,000 should be provided within three weeks.

- By December 2004 it was intended that all equipment should be provided within one week and all other services should be provided within a month of the completion of the assessment.

Carers and their needs

- The guidance issued in connection with community care acknowledges that it is not only the authorities who provide care for older people but that a large measure of care is carried out by 'lay' carers in the guise of relatives, friends and neighbours. Under a 1995 Act of Parliament it is provided that where a local authority is assessing (or re-assessing) an older person's needs then a carer who is providing or intends to provide what is described as a 'substantial' amount of care on a regular basis may, at the same time, ask the local authority to assess his or her ability to provide and continue to provide that care. It must be stressed that under this Act the carer has no separate right to an assessment. It only follows on from the assessment of the older person. It must further be emphasised that there must be a substantial amount of care to be provided and it must be on a regular basis.

As a result of an Act in 2000 the right of the carer to his or her own assessment is extended. It is possible that an older person may refuse an assessment or does not wish to have Community Care Services in which event under the 1995 Act the carer would not themselves be entitled to have an assessment.

The 2000 Act, however, entitles an informal carer in his or her own right to their own assessment of his or her ability to provide care for another person and also empowers local authorities to provide 'carer services' direct to the carer. Perhaps the main 'carer service' would be the provision of respite care. This would either be by the provision of temporary home care for the older person, or for residential care for the older person but all designed to give the carer a break. It should be noted that carers may be charged for the provision of these services.

Carers should be aware that they may be entitled to a 'carer's allowance' from the Department for Work and Pensions. Carers should also be aware that in some circumstances the receipt by them of a carer's allowance may reduce the benefits received by the older person.

- One important point for the layman to understand is that, whilst to him or her where money comes from to pay for care is immaterial as long as it does not come out of the pocket of the service user, to the 'authorities' it is very important. Each organisation (NHS, the Department for Work and Pensions and the local authority social services departments) have their own budget and have to maximise that budget. In consequence, wherever they can off-load a liability onto another authority they will do so. Therefore, a local authority will require a service user to claim state benefits such as pension credit since that will reduce the amount the local authority has to find from its budget for a residential care placement. Similarly if one local authority can use the rules to put on another local authority the cost of residential care they will do so. To the layman this may seem strange but it is a fact of life and if kept in mind will explain some of the complexity of the rules or at any rate put them into context.

Special issues on discharge from hospital

- Specific guidance has been issued by government relating to the discharge of older people following a period in hospital.
- Where he or she is going to need long-term support the discharge must be preceded by a multi-disciplinary assessment of his or her social and health care needs, whether in the community or in residential care, and which will involve input from nurses, occupational therapists, social workers, probably a geriatrician or psycho- geriatrician, the patient (if possible) and family and other prospective carers.
- The decision will include issues of whether the patient needs intermediate care funded by the NHS and also how the patient's long-term care is to be funded. The consultant will also consider whether the patient meets the criteria for continuing NHS health care and since each Primary Care Trust (PCT) sets down it's own eligibility criteria the consultant may well have

to be familiar with the criteria for a number of PCTs especially where patients are drawn from a wide area.

- A decision on whether a patient's future care will be fully funded by the NHS must be made before the patient leaves hospital.
- It is prudent on the part of patients and their representatives to ensure that all decisions, plans and considerations are set down in writing and are concluded before discharge. Once the patient is out of hospital the negotiating position in respect of the care package and financial arrangements will have been significantly weakened. It should also be borne in mind that any voluntary carers are also entitled to an assessment of their needs (see above) and it should be reflected in the care package offered. The patient should be given benefits advice and the financial implications of the care package explained. The patient (or his representatives) should always consider whether the level of nursing care required is such that fully funded NHS care should be provided. Patients who do not have mental capacity to accept discharge are in a slightly difficult position since even if they have appointed an attorney or if a receiver has been appointed the attorney/receiver has no 'power over the person' and cannot make decisions on care.
- Patients have a right to a review of any decision on the provision of continuing NHS healthcare and this must be carried out within two weeks of the request. The request for review is usually considered by one officer who, if he feels there is a justification for a review passes the matter to a review panel for decision.

ISSUES IN RESPECT OF SERVICES

As indicated there are two broad types of service that can be provided to older people by Social Services or which are arranged for them or can be arranged for them by Social Services:

1. Residential services (that is, residential care)
2. Non-residential services

I will look at some issues relevant to them.

CHARGES FOR NON-RESIDENTIAL SERVICES

- Local authorities are permitted by law to charge for most of the services they provide. Some exceptions to this are for social work advice, occupational therapy (which is, of course, not limited to those of working age) and assessments. One further important exception to the power to charge is for those who receive after-care services after being compulsorily detained under the Mental Health Act.

- Each local authority is effectively permitted to make its own charging guidelines but it must lay down clear guidelines and they must be reasonable and fair. It should be noted that the fact that an individual is in receipt of state benefits does not exclude them from having to pay for services provided. Appeals procedures exist.
- It should be noted that the law is unclear as to whether the financial resources of a husband or wife or partner are to be taken into account in deciding whether a service user should pay for services received.
- Where someone is shown to be in need of a particular service the local authority is not allowed not to provide that service because the service user refuses to pay the assessed charge. The local authority must pursue the debt through the courts.

RESIDENTIAL CARE

A few basic facts

- Residential care is provided in what are now generically known as 'care homes' and in general terms these can be sub-divided into:

    1. 'residential' where the care provided is essentially personal care as distinct from nursing care, and
    2. 'nursing' which provides personal care but on top of this nursing care is also provided
    3. 'mental nursing'.

- Some homes are '*Dual registered*' which means that they have some beds which are solely residential and some which are nursing. The advantage of a dual registered home is that if a resident initially needs only personal care but later progresses to a point where he or she needs nursing care as well there is no need for the resident to move to a separate/new home.
- Whilst there are still some homes actually owned and run by local authorities most local authorities have reduced the number of homes they provide substantially in recent years. Most homes are now provided by commercial entities of varying sizes and some by voluntary organisations.
- The local authorities now tend therefore to purchase care for service users in homes operated by others rather than providing care in the homes that they operate.
- Fees in a residential home will be less than in a nursing home
- Fees vary according to the area of the country involved.
- All homes are now regulated under the Care Standards Act 2000 that came into force in 2002. This act applies to homes run by the local authority, the private sector and the voluntary sector. It also applies to the services of non-residential care providers (see Chapter 19). The homes are

inspected by the Commission for Social Care Inspection (in England) (formerly the Care Standards Commission) and in Wales by the Care Standards Inspectorate for Wales.

- As has been seen in Chapter 17, National Minimum Standards have been laid down for all homes and these can be found via the Internet at **www.csci.gov.uk**

Arrangements for and choice of residential care

- The arrangements for going into care depend on whether a service user is '*self-funding*' (that is, paying all his or her home fees from their own resources – including pensions) or whether the service user is being paid for in whole or part by the local authority (see below).
- If someone is '*self-funding*' then the local authority (whilst possibly assisting with the making of arrangements for going into care following an assessment – as to which see below) do not actually purchase the care or enter into a contract with the home for the care. The contractual and payment arrangements are entirely between the service user (or their representative) and the home. The service user is completely free to choose the type of home into which they go even if the home provides a level of care over and above that which they actually need. They could, however, have a problem if they go into a level of care in excess of that which they need and then run out of money. The local authority could then require them to move out of the original home and into a home more suited to their needs. It is therefore prudent, where that could arise, to be assessed first by the local authority and ensure that the care provided is right for the individual.
- If, however, the service user is being funded in whole or part by the local authority from the outset then it follows from the above that they have to be assessed before they go into care and the level of care which they need determined. The authority will not pay for care at a level above that which is necessary.
- Where someone is funded from the outset by the local authority in whole or part then the arrangements for them to go into care will be made by the local authority and the local authority will enter into the contract with the home.
- It should be noted that if someone is initially not self-funding but later becomes so on account of, say, having sold their house or otherwise having 'come into money' then the local authority is entitled to drop out of the picture and someone else (the service user themselves or their representative) takes over the responsibility, both contractual and practical.
- As indicated above normally where someone is to be self-funding they

must make their own arrangements for going into care. However, there is an exception to this in that the local authority must still make those arrangements in those cases where someone is self funding but who is unable to make his or her own arrangements and where there is no one else (friend, relative etc) who is willing and able to make those arrangements.

- Anyone who is initially self-funding and who later ceases to be self-funding will have to be careful to set in train arrangements for the local authority to take over arrangements for care at the appropriate point when their financial resources reach a point where they cease to be self funding. This will apply also to those acting on behalf of service users such as attorneys and receivers. The responsibility will also extend to applying for appropriate state benefits at all times but in particular when the service users financial resources drop to a point where they are entitled to claim pension credit. The law permits an application to be made for pension credit up to four months before a resident will qualify for benefit. Service users need to have this provision in mind since it is apparent that some social security offices are unaware of the rule and may reject applications where it is made before the capital level falls below the threshold to justify a claim albeit that the capital resources are just above the threshold at the time the application is made. Quote Regulation 13 D of the Social Security (Claims and Payments) Regulations 1987 (S.I. 1987/1968) (as amended)'

- Where someone makes their own arrangements for care and is going to pay for it there is no problem as to which home they go into and where it is situated. There can, however, be problems where a person requires care that is going to be funded by the local authority. The position is governed by Regulations. Updated guidance on the regulations was issued in October 2004 and was aimed at clarifying the position and ensuring that service users have maximum choice. The following points emerge:

  o If the service user **expresses a preference** for particular accommodation (known as 'preferred accommodation') within England and Wales then the council **must** arrange for care in that accommodation subject to four conditions. If the authority decides not to comply with the users wishes then it must have clear justification for not doing so and be prepared to provide a full explanation in writing.

  The four conditions are as follows:

    (a) The accommodation is suitable for the service users needs decided by the assessment. The mere fact that a home meets the registration requirements is not of itself enough. It must actually be suitable to meet the needs of the particular individual. However, if it does not meet registration standards it will definitely not be suitable.

(b)It must not cost the council more than it would usually expect to pay for someone with the assessed needs (called 'the usual cost'). A council may have several 'usual costs' dependent upon the type of care provided. As long as an individual has not expressed a preference for more expensive accommodation then, if because of insufficient places being available at the usual cost to meet the assessed needs of individuals, the council must pay for more expensive accommodation and without any 'top-up' being required. Only when a service user requests more expensive accommodation can the council ask for a top-up. The moral must therefore be: see what is offered. Before requesting particular accommodation find out what it costs and whether the council will pay that cost. Only then request it.

It should be noted that the guidance says that there may be situations where there may be higher costs incurred in providing care. This may be where specialist care is needed for specialist user groups with high levels of need or where necessary to prepare special diets or provide additional facilities for medical or **cultural** reasons. The guidance says "councils should be prepared to meet these higher costs in order to ensure an individual's needs are appropriately met."

(c)The accommodation must be available.

If there is insufficient accommodation available then the service user may have to wait for it to become available. In that event the council should make arrangements for the service user's needs to be met on a temporary basis. This may involve moving to another care home. If the service user decides to stay there even when a place becomes available in the preferred accommodation then, if the cost in the care home is more than in the preferred placement and is more than the council is prepared to pay, a top up payment can be required. However, this possibility should be spelled out to the service user before they go to the temporary placement in the first place.

(d)The home is prepared to accept the council's usual terms

and conditions. However some flexibility is expected of councils particularly when dealing with homes outside their area.

o Where **the council chooses** to place someone in accommodation more expensive than the usual cost then they cannot require a top-up payment to be made.

o If a top-up is required (to meet the service users choice of preferred and more expensive accommodation) then the council will still be required to pay the full costs but with the right to recover the top-up from the resident or third party. Accordingly, the council will need to ensure that the third party can meet the top-up into the future and also can meet increased top-ups when costs rise. The service user and the third party should have it spelled out that if the top-up is not paid then the service user may have to move to less expensive accommodation with all the upset that may accompany such a move.

o It should be noted that 'liable relatives' cannot be third parties for top-up purposes where they are already actually contributing to the costs of maintaining the service user.

• Where a person cannot express a preference for accommodation themselves, then the council is entitled to act on the preferences expressed by their advocate, carer or legal guardian unless such wishes would be against the interests of the service user.

• Councils are required to make clear to service users the effect of the regulations and the choices open to them.

• One problem can arise if a service user lives in one local authority area but wishes to go into a home in another local authority area. Essentially, the cost of their care will fall on the local authority in whose area they 'ordinarily' resided rather than the authority into whose area they are moving. Disputes can arise between local authorities, say for example, where a service user moves away from their own home area for a time, say, to stay with relatives and then requires residential care. The local authorities may argue as to which of them is to pay for the care. Such a squabble can cause upset for the service user and families at a critical time and is clearly best avoided by, wherever possible, thinking things through in advance and making firm plans, where possible, in good time. It should be noted that where the NHS funds residential care it will be at the cost of the Primary Care Trust into whose area the patient moves and that will be based on registration with a GP.

• Local authorities produce lists of homes that they recommend. The fees charged by the homes may well influence these lists. Subject to the home providing the care which the service user is assessed as needing, there is nothing to stop a service user going into another home not on the list (and indeed in another authority area) even if the fees are more than the local authority are prepared to pay for that type of care, as long as someone is prepared to pay 'top-up' fees. A top up fee is the difference between what the home charges and what the local authority are prepared to contribute, after taking into account, of course, the contributions from benefits etc. from the service user. This may involve a third party, usually a relative, paying the top-up. Since it will be the local authority that will be entering into the contract with the home to provide the care the authority will need to be satisfied that there are resources and commitment to paying the top-up fees. To place a service user in a home and then have to move them because the third party would no longer be willing or would be unable to pay the top-up would be unacceptable. The service user is not permitted to pay the 'top up' from their own capital or from their personal allowance except in certain very limited circumstances.

- Wherever possible it is preferable for the local authority to make the arrangements for the care to be provided and enter into the contract with the provider. This is likely to result in a substantial reduction in cost to the service user than if he or she makes his or her own arrangements. Many homes feel justified in charging what amounts to a self-funding premium. This is done because providers feel that fees paid by the local authority are insufficient and take the opportunity to make up shortfalls by charging self-funders more.

Where someone is self-funding and makes their own arrangements then they pay to the home whatever fee they and the home have agreed is appropriate.

Charges for residential care

- If the service user is being discharged under Section 117 of the Mental Health Act 1983 then it is likely that the after care (including residential care) will be paid for in full by the National Health Service.
- On the assumption that Section 117 Mental Health Act does not apply then in all cases where someone is assessed as needing residential care the first question will be do they need continuing nursing care? If they do then their care will be paid for wholly by the NHS Primary Care Trust.
- If, however, they do not meet the criteria for continuing nursing care and therefore be entirely paid for by the NHS then if it is assessed that they do need an element of nursing care (as distinct from social care) then the NHS will make a contribution to the cost irrespective of whether they are self-funding. This is called Registered Nursing Care Contribution (RNCC). Any other cost over and above the nursing element will be subject to means testing to determine whether the service user should pay in whole or part for his or her care.
- If he or she needs no element of nursing care then again, means testing

will apply to determine whether the service user should pay the whole or part of the cost of his or her care.

- The regulations for determining whether a person pays for his or her care in a home and, if so, how much, are complex. They are set out in the CRAG (Charging for Residential Accommodation Guide). The CRAG is amended at intervals. The most recent amendment was Number 22 October 2004. The CRAG contains at present some 99 pages. The CRAG is very similar to the National Assistance (Assessment of Resources) Regulations 1992 and decisions of the Commissioners where appeals have been decided under the National Assistance Regulations in Income Support matters are useful in interpreting the CRAG.

  The CRAG can be found via the Internet at **www.dh.gov.uk**

- **The first calculation** to be made is whether the resident has *capital* that exceeds the upper limit that is currently set at £20,000 (£20,500 in Wales). If the answer to that question is 'yes' then the resident pays for his or her own care (but with a contribution towards nursing care from the NHS of an amount as set out below if an element of nursing care is required This is the RNCC referred to above). In arriving at the figure for capital the CRAG provides in some detail for which assets are disregarded in the calculation and how other assets are valued. This includes issues such as what interest in jointly owned assets and assets held in trust are taken into account. I have set out below some particular points of interest (see points on Capital Assessment).

- **The second calculation** is as to whether, whilst having capital below the upper threshold, the resident has capital above the lower limit which is currently set at £12,250 (£13,500 in Wales). In other words, they have more than £12,250 but less than £20,000 (£13,500 but less than £20,500 in Wales). If this is the case then whilst the £7,750 (£7,000 in Wales) difference is disregarded as capital, it is treated as generating additional income for the resident and which is known as 'tariff income'. This is calculated as £1 per week for each £250 or part thereof above £12,250 (In Wales £13,500). Thus, a resident with capital of £15,350 will be treated as having a tariff income of £13 per week (in England) and which will be taken into account in the third part of the calculation as set out below. The tariff income applies even though the income actually produced by the asset, even on the assumption it produces an actual income, may be far less than the tariff income calculated.

- **The third calculation** is as to what income the resident has. If the resident's income is (unusually) equal to or exceeds the cost of care then they are self-funding. If it is below the cost of care then (after taking into account funding for any nursing care being provided by the NHS (the RNCC)) the resident will be funded for the difference by the local authority. As with capital, some types of income are disregarded in whole or in part. On the other side of the coin, the resident may be treated as

199

having notional income, that is income that they do not actually receive. An example of this is the tariff income referred to in the second calculation above. I have set out below some particular points on issues of income calculation (see points on Income Assessment).

- There is no satisfactory appeal procedure against the assessment since the panel appointed by the local authority to conduct reviews can only make recommendations. The Director of Social Services makes the actual final decision. This has however recently been challenged under the Human Rights convention.
- Generally, the duty is on the service user to prove that he or she cannot pay for accommodation. Failure to supply full information may well lead to the service user being charged the full cost. Residents must therefore produce such things as passbooks, bank statements etc.

Points on capital assessment

- Valuation of capital assets can be complicated – depending on the asset concerned and who exactly owns it.
- Capital assets are valued at market value less 10% as a notional and arbitrary figure for the costs of disposal. If the asset is actually disposed of then its value will be the **actual** price realised less the **actual** disposal costs. If on a disposal the asset realises sufficient to make the service user self funding by a significant amount then the local authority may drop out of the picture and the service user may have to assume responsibility for their own arrangements and this may lead to the home increasing the fees charged.
- Where an asset is in joint names it is generally treated as being owned equally between the co-owners even if the owners regard it as owned in different proportions. If they do not want this situation to arise then they should split the asset up between themselves in the proportions that they consider they own it. The exception to this rule is where land or buildings is involved in which case the asset is treated as owned in the proportions in which it is actually owned by the co-owners. This will be a matter of evidence (and it is for this reason that it is prudent for owners to document ownership wherever possible). This differs from the way in which joint assets are treated by the Department for Work and Pensions for income support purposes. They treat all assets of any type as owned equally by the joint owners irrespective of the true and, possibly, documented position.
- Some assets are totally disregarded in the assessment. A full list of these is set out in Schedule 4 to The National Assistance (Assessment of Resources) Regulations 1992 (Number 2977). The most significant exception is personal possessions such as jewellery, furniture or works of art unless it can be shown that they have been purchased with the

200

intention of avoiding charges or unless it can be shown that these are actually trade items. Prudent potential service users will draw their own conclusions from this.

- On the other side of the coin there may be some assets that a service user does not have but which he will be treated as having. This will particularly be the case where the service user has tried to dispose of assets to claim benefits. This can either be where the service user has given the item away or where they have 'sold' it at an undervalue. These assets will be treated as still belonging to him or her in assessing liability for fees. Whilst the local authority will not be able to stop paying fees for the service user, if this is discovered there are various powers given to the local authority to try to recoup the fees which would have been payable and these include:

  o Where the asset has been disposed of less than six months before the assessment, seeking an order for its return from whoever has it if they have not paid full value for it.
  o Instituting bankruptcy proceedings against the service user and then seeking to recover the asset from whoever has it if they have not given full value to the service user for it. In general terms this power can be used for up to five years from the date of disposal.
  o A simple action for debt (if the authority is satisfied that the resident has assets out of which the debt can be met).

Particular points on capital assessment in respect of the resident's former home

- Most people are desperate to preserve their home to pass on to relatives or friends even if all other assets have to be used to pay fees. However, the house is a capital asset and where appropriate it will need to be sold and the proceeds used for the resident's home fees.

- When someone becomes a permanent resident in care then the home is disregarded in determining their capital for a period of twelve weeks from the date they become permanent. (It must be stressed that this does not mean that fees are not charged; it means that the value of the house is not taken into account for twelve weeks but any other assets are still counted.) I deal elsewhere in this section in more detail with issues of temporary residence. In consequence, if the service user has no other resources to make them self-funding for the first twelve weeks, the local authority will make the arrangements with the care home and pick up the bill subject to any contribution from the resident. Once the twelve week period has expired the resident becomes self-funding and the resident will then be responsible for their own care arrangements and will in consequence have to take steps to pay their own fees (resulting in the effectively forced sale of the house) unless the local authority is prepared to enter into a *deferred payment agreement* (a DPA). A DPA is where the local authority continues to fund the care but on the basis that the local authority takes a *charge* on the home and will recover the outlay on fees when the property is sold. It needs to be borne in mind that this will place a burden on local authorities for the time that the fees are outstanding.

- A DPA may affect state benefits. Whilst attendance allowance/disability living allowance can be claimed where a deferred payment agreement is in force, pension credit may not be claimed since there is a requirement that for pension credit to be paid the property must be on the market. If it is on the market then the property can remain unsold for up to twenty-six weeks at which time pension credit will cease to be paid unless the DWP is satisfied that determined efforts to sell are taking place in which event the property may continue to be disregarded and pension credit paid.

- The house is disregarded also if the resident is in care permanently but the house is occupied by a spouse or partner (unless estranged/divorced) or by a relative of the resident or by a member of his family who:

  o Is aged sixty or over; or
  o Is aged under 16, and is a child whom the resident is liable to maintain; or
  o Is incapacitated

Relative is defined as: parent (including an adoptive parent); parent-in-law; son (including an adoptive son); son-in-law; daughter (including an adoptive daughter); daughter-in-law; step-parent; step-son; step-daughter; brother; sister; grandparent; grandchild; uncle; aunt; nephew; niece; the spouse or unmarried partner of any of the following : parent (including an adoptive parent); parent-in-law; son (including an adoptive son); son-in-law; daughter (including an adoptive daughter); daughter-in-law; step-parent; step-son; step-daughter; brother; sister.

The term "family" above is said by the CRAG to include any of the following:

(a) a married or unmarried couple and any person who is:
  o a member of the same household **and**
  o the responsibility of either or both members of the couple **or**

(b) a person who is not a member of a married or unmarried couple and who is:
  o a member of the same household **and**
  o the responsibility of the resident

The meaning of 'incapacitated' above is not defined in the regulations but the CRAG states that it will be reasonable to conclude that a relative is incapacitated if either of the following conditions applies:

(a)   the person is receiving one (or more) of the following social security benefits: incapacity benefit, severe disablement allowance, disability living allowance, attendance allowance, constant attendance allowance, or an analogous (similar) benefit;

or

(b)   the person does not receive any of the benefits listed in (a) but the degree of incapacity is equivalent to that required to qualify for any one of those benefits. Medical or other relevant evidence may be needed before a decision is reached.

Once the person (that is, the relative etc. of the person in care) ceases to live in the property the disregard ceases and the property is then taken into account.

- The house is also disregarded if occupied by a lone parent who is the claimant's estranged or divorced partner. This is with effect from 1 April 2003.
- The property can also be disregarded, in the discretion of the local authority, if occupied by any other third party who does not have one of the prescribed relationships with the resident. However, this disregard, if applied, will not necessarily be permanent. The local authority should have a policy statement available on this topic. They should be asked for their policy statement on Paragraph 18 of Schedule 4 of the NA (AR) Regulations 1992. It should be noted that the DWP has no such discretion.
- If the resident shares **ownership** of the property with one or more other people (who are not themselves within the favoured categories above) then the resident's interest will be taken into account in the calculation of his or her resources. However, what is that value? The value is only what someone is willing to pay for it and it is unlikely that anyone other than the co-owners would be willing to buy it and unless they are prepared to do so (or they could be made to do so under land law) the value of the resident's share could well be nil. This possibility is acknowledged by the CRAG. Legal advice may well be necessary to try to resist the inclusion of the resident's share in the calculation – as will a very 'difficult' co-owner! It may well be that the problem could be resolved by the co-owner agreeing to buy out the interest of the resident – albeit at a much reduced figure.
- Where a *charge* is placed on a resident's property to ensure the local authority are repaid when the house comes to be sold, it should be noted

that no interest is payable on the sum outstanding until the resident's death. Depending on exactly how the charge has been registered the interest may not start to run until fifty-six days after the resident's death.

Points on income assessment

- Essentially all sources of income are included in the assessment
- Have in mind also that there may be a 'notional income' derived from savings where those savings exceed £12,250 (£13,500 in Wales) and are below £20,000 (£20,500 in Wales) (see above).
- There may also be other types of 'notional income' which the service user does not actually receive but which he or she is treated as having. In general terms this would be income which the service user is entitled to receive but which he or she voluntarily gives up or does not bother to claim. It is important that where service users are entitled to state benefits that they should claim them including pension credit.
- Some types of income are, however, wholly or partially disregarded. These are set out in Schedule 3 to the NA (AR) Regulations 1992. For example the mobility component in DLA and War Widows Special Payments are totally disregarded. War Disablement Pension and War Widows Pension are partially disregarded up to a total of £10 per week.
- The service user is entitled to retain a 'personal allowance' from their income for their own uses. This is currently (December 2004) £18.10 per week (£18.40 in Wales) and is disregarded in calculating available income. (A careful watch should be kept by those who may be looking after a resident's financial affairs to make sure the resident does actually get this sum and that it is not surreptitiously swallowed up by a home in allegedly paying for things which are already covered by fees from the authorities or by 'top up' fees. Similarly where a resident is self funding the contract should be checked carefully to see what is or is not included in fees and which if not included in fees may have to be paid for by the resident possibly out of the personal allowance.) It should also be noted that the local authority does have discretion to increase the amount of personal allowance where they consider it appropriate to do so. This would be particularly applicable where the resident could benefit from some activity or service not included in the care plan. One could imagine that this might include trips to the theatre or the provision of aromatherapy sessions.
- Couples, married or unmarried, are assessed separately whether one or both of them go into care. The one exception to this is in the case of married couples only, where one is entitled to a pension which would normally be treated as intended to benefit them both. In this case one half of the pension is disregarded where it is **actually** paid to the other party

who is not residing with him or her. Even if the couple are not married there is nothing to stop an approach being made to the local authority to raise the personal allowance of the one in care and in receipt of the pension so as to provide for the one not in care.

Nursing care

- Where a resident requires nursing care in a care home (but is not entitled to continuing nursing care resulting in payment of all fees) then the NHS funds that care (but remember not the social or personal care). The level of care required falls into three bands (high, medium and low) and depending on the level of care required, a non-means-tested payment will be made towards their care by the NHS. This is known as the Registered Nursing Care Contribution (RNCC). The assessment of the level of care will be made by designated registered nurses. It is regrettable that there is no guarantee that this contribution that is received from the NHS will actually be passed on to the resident by the home in reduced fees. It is apparent that those responsible for placing a person in care will need to check whether the RNCC is deducted from fees payable. There is nothing to stop a home from bumping up its fees only to appear to reduce them by seeming to pass on the RNCC. Complaints about the assessment are dealt with initially in the local primary care trust by a Nursing Care Co-ordinator. Reviews of the level of care needed are conducted three months after going into care and every twelve months thereafter unless there is a significant change in between programmed reviews.

The current weekly payments for the RNCC (from 1 April 2004) are:

High – £125.00
Medium – £77.50
Low – £40.00

These will rise from 1 April 2005 to:

High – £129.00
Medium – £80.00
Low – Will remain at £40.00.

It should, however, be noted that PCTs do have flexibility to decide on a case by case basis to pay an amount between low and medium band dependent upon need.

- The definition of the various bands is as follows:

o   High needs;

People with high need for registered nursing care will have complex needs that require frequent, mechanical, technical and/or therapeutic interventions. They will need frequent intervention and re-assessment by a registered nurse throughout a twenty-four hour period, and their physical/mental health state will be unstable and/or unpredictable.

o   Medium needs;

People whose needs for registered nursing care are judged to be in the medium banding may have multiple care needs. They will require the intervention of a registered nurse on at least a daily basis, and may need access to a nurse at any time. However, their condition (including physical, behavioural and psychosocial needs) is stable and predictable, and likely to remain so if treatment and care regimes continue.

o   Low needs;

The low band of need for nursing care will apply to people who are self-funding whose care needs can be met with minimal registered nurse input. Assessment will indicate that their needs could normally be met in another setting (such as at home, or in a care home that does not provide nursing care, with support from the district nurse), but they have chosen to place themselves in a nursing home.

Miscellaneous points

- One spouse (but not one of a cohabiting couple) is in law treated as liable to maintain the other under the National Assistance Act 1948 and technically the one who is supposed to do the maintaining (the liable relative) can be called upon to make 'reasonable maintenance' for the one in care. This can be enforced through the magistrates. Whether a local authority would attempt this in an ordinary case is doubtful given the bad publicity that would attach to it. In any event, it must be noted that that whilst one party may be liable to maintain the other there is no obligation on the maintaining party to give any information about his or her assets or means. Without that information the local authority would be hard put to make an assessment of whether maintenance should be paid. **Spouses should not therefore give any information about their own means.**
- Subject to assessment, continence pads are now provided free of charge for all older people who are in residential care.

Temporary Stays in care

- Where someone goes into care on a temporary basis (whether for respite care or on a trial basis) for up to eight weeks, then the local authority does not have to do a full financial assessment but can charge a 'reasonable' sum which may or may not be the full and normal cost. However, it should be noted that short periods of respite care in a care home providing nursing care of less than six weeks, qualify for NHS funding and without an RNCC determination. If a person is self-funding for respite care and there are no records to determine which NCC banding they fall in, then they would normally be treated as falling in the middle band. If a higher band is considered necessary then an RNCC determination will be needed.

- The fact that the stay exceeds eight weeks does not mean that it is not temporary. However, a full assessment would then have to be done but the value of the resident's house would be excluded.

- The use of the word 'temporary' is quite important in this and other contexts, since once the stay ceases to be temporary and there is no possibility of the person returning to their home the value of the house falls to be included in the assessment. The regulations define 'temporary resident' as one whose stay is unlikely to exceed fifty-two weeks. There can be some slight flexibility in that period. It follows therefore that the longer a resident can be considered as 'temporary' the longer the property can be excluded from the calculations. Those responsible for the finances of an older person should resist pressure for the placement to be considered as no longer temporary as long as possible where there is any prospect at all of the resident returning home. There is a downside to this in that until someone becomes permanent in residential care, Council Tax on their own home continues to be payable even where it is unoccupied.

- It should be noted that for the purposes of claiming pension credit to part fund a temporary placement the threshold for capital is £12,000 and not £16,000 where the stay is permanent. Accordingly, the sooner a resident becomes permanent the sooner the higher threshold figure kicks in and the sooner the resident can claim pension credit and the sooner the local authority's contribution is reduced.

Benefits issues

- Overall it should be remembered that some state benefits are payable even if someone is in residential care and whether funded by the local authority or not. Some are payable only if the person in care is self-funding.

- The rules on when benefits are payable to those in care, the interaction between benefits and the regulations on charges for care and the interaction between benefits is complicated. It is critical that anyone going into care should seek advice on benefits from an appropriate source such as the local authority welfare benefits adviser, Citizens Advice Bureau, solicitor etc.

- I have, however, set out below some basic points on the most common benefits available namely, Attendance Allowance and the Disability Living Allowance (care component), Disability Living Allowance (mobility component) and Pension Credit.

- Attendance Allowance (AA) and Disability Living Allowance Care Component (DLACC) are payable to those who need personal care. AA is payable only to those over the age of sixty-five. DLACC is payable to anyone under sixty-five. Once a benefit becomes payable it is paid for life unless the circumstances of the person change. They are non-contributory and are not means-tested. It is payable at two rates. The rules for claiming are almost identical. The following points are relevant to those in residential care:

   o It is payable to those in care who self-fund.
   o It is not payable to those in hospital or in a fully-funded nursing home bed paid for by the NHS.
   o It is payable to those who receive only the RNCC.
   o It is not payable (apart from the first twenty-eight days in care if the service user was already in receipt of benefit at the time of admission into care) to those placed in local authority owned or managed accommodation unless they are self-funding.
   o It is not payable (apart from the first twenty-eight days in care if the service user was already in receipt of benefit at the time of admission into care) where a local authority has arranged a place in a private home but only where the authority accept financial responsibility for the placement by entering into the contract with the provider. If the authority do not make the arrangements or do not accept responsibility for the cost by entering into the contract then it is payable.
   o If a service user has made their own arrangements for care and is therefore initially self-funding and later has to turn to the local authority for support then it ceases to be payable.
   o If the local authority make arrangements for care (because the service user lacks capacity to do so and there is no one else willing and able to make the arrangements on his or her behalf) but the service user is self-funding then, after some doubts, it appears that the DWP accept that although the local authority entered into the arrangement and are technically responsible for the financial aspects of the placement, AA is still payable. There is also a distinct advantage for the resident if the local authority enters into the arrangement in that the home fees are likely to be less because the local authority enters into the contract

with the home because of their negotiating power. Accordingly, wherever possible, the local authority should try to be encouraged to make the arrangements rather than the service user or his or her representative doing so. The local authority is, however, likely to try to resist this except where it is clear the service user cannot make his or her own arrangements. It is perhaps also appropriate to warn service users and their representatives that if they subsequently enter into the contract with the home the home may then seek an increase in fees in view of the fact that the local authority have dropped out of the picture.

o   As indicated earlier where there is a DPA (or any other arrangement whereby the service user will have to refund the cost of care paid out by the local authority) in force, AA will be payable and must be claimed at the earliest possible date since claims cannot be back dated. However, where the twelve week disregard in respect of the resident's property is in force then AA is not payable during that twelve week period since the local authority are providing funding which will not have to be repaid.   At the end of the twelve week disregard AA becomes payable.

o   Disability Living Allowance Mobility Component (DLAMC) is payable to people who are unable to walk or who have difficulty walking. The difficulty may be due to mental or physical causes. It may be payable along with AA or DLACC. It is non-contributory and is not means tested. It must be claimed before the person reaches sixty-five and is payable until death or until the disability ceases. It is paid at two rates.   It remains payable to someone who goes into residential care or into a hospice but usually ceases after someone is admitted to hospital care after twenty-eight days. This cannot be set off by the authorities against the cost of care.   It is therefore a valuable benefit.

•   Pension Credit.   This is, for many of us, a mysterious benefit involving complicated calculations. It seems to have been designed to be as complex as possible. It is a means tested benefit.   It is available for those whose income falls short of a figure referred to usually as "the appropriate amount". Usually, this will be a "standard amount" of money but it may be supplemented for certain individuals.

The standard amount for an older person going into care is currently £105.45 (December 2004).   The benefit will increase the person's income to that figure.   There is, additionally, a savings credit which is available to people of 65 and above and is designed to reward those who have saved.

The important point to note is that if you are in care you may be entitled to it and if the Local Authority is funding your care, they will expect you to claim it from the Department for Work and Pensions in order to reduce the amount the Local Authority has to find.

CHAPTER 19

DOMICILIARY CARE

KEY POINTS

- By domiciliary care is meant care provided for people in their own home.

- Since April 2003 all agencies providing domiciliary care (whether private, NHS or local authority) are regulated by the Commission for Social Care Inspection (CSCI) and have to comply with National Minimum Standards (NMS).

- The NMS detail what information a service user has to be provided with; the assessment which must be carried out before care is provided and during the provision of care; the way in which care should be provided; rules for the protection of the service user (and the care worker); and the way in which the agency is run.

CHAPTER 19

DOMICILIARY CARE

ISSUES

As we have already seen, an alternative to going into care (and possibly a preliminary to it) is the provision of support in their own home for an older person. This may comprise:

- a full time nurse or other carer;
- a night-sitting service;
- home care for doing such things as shopping, getting pension, getting dressed etc. involving one or more daily visits from a professional carer;
- a cleaner;
- respite care whilst normal voluntary carers are on holiday or take a few hours off;
- meals on wheels;
- laundry services;

or many other types of support either alone or in combination.

The support available varies from area to area and contact will need to be established with the local social services department to see what package of support they can arrange if it is that the older person cannot organise such services for themselves. As we have seen the fact that a local authority may arrange such support does not mean that it will be free nor indeed even subsidised. Generally service users can expect to pay for such services and possibly at a commercial rate. As with residential care, what package of support can be instituted by the local authority will largely depend on the assessment of needs which is carried out either by social services or by the multi-disciplinary team if this follows on from hospital discharge.

Many of the services which will be provided will involve older people being visited in their homes by carers. Until April 2003 there was little if any regulation of carers and the agency by which they were employed. From 1 April 2003 all that changed. As with care homes, agencies providing what is described as domiciliary care (and this includes local authority provision and that by NHS Trusts) now have to comply with National Minimum Standards laid down by the Commission for Social Care Inspection (CSCI) under the Care Standards Act 2000 (CSA). Those agencies now have to register with the

CSCI and compliance with the Standards will form the basis on which the CSCI will decide to register an agency or reject its application and at later stages decide whether a registration should be cancelled. The CSCI will have power to enforce the NMS if need be by prosecution.

WHO HAS TO REGISTER?

'All agencies which provide personal care for persons living in their own homes who by reason of illness, infirmity or disability are unable to provide it for themselves without assistance' must register and the term 'agency' includes 'all providers of personal domiciliary care services in the private, voluntary and public sectors including the local authority's own services, and NHS Trusts and supported housing or living schemes where applicable.' The CSA does not define personal care but it certainly includes assistance with bodily functions such as feeding, bathing and toileting and any other care involving intimate touching, including activities such as helping a person get out of a bath and helping them to get dressed. However, it may cover a wider range of activities.

WHAT DO THE STANDARDS AFFECT?

Effectively the whole operation of an agency is governed by the Standards including who runs it, the training of its staff, its administration etc. However, certain of the Standards will directly affect service users and I propose to summarise those so that an older person and their representative know what they can expect. It is perhaps appropriate to say that some agencies will have few problems in meeting the Standards. Many will already operate to similar levels and will welcome the Standards. Rochdale Community Support Trust (a mental health charity of which I am a trustee and which provides support for older people with mental health problems) is one such agency and which sees the Standards as a means of providing a level playing field for such agencies on which to operate. Some agencies will, however, have great difficulty in complying with the regulations and some will inevitably be forced out of operation.

WHAT CAN THE SERVICE USER EXPECT?

Supply of information

- As is the case with those going into residential care, the provision of information to the service user from the outset is important and Standard 1 requires the agency to publish a Statement of Purpose and a Service User's Guide for existing and prospective users and their relatives. These must be written in plain English and must be available in an appropriate format such as braille or large print. In appropriate cases the documents should be available in other languages.

- **The Statement of Purpose** must include the following:

  o The aims and objectives of the agency.
  o The nature of the services which the agency provides.
  o The name and address of the registered provider and of any registered manager.
  o The relevant qualifications and experience of the registered provider and any registered manager.
  o The range of qualifications of the domiciliary care workers supplied by the agency.
  o The complaints procedure established in accordance with the regulations.

- **The Service User's Guide** must be provided to all service users, their carers and prospective service users and must include:

  o The aims and objectives of the agency.
  o The nature of the services provided, including specialist services.
  o People for whom the service is provided.
  o An overview of the process for the delivery of care and support from initial referral, through needs and risk assessment and development of the service user plan to review of the care and reassessment of need.
  o Key contract terms and conditions.
  o The complaints procedure.
  o The Quality Assurance process.
  o Specific information on key policies and procedures.
  o How to contact the local office of the Commission for Social Care Inspection (CSCI), social services, health care authorities and the General Social Services Council (GSCC).
  o Hours of operation.
  o Details of insurance cover.

- **A copy of the most recent inspection report should be made available.**

- **Contract.** If a service user is self–funding then he or she must be provided (Standard 4) with a written contract within seven days of commencement of service. The service user and/or their relatives or representative and the agency must each have a copy of the contract which is signed by the service user (or their named representative on their behalf) and on behalf of the agency. It must include (unless they appear in other documents):

214

- o Name, address and telephone number of agency.
- o Contact number for out of hours and details of how to access the service.
- o Contact number for the office of regular care workers and their manager.
- o Areas of activity which home care or support workers will and will not undertake and the degree of flexibility in the provision of personal care.
- o Circumstances in which the service may be cancelled or withdrawn including temporary cancellation by the service user.
- o Fees payable for the service, and by whom.
- o Rights and responsibilities of both parties (including insurance) and liability if there is a breach of contract or any damage occurring in the home.
- o Arrangements for monitoring and review of needs and for updating the assessment and the individual service user plan.
- o Process for assuring the quality of the service, monitoring and supervision of staff.
- o Supplies and/or equipment to be made available by the service user and by the agency.
- o Respective responsibilities of the service user and of the agency in relation to health and safety matters.
- o Arrangements to cover holidays and sickness.
- o Keyholding and other arrangements agreed for entering or leaving the home.

Assessments

For every service user a care needs assessment must be carried out prior to the provision of care service or in exceptional circumstances within two working days of commencement. In the case of those who may be funded by a public authority this will be carried out by the local authority, health or primary care trust. A summary of this must be obtained by the agency. In the case of a service user who is self-funding the assessment must be carried out in the service user's own home by a competent manager from the agency and must cover the delivery of the services agreed including:

- Personal care and physical well-being.
- Family involvement and other personal and social contacts.
- Sight, hearing and communication.
- Continence.
- Mobility, dexterity and the need for disability equipment.
- Mental health and cognition.

215

- Medication requirements.
- Personal safety and risk.
- Specific condition-related needs and specialist input.
- Dietary requirements and preferences (if appropriate).
- Social interests, religious and cultural needs (if appropriate).
- Preferred method of communication.
- Method of payment.

- Information from the assessment must be provided in writing to care and support workers and procedures must be put in place to report changes of needs or circumstances.

- The particular requirements and preferences of any minority ethnic communities, social/cultural or religious groups should be identified, understood and entered into a plan for the service user.

- Following on from the various assessments and the service contract etc. a Personal Service User Plan outlining the delivery arrangements for care must be developed (Standard 7). This must be prepared with the involvement of the service user whenever possible and if not then with their representative, relatives, friends and other professionals. It will form the basis of care to be delivered. It must be reviewed at least annually or at the request of the service user. The plan will set out in detail the action that will be taken by care and support workers to meet the assessed needs, including specialist needs and communication requirements and identifies areas of flexibility to enable the service user to maximise their potential and maintain their independence. It will be signed by the service user or their representative. It will be in a language and format that the service user can understand and a copy will be left with the service user unless there are 'clear and recorded reasons' not to do so.

- Before a care worker commences work an appropriately trained person from the agency must carry out a risk assessment of the potential risks to service users and staff associated with the provision of care. This must include an assessment of the risks for service users in maintaining their independence and daily living within the home. This would include an assessment of whether the service user is able to take responsibility for his or her own finances. The assessment should take into account the views of service users and their relatives. A separate assessment must be carried out so far as moving and handling of service users is concerned.

- The assessments having been carried out, a plan to manage risks must be devised in consultation with the service user and their relatives or representatives. A copy of this must be kept in the home. The assessments and plan must be reviewed at least annually.

In practical terms what can be expected?

- The Standards set out in some detail what sort of standard of care a service user can expect. Overall, care workers should treat others as they would wish to be treated themselves

- Standard 8 sets out that the service must be provided in a way which maintains and respects the privacy, dignity and lifestyle of the person receiving care at all times and with particular regard to assisting with:

  o dressing and undressing;
  o bathing, washing, shaving and oral hygiene;
  o toilet and continence requirements;
  o medication requirements and other health related activities;
  o manual handling;
  o eating and meals;
  o handling personal possessions and documents (which presumably means seeking the consent of the service user before rooting around in drawers or looking at documents etc.);
  o entering the home, room, bathroom or toilet (which presumably means that barging in without knocking and/or waiting to be invited in is unacceptable).

- The standard requires that care must be provided in the least intrusive way at all times; that service users, their relatives and their representative are treated with courtesy at all times and that service users are addressed by the name they prefer at all times. The days of calling everyone by their first name, irrespective of age or status, without their consent have gone.

- Workers must be sensitive and responsive to the race, culture, religion, age, disability, gender and sexuality of the people receiving care, and their relatives and representatives.

- Carers communicate with the service user in his or her preferred language (Standard 9).

- Standard 9 establishes the principal that service users should be encouraged to maintain their independence as much and wherever possible. This includes:

  o Being encouraged to control their own finances.
  o That carers carry out tasks with the service user and not for them.

o   Limitations on the chosen life style or human rights to prevent self harm or self neglect, or abuse or harm to others, must be made only in the service user's best interests and consistent with the agency's legal responsibilities. Any limitation must be recorded in the risk assessment and the plan for managing those risks and must be entered on the service user plan.

- Standard 10 deals with issues of medication. A key worker, generally a health care professional from one agency who visits on a regular basis must be identified as responsible for taking the lead on medication. The Standard provides that staff provide assistance with taking medication and other health related tasks only when it is within their ability and they have been properly trained and it is:

  o   with the informed consent of the service user or their relatives or representative;
  o   clearly requested on the care plan by a named assessor;
  o   with the agreement of the care or support workers' line manager, and
  o   not contrary to the agency's policy.

- Staff must leave medication at all times in a safe place which is known and accessible to the service user or, if not appropriate for the service user to have access, where it is only accessible to relatives and other personal carers, health personnel and domiciliary care staff.

- Care workers must record, with the user's permission, observation of the service user taking medication and any assistance given, including dosage and time of medication and undertaking any other health related tasks, on the record of the care visit kept in the home and/or the Home Care Medication record and the personal file of the service user held in the agency. Any advice to the service user to see or call in their General Practitioner or other health care professional must also be recorded. The record must be signed and dated by the care worker and the service user or their representative.

- Service users are reminded that **they have an obligation to ensure that their premises are safe for the workers entering and working in the home**.

- Protection (in all manner of ways) of the older person (and in many situations protection of care workers) is a key consideration and Standards 13 to 16 deal extensively with financial protection, personal protection, security of the home and record keeping.

- The Standards require care agencies to have policies and procedures for the safe handling of service user's money and property and these will include: payment for the service/service user's contribution (if appropriate); payment of bills; shopping; collection of pensions; safeguarding the property of service users whilst undertaking the care tasks; reporting the loss or damage to property whilst providing the care.

- There will also be guidance on NOT:

  o accepting gifts or cash (beyond a very minimal value);
  o using loyalty cards except those belonging to the service user;
  o making personal use of the service users property, (for example telephone);
  o involving the service user in gambling syndicates (for example national lottery, football pools);
  o borrowing or lending money;
  o selling or disposing of goods belonging to the service user and their family;
  o selling goods or services to the service user;
  o incurring a liability on behalf of the service user;
  o taking responsibility for looking after any valuable on behalf of the service user;
  o taking any unauthorised person (including children) or pets into the service user's home without permission of the service user, their relatives or representative and the manager of the service.

  It must be assumed that when the Standards talk of guidance on these issues they mean prohibition of such conduct just as the Standard explicitly provides that the agency's policies and practices regarding service users wills and bequests must prohibit the involvement of any staff or members of their family, in the making of or benefiting from service users wills or soliciting any other form of bequest or legacy or acting as witness or executor or being involved in any way with any other legal document.

- As a measure of protection for all parties the Standard provides that the amount and purpose of all financial transactions undertaken on behalf of the service user, including shopping and the collection of pensions, is recorded appropriately on the visit record held in the service users home (see Standard 16) and signed and dated by the care and support worker and by the service user, if able to do so, or their relatives or representatives on their behalf.

- The physical security of the service user and the service user's home are clearly vitally important and the Standards require the agency to have clear procedures in relation to entering homes including: knocking/ringing bell and speaking out before entry; written and signed agreements on keyholding; safe handling and storage of keys outside the home; confidentiality of entry codes; alternative arrangements for entering the home; action to take in case of loss or theft of keys; action to take when unable to gain entry; securing doors and windows; discovery of an accident to the service user; other emergency situations.

- Agencies must provide Identity cards for all care staff entering the home of service users and these must display a photograph of the member of staff, the name of the person and employing organisation in large print, the contact number of the organisation and the date of issue and an expiry date which should not exceed thirty-six months from the date of issue. They should be available in large print for people with visual disabilities and laminated or otherwise tamper proof.

- The keeping of records is a recurring theme in the Standards. The written records kept must be legible, factual, signed and dated and kept in a safe place in the home. They must be kept in the home for one month or until service is terminated when they should be transferred to the agency or, say, to the local authority for safekeeping. If a service user or their representatives refuse to have records kept in the home then they must sign and date a statement confirming the refusal. Standard 16 makes provision that, with the consent of service users, care workers record on records kept in the home: the date and time of every visit to the home; the service provided and any significant occurrence. They should include details of assistance with medication including time and dosage; other requests for assistance with medication and the action taken; financial transactions undertaken on behalf of the service user; details of changes in the users or carers circumstances, health, physical condition and care needs; details of any accidents however minor whether to the service user or care worker; any other untoward incidents; any other information which would assist the next health or social care worker to ensure consistency.

- The service user and their relatives/ representatives are told about what is written and have access to it. This includes their personal records kept in the premises of the agency in accordance with the Data Protection Act.

- Staff should be reliable and dependable (Standard 6).

- Staff should arrive within the time band specified and work for the full amount of the time allocated.

- On arrival they should ask the service user if there are any particular personal care needs or requirements they have.

- Continuity of care should be ensured and care or support workers are only to be changed for legitimate reasons. Whenever possible the service user, relatives and representatives should be consulted in advance.

- Service users should be kept fully informed on issues relating to their care.

Miscellaneous

- Service users must be encouraged to use the complaints and compliments procedure (and, yes, it is perfectly permissible for service providers to be complimented on the service that they provide!) and where a complaint is made users should be kept informed at each stage of the investigatory procedure and should be given information on appeals procedures and how to refer a complaint to the regional office of the CSCI.

CHAPTER 20

OVERALL

- Plan early. Older people and their family need to give forethought to how things may develop. Discuss and plan for the unthinkable.

- Put in place the basic documents and keep them up to date and in such a place that they can be found and cannot be destroyed. These key documents are:

  - A will;
  - An Enduring Power of Attorney;
  - Possibly a living will and Statement of Values;
  - A list of assets;
  - Basic information;
  - Details of any 'skeletons';
  - Your deeds and securities.

- Ensure that each older person has a current (cheque) account and, if possible, a deposit (high interest earning) account at a mainstream bank. That is, a bank which offers the full range of banking facilities. These accounts should be opened at a time when the older person is able to get to the bank and produce any necessary evidence of identification etc. and when they are still likely to have available such documents as passports, driving licences etc.

- Generally, regularise your finances.

- Consider disposing of assets but only dispose of those when you know for certain that you will not need them or will not be affected by the loss of control. Ensure that you do not fall foul of the deliberate deprivation rules nor the pre-owned property tax rules.

- Establish a good relationship with the solicitor who generally looks after your affairs.

- Familiarise yourself with services that are available in your area or in the area to which you may be planning to move. This will be in terms of the housing, residential care, non-residential care, support systems etc.

- Try to keep up-to-date with the financial rules governing care.

- Put in place security systems, perimeter security, emergency call equipment and aids at an early stage and on the principle of not having to shut the stable door after the horse has bolted.

- Obtain accurate information from authoritative services (not the bloke in the pub or from Mabel next door or from generalised comment on TV, radio or in the press).

- Spend some of the money you have put away for a 'rainy day' now to ensure your comfort and safety. Perhaps now is the rainy day. Remember the old saying that 'shrouds do not have pockets'.

APPENDIX 1

EXPLANATION OF TERMS
(GLOSSARY)

Abuse	
Administrator	The person who deals with the estate of someone who has died and who has either not left a will or has left a will but where, for some reason, the executors named in the will are unable or unwilling deal with the deceased's affairs.
Advance Directive	An expression of wishes as to what medical treatment a person would or would not be prepared to undergo if he or she were not capable of expressing a view at the relevant time. Very similar to a Living Will.
AID	Artificial Insemination by Donor
Appointeeship	The appointment of one person to receive state benefits on behalf of someone else who is mentally incapable. The appointment is made by the Department for Work and Pensions.
Assessment	Usually used in the context of reviewing the needs of an older person in order to decide what, if any, need they have for community care services, and how best to provide such services and how they should be paid for. This usually involves a review of the older person's finances to assess income and capital.
Assets	An asset is any item of any value which belongs to a person. It would, depending upon its context, include property, bank and building society accounts, premium bonds, stocks and shares, savings and any personal items such as furniture or articles of household use or ornament, jewellery etc. It can also extend to include sources of income.

Attorney	In a British context, an attorney is a person appointed by another (the Donor) to manage some or all of the Donor's affairs. It does not necessarily mean someone with legal qualifications as in the American context.
Beneficiary	The person who receives or is entitled to receive a gift or some form of benefit
Capital	Any financial asset other than income. It is likely to include such things as property, savings at the bank, investments, etc.
Care home	The modern collective name for residential and nursing homes.
Care Manager	A person, usually a social worker, who helps older people and their carers to assess what needs they have and make a care plan and then review any services that the older person may use, and who will then take steps to organise the services required.
Care Plan	A form that tells an older person, in writing, what services will be given to him or her after his or her needs have been assessed.
Certificate of Service	A certificate which is signed by a person who has served a document on another person. In this book, used where someone serves a Court of Protection document on someone who is mentally incapable.
Charge	A form of 'mortgage' registered against a property belonging to one person by someone to whom the owner owes money. Often used by local authorities to protect money due to them from a resident in residential care.
Codicil	A document which alters or adds to the provisions of a will. It has to be signed and witnessed with the same formality as a will itself. Because of the advent of word processors and the ease of 'running off' a new will, codicils are increasingly rare.
Commission for Social Care Inspection	The regulatory body which now supervises most Social Care provision and carries out inspections. Inspection Reports are available to the public. These can be found on the internet or copies can be purchased.
Common Parts	Parts of a building which are shared by occupiers. This would, in the case of a block of flats, include the entrance hall, staircases, grounds etc.
Court of Protection	A branch of the Supreme Court of England and Wales which deals with the affairs of the mentally disordered.
CSCI	See Commission for Social Care Inspection

Deferred payment agreement (DPA)	An arrangement entered into by an older person with the local authority under which the local authority agrees to fund the care of the older person, but on the basis that the cost will later be recovered from the older person's assets, usually on the sale of a property. It may well involve the registration of a charge against the older person's property, either in the local Land Charges Department or at the Land Registry.
Delegate	To appoint someone else to undertake some task on behalf of yourself.
Department for Work and Pensions	The Government body responsible for, amongst other things, payment of state benefits. Part of it used to be the Benefits Agency or Social Security.
Discretionary trust	A gift of money, usually in a Will, given to Trustees for them to use the capital and/or income in such a way as the Trustees think fit, for the benefit of one or more individuals. Usually the people to be benefited have a mental or physical disability and are or may be in receipt of state benefits which would be affected if they were to receive the gift in their own right. Alternatively, the person or persons to be benefited may not be able to manage their own affairs or may not be able to manage their financial affairs wisely and free from pressure
Donor	A person who gives something to someone else. This may be a gift of money or, in the context of Enduring Powers of Attorney the person who appoints someone else to act on his or her behalf.
Dr Shipman	A doctor in the north of England who was found to have murdered many of his elderly patients over a number of years. He was caught after he forged the will of a patient he had murdered. He was convicted in January 2000 of fifteen counts of murder and one of forgery and was sentenced to fifteen life terms. He committed suicide in prison in January 2004. See **www.the-shipman-enquiry.org.uk**
Dual registered	A care home which is registered with the Commission for Social Care Inspection as both a residential care home as well as a nursing home.
Electoral record/roll	The list kept by local authorities of the people in their area entitled to vote. Sometimes called the Voters List or the Burgesses roll. It can usually be viewed at the Town Hall, a local library or the local Post Office.

Enduring Power of Attorney	A document signed by one person (the Donor) appointing one or more other people (the Attorney or Attorneys) to act on his or her behalf in respect of (depending upon the terms of the Power of Attorney) some or all of his affairs. It can continue to operate even if the Donor becomes mentally incapable.
Estate	Depending upon the context this will mean the monies or property which a person has available to them during their lifetime or the monies or property which they leave behind on death.
Estate and Distribution Account	The accounts prepared (usually by solicitors) at the end of the administration of the estate of someone who has died, showing what assets have been received, what liabilities have been paid and how the balance is to be distributed.
Exhumation	The digging up of a body of someone who has died and previously been buried. Exhumations often taken place where further investigations into the cause of death arise because of some suspicious circumstances. In the context of this book where someone has been buried and their family etc. subsequently decide to change the place of burial.
First General Order	This is usually the first order to be issued by the Court of Protection following an application for Receivership (unless Interim Directions have been issued in respect of specific issues) and will set out the obligations of the Receiver and the powers which have been granted to the Receiver by the Court.
Grant of letters of administration	The legal document issued by the High Court authorising a person or persons to deal with the estate of someone who has died where that person had died without leaving a valid will or having left a valid will has not appointed executors or where the executors appointed cannot or will not apply for the grant.
Grant of probate	The legal document issued by the High Court authorising the Executor or Executors of someone who has died to manage the affairs of the person who has died and where that person left a valid Will naming an Executor or Executors.

Ground rent/rentcharge/chief rent	Ground rent is the payment of (usually a small) rent paid by the occupier of property held on a long lease. Rentcharge/chief rent is a similar payment but which is paid by the owner of a freehold property usually to a previous owner of the land.
Half Blood	A person related to another who have only one parent in common. Usually brothers or sisters.
H. M. Inspector of Anatomy	An appointment under the Anatomy Act 1984 of an Inspector whose role is to ensure that human cadavers (bodies) donated to Anatomy Departments in British Medical Schools, are treated in compliance with the law.
Home	This could mean a Nursing Home or Residential Home. They are collectively known as Care Homes.
Incest	Sexual intercourse between people regarded as too closely related to have such intercourse. For example mother and son, brother and sister, father and daughter.
Informed Consent	Where someone agrees to some course of action affecting themselves or others after the proposed course of action has been explained to him or her and they have a sufficient level of understanding to be able to appreciate the proposed course of action and its consequences.
Interim Directions	These are Orders made by the Court of Protection prior to the making of the First General Order and empower the proposed Receiver or solicitors involved to take certain steps. For example to have mail re-directed or to draw monies in order to pay Care Home fees etc.
Intermediate care	A short period (normally no longer than six weeks) of intensive rehabilitation and treatment to enable service users to return home following (or to avoid) hospitalisation, or prevent admission to long-term residential care.
Intestacy	Where a person has not made a valid will. A partial intestacy is where a person has made a valid will but it does not dispose of the whole of his or her estate.
Joint Tenancy	One of two ways in which property can be held by two or more people together. It usually has nothing to do with Landlord and Tenant Law. Where there is a joint tenancy if one joint tenant dies the property passes to the other automatically irrespective of the will of the one to die or the Laws of Intestacy if there is no will. The opposite of a Joint Tenancy is a Tenancy in Common.

Lasting Power of Attorney	A replacement for the Enduring Power of Attorney. It is likely to be capable of creation when the Mental Capacity Bill has become law. In addition to empowering an Attorney to manage a person's financial affairs, it can permit the Attorney also to have an involvement in health care decisions.
Mental Incapacity	Where a person does not have sufficient understanding to be able to carry out a particular task or tasks. Different levels of mental capacity apply to different tasks. Usually used in this book in the sense of a person not having sufficient capacity to manage his or her own affairs.
Money Laundering	The process by which money which has been obtained through some unlawful activity such as tax evasion or drug dealing (or other criminal activity) is turned into apparently legitimate money by various transactions designed to conceal its origin, such as, by being passed through one or more bank accounts.
Notification Letter	In the context of this book a letter by which a person is notified that a relative or friend is the subject of an application to the Court of Protection for the appointment of a Receiver.
Occupational Pension	A pension derived from a person's employment as opposed to state retirement pension.
Office Copy	An office copy usually refers to an official copy of a document and which is provided by a public authority. The Court of Protection provides office copies of Order made by it. These are shown to be office copies by having the impressed seal of the Court on them. The Land Registry supplies office copies of registers of Title. These are definitive versions of the state of the Title at the particular time.
Officiant	In the context of this book a person who officiates at a funeral whether this be a clergyman, a friend or a relative of the deceased

Panel Receiver	A person appointed by the Court of Protection to be the Receiver of someone who is mentally incapable of managing his or her own affairs and who has been selected by the Court from a group of professional people who are willing to take on the role of Receiver. Many solicitors are panel receivers.
Partially intestate	See Intestacy
Patient	In the context of this book a person who because of mental incapacity has become subject to an Order of the Court of Protection
Pecuniary legacy	A specific sum of money left under the terms of a Will, for example £50.00 or £2,000.00 etc.
Pension credit	A means tested welfare benefit for older people
Personal Chattels	The personal items belonging to someone such as furniture, jewellery, clothes etc. The term 'Personal Chattels' is defined by Section 55(1)(x) of the Administration of Estates Act 1925 in detail. See Chapter 9 for full definition.
Power of Attorney	A document by which one person appoints one or more other people to manage some or all of his affairs. See also Enduring Powers of Attorney and lasting Powers of Attorney.
Prescribed Form	Some document the form of which is laid down by law.
Pressure sores (otherwise known as pressure ulcers or bedsores)	An area of skin that breaks down when a person stays in one position for too long without shifting their weight. This often happens if a person uses a wheelchair or is bedridden even for a short period of time. The constant pressure against the skin reduces the blood supply to that area and the affected tissue dies.
Primary Care Trust	Primary care is the care provided by people you normally see when you first have a health problem. For example your GP or the local NHS walk-in centre. These services are managed by a Local Primary Care Trust. The PCT will work with local authorities and other agencies that provide health and social care locally to make sure that local community needs are being met.
Prove the will	The legal process by which a will is accepted by the High Court as being a valid will of someone who has died. It results in a Grant of Probate or sometimes of a Grant of Letters of Administration with Will annexed.
Receiver	In the context of this book the person appointed by the Court of Protection to manage the affairs of someone who is mentally disordered under the supervision of the Court of Protection.

Receiver's declaration	A form completed by a proposed Receiver confirming to the Court of Protection certain facts about themselves and confirming that he or she will properly carry out the duties of a Receiver
Receivership Bank Account	All Receivers under Orders of the Court of Protection are required to open one or more Receivership Bank Accounts into which monies of the patient will be paid.
Registered Nursing Care Contribution (RNCC)	Where a person is not entitled to have their residential fees paid because they require full continuing nursing care, they may be entitled to a contribution towards the nursing element of their care. It is paid by the NHS and falls into three bands, dependent upon the amount of nursing care required.
Registration of EPA	This can mean two things. Where a person has made an Enduring Power of Attorney the person appointed as Attorney will need to register the Power of Attorney with any financial institution with which the Donor has dealings so that the financial institution can act on the instructions of the Attorney. The second meaning is where an Enduring Power of Attorney has to be registered with the Court of Protection at the point where someone who has made the Enduring Power of Attorney has become or starts to become mentally incapable of managing his or her own affairs.
Renounce	An executor is said to renounce probate where he or she formally decides that he or she does not wish to deal with the administration of the affairs of someone who has died and where he or she had been appointed the executor in the will.
Residential Care Services	The placement of a person in a care home.
Residuary Beneficiary	A person who receives that part of the estate of someone who has died after all the specific bequests and pecuniary legacies have been paid out.
Residuary estate	That part of the estate of someone who has died which is left over after all specific bequests and pecuniary legacies etc. have been paid out. In almost every case where someone dies there will be some 'residue'. A will should always contain a gift of residuary estate.
Residue	Effectively the same as Residuary estate.
Self funding	A person who is wholly responsible for payment of their own residential care fees.

	A politically correct term for someone who uses a particular service. It covers a wide range of people and services.
	A birth certificate which shows only the name of the person born, the date of birth and the place of birth and the place where the birth was registered.
Specific bequest	A gift in a will of a particular item. For example a ring, a table, a car, a stamp collection etc.
Spouse	A husband or wife.
	The main document which is submitted to the Court of Protection when an application is being made for the appointment of a Receiver. It sets out full details of the Patient (see above) and his or her finances and other matters.
	This is what is often referred to as 'secondary' legislation. It is law which is not actually contained in an Act of Parliament but is made by Government acting under Authority given by Acts of Parliament. Until the advent of the internet, secondary legislation was often very difficult for lawyers (let alone the layman) to locate.
	A Will made on behalf of someone by the Court where he or she is unable because of mental incapacity to make his or her own Will. It can be made either where someone has made an Enduring Power of Attorney which has been registered with the Court of Protection or where an application has been made to the Court of Protection for the appointment of a Receiver.
	One of two ways in which property can be held by two or more people together. It usually has nothing to do with Landlord and Tenant Law. Where property is held on a Tenancy in Common each co-owner is treated as owning their own distinct share in the property which they can leave under the terms of their will or which will pass under the Laws of Intestacy if there is no will on their death. Usually, the purchase deed will have declared what proportions the respective owners have in the property. It is the opposite of a joint tenancy.
Testamentary capacity	The mental capacity or mental ability required by someone to be able to make a valid will.
Testator	The person making a will.
	The professional body of solicitors. It theoretically fulfils the role of the solicitors trade union and is also responsible through the Office for the Supervision of Solicitors for the control of solicitors.

The prohibited degrees	Those people who cannot marry each other either because they are related by blood or marriage. For example brother and sister, parent and child, child and grandparent etc.
Threshold	A level (usually a sum of money) above or below which a service will or will not be provided free of charge or subject to a contribution. For example in England the threshold for a person's savings above which sum they will not receive any contribution to residential care fees (except in some circumstances) is £20,000. The threshold figure below which the service will be provided entirely free is £12,250.
Trustees	Persons who are appointed to manage over a, perhaps lengthy, period money or property which has previously belonged to some other person. They may be managing that money or property following the death of the person to whom it has belonged, or because it has been transferred to them during the lifetime of the person to whom it previously belonged to be held in trust by them.
University Medical School	The department of a university which trains doctors. In the context of this book it is used in respect of donations of bodies for medical training and research.
Valid objection	There are only five grounds for objecting to registration of an Enduring Power of Attorney as follows: a) The power is not valid. b) The power no longer subsists. c) The Donor is not yet becoming mentally incapable. d) Fraud or undue pressure has been applied to the Donor in making the Enduring Power of Attorney. e) The attorney is unsuitable.
	See Electoral Record/Roll
	A person related to another and each having the same parents. Usually brothers and sisters.
Will	In popular usage this means a document under which a person expresses who he wants to have his money or property when he dies.

APPENDIX 2

SOURCES OF INFORMATION

Name of Organisation	Address, Telephone Numbers of Organisation	Website and email information	Nature
Action for Blind People	14–16 Verney Road, London SE16 3DZ Tel: 020 763 54800 Fax: 020 76354900	Website www.afbp.org Email info@afbp.org	Enabling blind and partially sighted people to transform their lives. Offering a wid range of services to visually impaired peopl their family, advocates, professionals and the public.
Action on Elder Abuse	Astral House, 1268 London Road, London SW16 4ER Tel: 020 876 57000 Fax: 020 867 94074 Whistleblowing Hot Line: 0800 169 4312 (for workers in care homes or domiciliary care who want to whistleblow) Elder abuse helpline: 0808 808 8141	Website www.elderabuse.org.uk Email enquiries@elderabuse.org.uk	National organisation which aims to prevent the abuse of older people by raising awareness, encouraging education, promoting research and collecting and disseminating information. The website ha a superb sectio on indicators o abuse.

zheimer's ciety	Gordon House, 10 Greencoat Place, London SW1 P1PH Tel: 020 730 60606 Fax: 020 730 60336	Website www.alzheimers.org.uk Email enquiries@alzheimers.org.uk	Support and advice on Alzheimer's disease and other dementia and Creutzfeldt-Jakob disease (CJD). There are local branches.
rers tional sociation arers UK)	20–25 Glasshouse Yard, London EC1 A 4JT	Website www.carersuk.org/home	The website has a useful page on carers' assessments.
are andards spectorate r Wales	National Office Units 4/5, Charnwood Court Heol Billingsley Parc Nantgarw Nantgarw, Cardiff CF15 7QZ Tel: 01443 848450 Fax: 01443 848472	Website www.csiw.wales.gov.uk Email: csiw_national_office@wales. gsi.gov.uk	

Charity Commission	Harmsworth House, 13–15 Bouverie Street, London EC4 Y 8DP Tel: 0870 333 0123 Minicom: 08703330125	Website www.charity-commission.gov.uk Email enquiries@charitycommission.gsi.gov.uk	The regulator and registrar of charities in England and Wales. The Website is useful for verifying the existence of a charity and also for locating particular charities or types of charity and for locating local charities. Useful for locating charities when making a will.
Commission for Social Care Inspection	Head Office 33 Greycoat Street, London SW1P 2QF Tel: 020 797 92000 Fax: 020 797 92111 The CSCI also operates out of regional and local offices	Website www.csci.org.uk Email enquiries@csci.gsi.gov.uk	The CSCI regulates social care services relating to both adults and children through a process of registration and inspection. Inspection reports on care homes and domiciliary services and the website has links to legislation regulations and standards.

o-operative ineral ociety, ineral Care		Website www.funeralcare.co-op.co.uk	Has useful guide on How to Write a Euology.
uncil for gistered IS itallers ORGI)	1 Elmwood, Chineham Park, Crockford Lane, Basingstoke, Hampshire. RG24 8WG Tel: Various numbers but customer service is 0870 401 2300	Website www.corgi-gas-safety.com Email enquiries@corgi-gas.com	National watchdog for gas safety in the United Kingdom. Useful for locating a Corgi Registered installer in your area.
USE ereavemen Care	Cruse Bereavement Care, Cruse House, 126 Sheen Road Richmond Surrey TW9 1 UR Tel:020 893 99530 Fax: 020 894 07638 Day by day helpline: 0870 167 1677	Email helpline@crusebereavementc are.org.uk General email info@crusebereavementcare. org.uk	Information on bereavement and support for the bereaved.
epartment r Work id Pensions	See local telephone directory	Website www.dwp.gov.uk	Information about state benefits and services

Deaf Blind	Deafblind UK National Centre for Deaf Blindness. John and Lucille Van Geest Place, Cygnet Road, Hampton, Peterborough PE7 8FD Tel: 01733 358100 (voice/text) Fax: 01733 358356 (Information helpline 0800 915 4666)	Website www.deafblind.org.uk Helpline 0800132320 (voice or text a real person at the end of the line 24 hrs a day)	Assisting deaf, blind or dual sensory impaired people to cope with their disability and to lead as fulfilled and independent lives as possible. Offer comprehensive services to deaf blind people, their support assistants and other professionals.
Department of Health	Customer Service Centre, the Department of Health, Richmond House, 79 Whitehall Street, London SW1A2NL Tel: 020 721 04850 Minicom: 020 721 05025	Website www.dh.gov.uk Email dhmail@dh.gsi.gov.uk	A large organisation and large website dealing with a whole range of health service matters
Depression Alliance	35 Westminster Bridge Road, London SE17JB Tel: 0845 123 2320	Website www.depressionalliance.org	Information support and understanding for those affected by depression.

fcom ncluding dvisory ommittee n elecommun ations for isabled and lderly eople)	Ofcom Riverside House, 2A Southwark Bridge Road, London SE1 9HA Tel: 020 763 48773 Minicom: 020 763 48769 Fax: 020 763 48924	Website: www.ofcom.org.uk	This is stated not to be a helpline but will try to point people in the right direction to obtain the services they need.
isabled iving oundation	380-384 Harrow Road, London W9 2HU Tel: 020 728 96111 Helpline 0845 130 9177		Organisation working for freedom empowerment and choice for disabled and older people and others who use equipment or technology to enhance their independence. Offers a wide range of fact sheets for choosing a wide range of equipment and how to use equipment
ıga ırtnership	Customer Services Manager Eaga Partnership Ltd Freepost NEA1205 Newcastle upon Tyne NE21BR Fax: 0191 247 3801 Tel: 0800 316 2808	Website www.eaga.co.uk. Email Enquiry@eaga.co.uk	Information about grants for heating or insulation improvements.

Elderly Accommodat-ion Counsel	3rd Floor 89 Albert EmbankmentLondon SE1 7TP Tel: 020 782 01343	Website www.eac.org.uk Email enquiries@e-a-c.demon.co.uk (See also www.housingCare.org)	Information on housing, care and support for older people.
Facsimile Preference Service (FPS)	DMA House, 70 Margaret Street, London W1 W8SS Tel: 020 729 13330 Fax: 020 732 34226	Website www.fpsonline.org.uk Email fps@dma.org.uk fps registration line 0845 070 0702	Service to reduce unwanted faxe
Hearing Concern	4th Floor 275–281 King Street, London W6 9LZ Tel: 020 874 31110 Helpdesk low call number is 0845 074 4600 (voice and text)	Website www.hearingconcern.org.uk Email info@hearingconcern.org.uk	Charity dedicated to hard of hearing adults. Provid advice, suppor and informatio

elp the ged ngland	207–221 Pentonville Road London N1 9UZ Tel: 020 727 81114 Fax: 020 727 81116	Website www.helptheaged.org.uk Email info@helpthe aged.org.uk Email: infocymru@helptheaged.org. uk	Wide range of information available in respect of older people. Has a vast number of fact sheets available on various issues such as equity release schemes, choice of care homes, funding of residential care, state benefits, home repairs and improvements etc.
'ales	12 Cathedral Road, Cardiff CF11 9LJ Tel: 02920346550 Fax: 02920390898		
ome Share	Home Share International, 54 Christchurch St. London SW3 4AR	Website www.homeshare.org Email hi@homeshare.org	Homeshare is an exchange of services. A householder offers accommodation to a home sharer in exchange for an agreed level of help. Various programmes run by not for profit organisations around the country.

HousingCare .org	See Elderly Accommodation Counsel	Website www.housingcare.org	An umbrella website of a large number o housing etc. organisations led by Elderly Accommodatic Counsel to hel older people make decision about where to live and any support or care they need. It will help in maintaining, adapting or improving you home, finding care or home help services; moving to retirement or extra care housing, or to care home. A excellent site.
Housing Organisation s Mobility and Exchange Services (HOMES)	This organisation seems not to give a postal address. Suggest contact by telephone Tel: 0845 080 1089	Website www.homes.org.uk Email customer.services@homes.or g.uk	Puts Council and Housing Association tenants in touc with others wh might like to exchange their home.
Incontact (Action on Incontinence	United House, North Road, London N7 9DP Tel: 0870 770 3246 Fax: 0870 770 3249	Website www.incontact.org Email info@incontact.org	Organisation f people affecte by bowel and bladder problems

bcentre lus	Part of the DWP See local telephone directory.	Website www.jobcentreplus.gov.uk	Information etc. in respect of employment issues and in the context of this book, funeral payments.
ailing reference ervice 1PS)	DMA House 70 Margaret Street, London W1 W8SS Tel: 020 729 13310 Fax: 020 732 34226	Website www.mpsonline.org.uk Email mps@dma.org.uk MPS Registration Line 0845 703 4599	Reduction in junk mail.
emorials Artists	Snape Priory Snape Suffolk IP17 1SA Tel: 01728 688 934	Website www.memorialsbyartists.co.uk Email harriet@memorialsbyartists.co.uk	Memorials by Artists is a nationwide service which helps people to commission fine, individual memorials for churchyard, cemetery, garden or public space.
inilabels	Finches Yard, Mill Green Road, Haywards Heath, West Sussex, RH16 1XQ Tel: 01444 417259 Fax: 01444 417664	Website www.minilabels.co.uk Email sales@minilabels.co.uk	Suppliers of iron-on and sew-on clothing name labels

Ricability	30 Angel Gate. City Road, London EC1V 2PT Tel: 020 742 72460 Textphone: 020 742 72469 Fax: 020 742 72468	Website www.ricability.org.uk Email Mail@ricability.org.uk	Providers of information on products and services to make life easier for older or disable people
Royal National Institute for the Blind (RNIB)	105 Judd Street, London WC1H 9NE Tel: 020 738 81266 Fax: 020 738 82034 Helpline 0845 766 9999	Website www.rnib.org.uk Email helpline@rnib.org.uk	Information support and advice to peop with sight problems
Royal National Institute for Deaf People (RNID)	19–23 Featherstone Street, London EC1 Y8FL Tel: 0808 808 0123 (Freephone) Textphone: 0808 808 9000 (Freephone) Fax: 020 729 68199	Website www.rnid.org.uk Email Informationline@RNID.org. uk	Information support and products for deaf and hard o hearing people Extremely useful source o information on equipment for hard of hearing people.
Royal Society for the Prevention of Accidents (ROSPA)	Edgbaston Park, 353 Bristol Road Edgbaston, Birmingham. B5 7ST General Information Tel: 0121 248 2000 Fax: 0121 348 2001	Website www.rospa.com Email help@rospa.com	Charity dealing with the prevention of accidents and general safety information including safet in the home.

ANE	1st Floor Cityside House, 40 Adler Street, London E1 1EE Tel: 020 737 51002	Website www.sane.org.uk no email	Information on schizophrenia, depression, anxiety, phobia, obsession, alcohol, drugs and mental illness.
ENSE	11–13 Clifton Terrace, Finsbury Park, London N4 3SR Tel: 020 727 27774 Text No: 020 727 29648 Fax: 020 727 26012	Website www.sense.org.uk Email enquiries@sense.org.uk	Support and services across the UK to help sensory impaired people of all ages.
ociety for hiropodists d odiatrists	1 Fellmonger's Path, Tower Bridge Road, London SE1 3LY Tel: 020 723 48620 Fax: 020 723 78621	Website www.feetforlife.org. Email enq@fcpod.org.	Information on foot health and how to find a local state registered chiropodist/podi atrist.
lephone eference rvice PS)	DMA House 70 Margaret Street, London W1 W8SS Tel: 020 729 13320 Fax: 020 732 34226	Website www.tpsonline.org.uk Email tps@dma.org.uk TPS registration line 0845 070 0707	Reducing unsolicited sales telephone calls. For those troubled by calls where the phone rings but on answering there is no one there, register your number on silent call guard service on 0870 444 3969

Teletec International Ltd	Cranfield Innovation Centre, University Way, Cranfield Technology Park, Cranfield, Bedfordshire. MK43 0BT Tel voice: 01234 756026 Text: 01234 756027 Fax: 01234756028	Website www.teletec.co.uk	Company specialising in telecommunicat ons, equipmen for deaf and hard of hearin; or speech impaired peop
The Continence Foundation	307 Hatton Square, 16 Baldwins Gardens, London EC1N7RJ The helpline is 0845 345 0165	Website www.continence-foundation.org.uk The helpline email Continence-help@dial.pipex.com Administration continence.foundation@dial. pipex .com.	Provides information advice and expertise for those with bladder and bowel problem
The Family Records Centre	1 Myddelton Street, London EC1 R1UW Tel: 020 839 25300 Minicom: 020 839 29198	Website: www.familyrecords.gov.uk	Access to som of the most important sources for family history research in England and Wales. It is jointly run by the General Register Offic and The National Archives. (TNA).

he Natural eath Centre	6 Blackstock Mews, Blackstock Road London N4 2BT Tel: 0871 288 2098 Fax: 020 735 43831	Website www.naturaldeath.org.uk Email ndc@alberyfoundation.org.	A charitable project aiming to support those dying at home and their carers and to help people to arrange inexpensive, do-it- yourself, and environmentally friendly funerals. It has a general aim of helping to improve the quality of dying.
he Office of air Trading)FT)	Fleet Bank House 2–6 Salisbury Sq London EC4Y8JX Tel: OFT Enquiries 0845 722 4499	Website www.oft.gov.uk Email enquiries@ oft.gov.uk	General information on consumer issues. In the context of this book information is available on prepaid funeral plans and care homes. Included is information on whether terms for care home contracts are fair.

The Partially Sighted Society	Queen's Road Doncaster, South Yorkshire DM1 2NX Tel: 01302 323132	Website (use Google to locate searching for "partially sighted society") Email doncaster@partsight.org.uk	Information fo the partially sighted.
The Pension Service	Part of the DWP. See local telephone directory	Website: www.thepensionservice.gov. uk	Information on State Benefits
The Suzie Lamplugh Trust	PO Box 17818. London SW14 8WW Tel: 020 887 60305 Fax: 020 887 60891	Website www.suzielamplugh.org email info@suzielamplugh.org	A charity whic is the leading authority on personal safety Offers information an equipment for improving personal safe for the gener public includ disabled and disadvantage people.
UK Transplant	Fox Den Road Stoke Gifford Bristol BS 34 8RR Tel: 01179 757 575 Organ Donor Line: 0845 606 0400	Website www.uktransplant.org.uk	NHS Organ Donor Regist

APPENDIX 3

LIST OF INFORMATION AN OLDER PERSON SHOULD COMMIT TO PAPER

Basic and Family Information

Your full, correct and complete name?
Details of any other name you have at any time used or been known by.
Place (town and country) of birth.
Date of birth.
Parents names.
Is there anything about your origins or your past which anyone else might need to know? For example, were you adopted? What details do you have of your natural and adoptive parents? Do you have any genetic or hereditary conditions?

Is there anything in your past which you feel you need to admit or which might put someone else's mind at rest? Criminal activity, bigamy etc.

Marriage and children

How many times have you been married?
Full names of husbands/wives.
How and when the marriage ended – death, divorce?
Are any former husbands/wives still alive? Have they remarried?

Have you **any** children from **any** relationship? (This includes any illegitimate children.) If so, names and dates of birth of children and if female and married, give both maiden and married names.

If a child has died then give details of his or her date and place of death? Who was each child's other parent?

If any children have died did they leave children? If so, details.

Have you ever **legally** adopted any children? If so, when, who, date of birth, date of adoption, details of natural parents.
Are their any children you have informally adopted? If so, give details.

In the case of either legal or informal adoption have you any details of the medical history of the natural parents or their extended families including details of any genetic or hereditary conditions?

Have you ever given up a child for either **legal** or **informal** adoption? If so, give details of the child, the adoption and the adoptive parents.

Extended family

Names and addresses of any living relatives and their relationship to you?
Do you have any living brothers and sisters? Give details.

Personal information

Your last or main occupation.
Your late husband/wife's occupation? Was he/she retired at the time of his/her death?
Your religion.
Do you actively participate in religious activity?
Do you hold a driving licence? What is its number? When does it expire?
What is your National Insurance number?
What is the name and address of your tax office and what is your tax reference number?

Income

What state benefits do you receive? What are they and how are they paid to you?

Do you get an occupational pension from your previous employment? If so, from whom? What is the provider's name, address and reference number?

Do you get an occupational pension from any former husband or wife's previous employment? If so, from whom? What is the provider's name, address and reference number?

Other than from financial investments do you have any other sources of income? Give details.

Wills, Enduring Powers of Attorney and Living wills/advance directives

Have you made a will? Where is the original? Who are the executors?
Have you made any form of power of attorney? If so, is it an Enduring Power of Attorney? Where is the original? Who are the attorneys? What is/are their address/es?

Have you ever made a living will/advance directive? If so, when and where is the original? Do you still consider it as applicable?

If you have not made a living will, who would you like to be consulted about any health care decisions to be made for you?

Gifts

What gifts have you made in the last seven years? (This would include if you have released someone from a debt they owed to you.) Give dates, amounts, to whom and what for and if not money what was the item and how much was it worth?

Since 1986 have you made any gifts in the subject matter of which you have retained any interest (for example, given away a house but have continued to live there)? Give dates, amounts, to whom and what for and if not money what was the item and how much was it worth and how have you continued to benefit?

Does anyone owe you any money? If so, what was it for, what was the original amount, how much is outstanding, is there a written agreement, was interest payable and if so at what rate?

Have you paid any premium on any   life insurances which:

(a) were not for your own benefit or   (b) will not pay out to your /estate?

If yes, give details

Property and contents

Who has keys to your house?

List the addresses/location of any land or property which you own? Where are the title deeds? Is there a mortgage on any property and if so in whose favour is the mortgage?

So far as your house is concerned, are you satisfied that all land which you occupy is clearly marked on the deeds? Are there any bits of land which you occupy but which are not on the deeds?

Do you occupy a garage on separate land? Do you own that land or rent it? Who do you rent it from?

Where are the water and gas stop cocks?

Do you pay any ground rent on the property? Who do you pay it to?

Is there anything on rental (for example, television, video etc.) If so details of the rental company and your account number

To whom do your telephones belong?

Is there anything in your house which you have not fully paid for? For example anything bought from a catalogue company or double-glazing which is still being paid for.)

Is there anything in your house which you have borrowed or which does not belong to you (for example, items borrowed from social services or a hospital or from a neighbour or items belonging to any organisation to which you or your late husband/wife belonged (for example Masonic regalia)) ?

Do you have any special accounts/supplies such as internet, broadband, satellite television etc? If so, details?

Are there any safes in your house? Where are the keys? What is the code?

Is there an alarm? What is the code? Who maintains the alarm system? Is the alarm monitored by a central control? What is their telephone number? What is your code word for the alarm monitoring station?

Is there anywhere in your house that you have hidden, for example, any money or bank etc. books?

Are your house and contents insured? If so, with which company and for how much are they insured? Where is the policy and evidence of payment of the most recent premium? What is the annual renewal date?

Are there any items in your house of particular value and which might be overlooked?

Other assets

List in full any other financial assets which you may own and include account numbers and the names addresses of any financial institutions concerned? (This would include, for example, Timeshares, National Savings Certificates, Income Bonds, Deposit Bonds, Premium Savings Bonds, Shares, Bank Account, Building Society Accounts, Life insurance Policies, Business interests.) Give details of names and addresses and account/reference numbers and the location of the bank etc. books?

Do you have any items or documents in safe custody with a bank or with solicitors etc.? If so, what and with whom? (This would include any deed boxes that may be deposited with a bank or other organisation.)

Are there any items which you have lent to anyone else?

Are there any items, documents or money which you have given to someone else to look after for you? Give full details of what, when, who, why?

Details of any car that you own including which firm it is insured with and the policy number, where is the Vehicle Registration document and any MOT test certificate? Where is the vehicle kept if not in a garage at your house? Who bought (that is, paid for) the car? Is it on hire purchase etc.?

Do you have financial or other information stored on a computer which may need to be known about now or in the future? If so what is its nature? What are your passwords for the system etc. and if appropriate the document itself?

Are there any assets of any description which belong jointly to you and someone else? If so, what, who, why, value, how acquired etc.

Other people

Details of your accountant, solicitor, financial adviser, and insurance broker?

Details of your doctor (GP), dentist, chiropodist, optician, hospital consultant etc.

Details of your milkman, newsagent, window cleaner, gardener, cleaner.

Details of your electricity, gas, telephone service supplier.

Do you have meals on wheels, home care etc?

Miscellaneous

Have you guaranteed anyone else's debts?

Are you a trustee of any trust or an executor/administrator of any estate?

Are you a beneficiary under any trust or under an estate which has not been finalised?

Do you belong to any organisations? Do you wish to continue your membership in the future?

Private medical insurance details?

Have you pre-paid your funeral? Who is the plan with?

What are your funeral wishes?

APPENDIX 4

SOME WILLS CLAUSES

Clause restricting the rights of beneficiaries to information about the administration

I direct that neither my Executors nor any Solicitors employed by them shall be under any obligation howsoever imposed to supply any information to any beneficiary or prospective beneficiary as to the progress of the administration of my estate for a period of [   ] months from the date of my death unless my Executors shall in their absolute discretion think fit.

Clause restricting the rights of beneficiaries (usually charities) to require Tax Deduction Certificates to be produced

I direct that neither my Executors nor any Solicitors employed by them shall be under any obligation howsoever imposed to supply Certificates of Deduction of Income Tax to any beneficiary or prospective beneficiary unless my Executors shall in their absolute discretion think fit.

Clause requesting beneficiaries to act with decency

In making bequests under the terms of my Will it is because I wish the beneficiaries named in my Will to receive some benefit from my estate. It is however, my wish that those beneficiaries should behave decently following my death and should understand that the proper administration of an estate can take many months and sometimes a number of years to conclude. It is my wish therefore that such beneficiaries should not anticipate the bequest that I have left to them and should not press the Executors of my Will or any Solicitors employed by them to proceed with the administration of such estate in such a way that is unseemly. It is my wish that my beneficiaries should understand that they are receiving a benefit which they would not have obtained were it not for my death and should accordingly act in a decent manner.

APPENDIX 5

SUGGESTIONS FOR THOSE TO BE MENTIONED IN ACKNOWLEDGEMENTS

- Family, friends, neighbours who sent floral tributes or messages of sympathy.
- Those who attended the service and/or committal.
- Those who sent donations.
- Paramedics, police, fire service.
- The hospital/hospice staff.
- The GP.
- Professional carers e.g. Home care staff, Crossroads, the Macmillan nurses.
- Sheltered housing warden.
- Social workers.
- Community psychiatric nurses.
- District nurses.
- The coroner's staff.
- Meals on wheels.
- Solicitors.
- Any particular individuals who have given particular help or support before death and to the family after.
- The officiant at the funeral.
- The funeral directors.

APPENDIX 6

CHECKLIST OF INFORMATION REQUIRED/QUESTIONS TO BE ASKED PRIOR TO ADMISSION TO RESIDENTIAL CARE

The following are some of the things that should be looked for when visiting a Care Home with a view to admission of either yourself or a relative or friend. Some of them are general issues which are issues to be considered in choosing any home, such as accessibility, but many are points that need to be looked for in visiting a particular home.

This list should not be considered to be exhaustive. The fact that something is on the list does not necessarily mean that it is optional. As will be seen from studying Chapter 16 many of the points made are now required by the National Minimum Standards. However, many homes appear yet to have to implement some of the requirements of the Standards and accordingly it should not be assumed automatically that all the requirements will be met by a particular home.

(1) Accessibility/Location

- Are there any problems with the location of the home? For example:

  o Busy roads.
  o Public transport.
  o How convenient it is for the shops, post office, Church etc.?
  o Is it in a noisy location?

- How easy is it to enter, leave and move about inside the home (possibly with a wheelchair)?

- Is there a lift?

- What difficulties will people who want to visit you encounter? For example:

  o Getting there.
  o On a bus route.
  o Parking.
  o Seeing you in private.
  o Any restrictions on visiting hours?

- What is the view like?

(2) Accommodation

- How long does it take for the main door to be answered?

- What is your overall impression of the building?

  - Is it noisy; clean; well-maintained; well decorated?
  - What's the temperature like?
  - Is it comfortable and inviting?
  - Does it smell fresh?

- How will you be able to make use of the garden?

- What do you think of the bedroom?

- Will you have to share a room? If so, do you have a say on whom to share with?

- So far as the bedroom is concerned:

  - Is it too big or too small?
  - Can you personalise it?
  - What furniture of your own can you take in?
  - What facilities does it have; washbasin, bath, shower, mirror etc.?
  - Is it carpeted?
  - Is there enough cupboard space for all your clothes and personal belongings?
  - Are there bedside commodes? If in a shared room is there a privacy curtain or screen?
  - Is the bed comfortable?
  - How big is the bed?
  - What sort of bed linen is provided for example duvets or blankets?
  - What's the view like?
  - Will you have a key?
  - Do the staff knock on the door before entering?
  - Can you have your own telephone?
  - Are personal radios and televisions allowed in your own room?
  - Are there television aerial points in the room?
  - Is there an adequate 'nurse call' system?
  - Are pets allowed?
  - Is there somewhere lockable for personal papers/possessions to which only the resident has the key?
  - What is the lighting like?
  - Is there bedside lighting?

- Are there adequate electric sockets in convenient places?
- Is it centrally heated with temperature control within the room?
- Is there comfortable seating for at least two people?
- Is there a table at which to sit and a chair?

- How easy will it be to get to the bathroom/toilet?

  - What aids are there, for example lifting equipment?
  - How many other people use it?
  - How often is it cleaned?
  - How many bathrooms are there?

- What is the lounge like?

  - Is it comfortable; warm; noisy?
  - Who decides what to watch on TV?
  - Are people allowed to smoke? Is there a smoke free lounge?
  - Is there more than one lounge?

- What are the arrangements for the dining room?

  - Can you sit on your own?
  - Do people always sit at the same table?

- Is the kitchen spotlessly clean?

  - Is it used just for preparing meals, or are the residents' clothes and bed linen washed there too?

- How easy will it be to manoeuvre the stairs and corridors?

  - Is there a lift?
  - Are there handrails?

- If there isn't a phone in your room, what arrangements are there for you to make and receive calls?

  - Will you be overheard?
  - How will you pay for the calls you make?
  - If you wish, can you have your own phone installed in your room?

- What fire safety precautions are there?

- o Fire doors, alarms, smoke detectors, extinguishers, a fire escape?

- What security arrangements are there?

  - o What control is there over who enters the building?

- Is the resident's room lockable?

- Does the resident have a key to his or her room?

(3) Care

- Does each resident have an individual care plan?

- Will you be able to remain in the home if your health deteriorates?

- Can you retain your own GP? (Also check this with your own GP – some GPs are reluctant now to go outside very tightly defined areas.)

- How often is the home visited by a physiotherapist; chiropodist; hairdresser etc?

- Are there set routines for when residents get up and go to bed?

- Are you free to come and go to bed as you wish?

- What are the laundry arrangements?

- Who looks after your drugs and medicine?

- Can the home meet your entire medical, nursing, emotional and special needs?

- What social activities and entertainment are provided for residents? How frequently? By whom?

- Are family and friends encouraged to join in social events?

- Does the home have its own transport?

- What steps are taken to make sure that your own clothes always come back to you after laundering?

- Are there visiting dentists, opticians, hairdressers, chiropodists, physiotherapist, ministers of religion?

- What 'aids' are there?
  o Is there an induction loop (either fixed or portable) for those with hearing aids?

(4)   Catering

- What are the meal times?

  o Are they rigid or flexible?

- Is there a menu?

  o Is there much choice?
  o How often is the same menu prepared?
  o Do residents have any say in planning or preparing meals?

- Are special diets (especially religious or cultural diets) catered for?

- Is the diet appetising and well balanced?

- How many meals a day are provided?

- How many are cooked?

- Can you have a snack between meals?

- What happens if you fancy a cup of tea or coffee at any time?

- Is alcohol available?

- Can you have your meals in your own room if you wish?

- Can visitors join you for a meal?

- Is assistance with eating readily available, if required?

(5)   Finances

- What are the current fees?

  - When are they payable?
  - Are they paid in advance or arrears or a mixture of both?
  - How are they paid?
  - When and how are the fees reviewed?
  - To what extent have they increased over the last few years?

- What services do the fees cover?

  - What extras will you have to pay?

- What retainer will you have to pay if you leave the home temporarily while you're on holiday, visiting family or friends, or in hospital?

- What happens about fees when a resident dies?

- Are you allowed to retain control of your own pension book?

- What will happen if you become unable to pay the full cost of the fees?

- What money is received for personal use and who looks after it?

- Are top-up fees charged?

- Does the home attempt to recover top-up charges from the residents' own monies?

- Does the home attempt to put personal liability for residents' fees on members of the family or their receivers or attorneys?

(6) Management

- Is the home registered as a residential care home or nursing home or both?

- Who owns the home?

  - What qualifications and experience do they have?
  - Do they plan to sell up or retire in the foreseeable future?

- Will you be able to get on with the owner or manager?

- Are there any plans for extensions etc? Will it become impersonal?

(7) Policy

- What is the home's general attitude towards residents':

  o Privacy?
  o Dignity?
  o Independence?
  o Choice?
  o Rights?
  o Fulfilment?

- What are the procedures for dealing with:

  o Complaints?
  o Arrears?
  o Reporting faults in equipment?
  o Damage caused by residents?
  o Drugs and medicine?
  o Anti social behaviour?
  o Pets?
  o Smoking?
  o Alcohol?

- Are visitors encouraged at all times?

- Where would the resident see professional advisors?

(8) Residents

- How many residents is the home permitted to take?

  o How many are there at present?

- What is the age range?

  o Who has been there the longest?

- What is the proportion of males to females?
- How many are physically frail, mentally infirm, convalescent?

- Is there a residents' committee?

- How much say do the residents have in the way the home is run?

- Do they seem to be happy and well cared for?

- Will you be able to get on with the other residents?

(9) Staff

- How many staff does the home employ?

- How many are on duty at any time during the day or night?

- What hours and what shifts do they work?

- What is the proportion of male staff to female staff?

- Do the staff seem to treat the residents with respect and sensitivity?

- Are they constantly busy, or are they able to find time for chat?

- Do they look smart or slovenly?

- What is the home's record on staff turnover?

- Will you be able to get on with the staff?

- Do the staff address residents by their first names? Do they find out how you want to be addressed?

(10) Terms and Conditions

- Are there any particular criteria for admission?

- Can you stay for a trial period?

   o If so how long?

- Does the home give residents a written contract?

Make sure you are aware of:

- How much the fees are, and when and how they are paid

- Does the home attempt to put personal responsibility for fees and complying with the other terms of a resident's occupancy, upon the resident's relatives, receiver or attorney?

- The services included in the fees. In particular seek confirmation that no part of the fee covers continence aids since this is now paid for by the NHS for all care home residents from April 2003. (A continence assessment will be necessary before the home is paid for these for a resident.)

- The procedure for reviewing fees.

- The items you are expected to provide and pay for yourself.

- The retainer payable, if you are away from the home in hospital or on holiday.

- The period of notice you need to give the home.

- The period of notice the home has to give you.

- The circumstances in which you might be asked to leave.

- What items are covered by the home's insurance policy and what items you will need to insure for yourself?

- The facilities for looking after any cash or valuables?

- How to complain.

- What happens if you die?

(11) Activities

- Does the home have an Activities Organiser?
- What is his/her experience?
- What activities are organised?
- How frequently?
- What has been organised in say, the last month?
- Are there any photographs available?
- How are such activities paid for?
- If trips out are organised, how many staff go on the trips?
- Does someone bring in library books?

(12) Miscellaneous

- What steps does the home take to ensure that residents are on the *electoral register?*
- What steps does the home take to arrange for residents actually to vote?
- What insurance is in place for residents' belongings?
- What facilities are available for safe keeping of residents' valuables?

APPENDIX 7

FORTHCOMING CHANGES

At the time of writing the Mental Capacity Bill is passing through Parliament.

This Bill has significant impact on Enduring Powers of Attorney, the Court of Protection and Living Wills/Advance Directives.

It is unclear when the Bill will become law and in particular it is unclear when it will come into effect.

In summary, the Bill provides as follows:

- There is a starting point that a person has mental capacity unless proved otherwise and that all practicable steps must be taken to help the person to make a decision and that they should participate in decision making as far as possible. Any decisions that are taken must be in the person's best interests having in mind what they themselves would have wanted.

- Enduring Powers of Attorney will become known as Lasting Powers of Attorney and will allow a person to appoint an Attorney to manage not only their financial affairs but also to make welfare and health care decisions on their behalf if that is what they want. New procedures for making Lasting Powers of Attorney will be introduced to ensure that a person has capacity to make the Power of Attorney and is not doing so under any pressure.

- So far as Enduring Powers of Attorney made before the new Act comes into effect are concerned, these will continue to operate and although there is no reason for them to be replaced by a Lasting Power of Attorney it may be that a donor would wish to do so in order to extend the powers that they give to the Attorney.

- Receivers will be replaced by Court Appointed Deputies who will be able to take decisions, not only on financial matters but also on welfare and health care matters as determined by the Court of Protection.

- The Court of Protection will be re-vamped in order to allow it to consider applications for financial decisions and serious health care decisions which are currently dealt with by the High Court.

- A new Public Guardian will be appointed to act as the registering authority for Lasting Powers of Attorney and Deputies and will supervise Deputies appointed by the Court of Protection.

- The Public Guardian will work with other agencies, such as the Police and Social Services, and will respond to any concerns about the way in which an LPA is being operated.

- A Code of Practice will be established to provide guidance to those working with or dealing with those who lack capacity.

- Living Wills/Advance Directives will have their legal status confirmed but will become known as Advance Decisions.

- A criminal offence will be created, namely that of ill-treating or wilfully neglecting a person who lacks capacity with a penalty of up to five years imprisonment. It will also become a specific offence to destroy certain documents such as Advance Decisions.

It will be important for those who have made Enduring Powers of Attorney to keep an eye on the press for details of when the new Act will come into force in case they should wish to make a new Lasting Power of Attorney and in order to include health and social care decision making.

Until the new Act comes into force, people contemplating making an Enduring Power of Attorney should continue to do so and will probably be ill-advised to put off making the Enduring Power of Attorney until the new Lasting Powers of Attorney come into operation.

It is the writer's view that the procedures for making Lasting Powers of Attorney will be more complex than Enduring Powers of Attorney and will almost certainly involve greater expense because of the need to comply with the much stricter rules which will apply to ensuring that the Lasting Power of Attorney is made voluntarily and whilst the maker still has capacity to do so.

Printed in the United Kingdom
by Lightning Source UK Ltd.
104357UKS00002B/6